THE POETRY TOOLKIT

For Readers and Writers

William Harmon

A John Wiley & Sons, Ltd., Publication

This edition first published 2012
© 2012 William Harmon

Blackwell Publishing was acquired by John Wiley & Sons in February 2007.
Blackwell's publishing program has been merged with Wiley's global Scientific,
Technical, and Medical business to form Wiley-Blackwell.

Registered Office
John Wiley & Sons Ltd, The Atrium, Southern Gate, Chichester, West Sussex,
PO19 8SQ, UK

Editorial Offices
350 Main Street, Malden, MA 02148-5020, USA
9600 Garsington Road, Oxford, OX4 2DQ, UK
The Atrium, Southern Gate, Chichester, West Sussex, PO19 8SQ, UK

For details of our global editorial offices, for customer services, and for information
about how to apply for permission to reuse the copyright material in this book
please see our website at www.wiley.com/wiley-blackwell.

The right of William Harmon to be identified as the author of this work has been
asserted in accordance with the UK Copyright, Designs and Patents Act 1988.

Library of Congress Cataloging-in-Publication Data

Harmon, William, 1938-
  The poetry toolkit: for readers and writers / William Harmon
    p. cm.
  Includes index.
  ISBN 978-1-4051-9578-2 (cloth) – ISBN 978-1-4051-9577-5 (pbk.)
  1. Poetry–Authorship. 2. Poetry–Appreciation. 3. Poetics. I. Title.
  PN1059.A9.H37 2012
  808.1–dc23
                                                            2011037208

A catalogue record for this book is available from the British Library.

Set in 10.5/13pt, Minon by Thomson Digital, Noida

Printed in Singapore by Ho Printing Singapore Pte Ltd

1   2012

Contents

Preface

Nobody knows nothing about poetry.

If you can read well enough to understand that sentence, then you have been meeting poetry in some form for some years, and such meetings will continue throughout your life. Everybody knows something about poetry, but nobody understands everything about it, and everybody can always learn more. The more you know, the more you can enjoy reading and writing poetry.

Eventually you may master such terms as "antimetabole," "englyn," and "drottkvætt," but first you will need some rudiments. It is encouraging that, even without rudiments, you can still get genuine pleasure out of reading and writing poetry, but, if you will be honest with yourself, you may soon recognize that some frustrations, which come when reading and especially when trying to write, can be eased by learning more about the arts and techniques of poetry.

This book aims to exploit what people already know, in some sense, in order to increase their understanding and appreciation. This procedure of moving from the known to the unknown may not account for such things as whim, luck, guesswork, serendipity, and accident, but it does provide a reasonable basis for what we do.

In any process of learning, you will probably reach a point of suddenly exclaiming, "Oh! I get it!" A toolkit can hope only to furnish the materials for facilitating such leaps of intuition and illumination. Most readers begin with a vague unexplained liking for something; the liking may impel them to learn more and to try harder to explain and understand.

The first six chapters of this book follow a systematic division of the elements of poetry, considered in a certain order:

1. overall design (plot of action, story of some sort), along with rhetorical attitude;

2. character (the persons or other agents involved in an action);
3. thought, feeling, state of mind (the background and motivation of character);
4. diction – vocabulary and syntax – (the verbal expression of thought and feeling);
5. sound (the pronunciation of words);
6. graphic effects (the appearance of words on a page).

Those are not the only elements, and that is not the only order, but the approach remains sound, rational, and time-tested. The first three elements apply to almost any literary work, prose and poetry alike; the last three have been associated mostly with poetry to one degree or another. The seventh chapter takes up various ways in which one poem can interact with another, along with a measure of entertainment.

Some have begun writing by producing the sixth element first, that is, with a poem-*looking* object, which, as with many poems, has a more or less justified left margin and an unjustified right margin. But you will probably not know what the poem looks like until you know what it sounds like. Some, therefore, produce a poem-*sounding* object, with words that rhyme, for example, but they will not know what sounds to combine until they know what words they ought to use. They will not know what words to use until they know what thoughts and feelings are to be expressed, and they will not know much of that, in turn, until they know what characters are involved; and the characters in turn are a function of the overall story. Accordingly, it is best to begin with the governing elements.

Having encountered terms associated with poetry in one way or another – anapest, tragedy, poetic justice, irony, overstatement, braggart, stanza, subordinate clause, vulgarism, rhyme, metaphor – students might not have thought consciously about how certain kinds of characters belong in certain kinds of stories, or how certain levels of vocabulary or textures of syntax belong with certain kinds of character, or how any of those things relate to rhythm and meter. And much about the whole process will necessarily remain forever irrational, mysterious, and controversial. (That is part of the fun.) But at any rate the matters can be laid out in an orderly fashion that will, if nothing else, at least permit analysis and debate.

Learning the rudiments of reading often leads to a desire to write for oneself. Someone with hardly a clue may not know whether to say "autumn" or "fall" in a given situation, except that "it's just the word I wanted – to express myself spontaneously"; and, while that is not a strong argument, neither is it a wrong argument; sometimes it is all we can come up with. Every day we choose from "taxicab," "taxi," or "cab," "phone" or "telephone," "newspaper" or "paper," for some reason or another, and we do not always know why. On the matter of "taxi," one recent writer, the actor Peter Bull, went so far as to use "taximeter–cabriolet," a choice that can be explained historically as the primitive ancestor of "taxicab" but maybe not vigorously defended, except as a humorous affectation. Perhaps "taxicab" preserves the ghost or tissue memory of its earliest form.

Writers all began as readers, and, unless one is an exceptionally spontaneous genius, a writer can benefit by reason and reflection as well as whimsy and a sense of fun.

Learning most things involves a progression from ignorance to improvement, perhaps to the level of mastery. Many common activities – such as preparing a meal, playing a musical instrument, driving a motor vehicle, operating a computer, engaging in a sport or game – begin with one being interested, move on to first steps, when everyone is awkward, and on to some point at which the activity becomes "second nature" and may even look easy to a casual observer. Such activities may involve boring repetitive exercises, such as playing scales or performing calisthenics, which may not seem very interesting in themselves. It is important not to give up in frustration just because the early stages of a process are difficult or tedious. Running is natural, but many runners who exercise for a track team suffer a most discouraging affliction called "shin splints" that may even persuade some to give up.

Speakers cannot take the time to analyze what they are saying as they are saying it, so that much about rhetoric, diction, and prosody remains necessarily unconscious. If, in fact, you think too much about sounds, you will interrupt an order to a butcher – "A pound of ground round" – to notice that three of the words rhyme. Efficient speech demands that much remains habitual, unconscious, intuitive, unanalyzed, and invisible. Rhyme, alliteration, and other such devices may distract.

Some have preached sermons on the text, "Write the way you talk." That text is of very little practical value, since, paradoxically, much poetry emphasizes the very features of language that speakers and prose writers usually try to avoid. Instead of avoiding rhyme, alliteration, regular rhythm, and other kinds of repetition, the poet may court them to a peculiar degree. Such a departure from the norm seems to exempt the discourse from ordinary informal communication and moves it to an extraordinary formal realm of special things like ritual and ceremony. Even so, "Write the way you talk" may be extended to "Don't write the way you don't talk" – that is, don't write a word you would not use in speech.

The telling of a story, presentation of a character, and probing of thoughts and feelings all find their expression in language – spoken aloud, written down silently, or rehearsed mentally in the stream of consciousness – and the choices one makes in vocabulary and syntax depend on the overall situation. No diction is automatically poetic or unpoetic: poetic diction is appropriate to a situation. "Fall" is as poetic as "autumn," say, just as "We trust in God" is as poetic as "In God we trust": it all depends on the context. English depictions of Americans and American depictions of the English can go ridiculously astray on the basis of diction alone. John O'Hara once suggested that a good writer, as of about 1950, had better know whether an American character would say "half-dollar" or "fifty-cent piece." In some situations, expressions normally regarded as incorrect are perfectly appropriate, as when poems by Gerard Manley Hopkins say "What I do is me" or "My taste was me." Lord Byron could write, "Where burning Sappho loved and sung"; a few years later, Alfred Tennyson, who admired Byron, could write, "The blue fly sung in the pane" – even though both were aware that since about 1800 the standard past form of "sing" has been "sang." T. S. Eliot commented: "*The blue fly sung in the pane* (the line would be ruined if you substituted *sang* for *sung*) is enough to tell us that something important has happened." Possibly what has happened is that Tennyson, though young, was already mature and confident enough to depart from a convention.

True, some dictionaries classify items as "poetic": "alack," for example, qualifies as "Now arch., poet. or dial." in the *Oxford English Dictionary*: "archaic, poetic, dialectal."

As writers and readers, we will not know how to assess or present characters – that is, people – in literature or life, unless we know what is on their minds and in their hearts, since characters are motivated by thoughts and feelings – matters which, again, are subject to complete change: love can turn into hate and vice versa, or love and hate can co-exist in a volatile combination.

Although this book is in the third person and uses the first person mostly in the form of a general "we," the first-person author – I – is always present and may as well say something here *in propria persona*. I first heard poetry more than seventy years ago. My first published poems were in little magazines more than fifty years ago, and my first book of poetry appeared more than forty years ago. Those statistics mean what most statistics mean:

nothing. But they do testify to a long engagement, often involving frustration, disappointment, rejection, and demoralization, but just as often involving satisfaction and delight, and more than one surprise. They do not testify much to financial gain or professional advancement, but very little poetry has ever produced such returns. Unlike some people who arrive at poetry through circuitous detours of work in medicine, law, engineering, publishing, and banking, I was always an English major – even while serving in the Navy – and, after spending decades working in English and Comparative Literature, I became a "professor in the humanities." Like the statistics, that title means what most titles mean.

I know this: what I know is a drop, what I don't know is an ocean. But a single drop is like Walt Whitman: it contains multitudes. A drop of water contains five sextillion atoms, possibly including, as Antonie van Leeuwenhoek discovered more than three hundred years ago, thousands of living creatures. Knowledge is so baffling that public intellectuals are forever weighing in with maxims: "When you don't know that you don't know, it's a lot different than when you do know that you don't know." (Bill Parcells, head coach.) "There are known knowns. These are things we know that we know. There are known unknowns. That is to say, there are things that we know we don't know. But there are also unknown unknowns. There are things we don't know we don't know." (Donald Rumsfeld, secretary.)

Now for some good news: however talented you may be, there is little possibility that you will be a virtuoso, champion, or master on your first day of trying something. That applies to playing chess or the cello or to baking a delicious cake or repairing a car or computer. I can think of many tempting activities that I have attempted but failed to make any progress with. (I will just say one word: dancing.) Poetry is different. Chess or the cello involves concepts and operations remote from daily life. But anybody, even the newest amateur, has been telling stories and singing songs and using language for a long time, so that there really are not any beginners. You began long ago. You know all the elements, even though you may not know you know.

Once in a blue moon, a poet can write a poem quickly and be done with it. Most of the time, however, there is slow, difficult, protracted development, with many hazards and opportunities for failure. A thousand ideas will float into your head for every one that survives to a later stage, since most ideas are just unfit in one way or another. Of every thousand that do manage to get beyond the primitive stage, most just perish of one of many afflictions, including deficient originality as well as excessive originality. So it goes, from stage to stage, by winnowing and further winnowing until the original idea finds its answerable form in a word or image or maybe just a rhythm. Again the winnowing starts, and the words or whatever have held the germ fail, victims of another myriad afflictions. Thus far the whole process could have taken a few minutes or a few weeks, but the end is the same: nothing. (Relics and fossils may endure awhile, and the resourceful writer may revisit and revive materials that had once been abandoned – but usually the things die and stay dead.)

For economy's sake, we can skip over another twenty stages of trial and error until we arrive at the point when the poem ceases to exist only in your head and finds some outer form, either as speech or writing. Some poems are spoken but never written down; others are written down without ever having been spoken. (Be careful: some poets speak words they cannot spell, others write words they cannot pronounce.) Most poems that get written are put away and never seen again. Of those submitted to magazines, most are rejected, and some that are accepted never appear for some reason. Of those that do appear – and now we are talking about some fantastic figure on the order of 1% of 1% of 1% of 1% of 1% of 1% of 1% of 1% of 1% – most never reappear, and even those are subject to revision or even being repudiated by their author who has undergone a change of heart.

I can testify that poetry is fascinating and frustrating. I have never outgrown the excitement I felt when as a teenager I first read a speech from *Paradise Lost*, but I have never understood the springs of that excitement. The one thing I do understand is that poetry is never simple. For many people much of the time, and for some people all of the time, poetry amounts to a sort of comfort food for the soul – something offering relief and escape from the setbacks, harassments, complications, obscurities, difficulties, obliquities, worries, vexations, frets, and hassles of existence. And so it should be. Nobody should have to face unending excitement and incessant demands, and no constitution is equipped to withstand physical, mental, and emotional strain without interruption.

But nobody should have to face a life of nothing but leisure and relaxation. We all need a certain amount of physical, mental, and emotional strain for exercise, to stay in condition and prepare for challenges that are sure to come along. A diet of nothing but comfort food will soon lead to discomfort and malnutrition.

It makes sense to want things in life to be simple, easy, natural, straightforward, direct. Some teachers teach that the ideal poem is simple etc. And some pupils try to apply the lesson by approaching poems as ideally simple things with a good beat, which they like.

But, face it, nothing in life is really simple. Why should poetry be an exception? The earliest poems in anybody's memory will be enigmatic lullabies, nursery rhymes, hymns, and jokes that invade the mind with frightening images of a breaking bough, a falling cradle with a baby on board, a falling bridge, a lamb's bloodbath, a feather cryptically called "macaroni," an old woman living in a shoe with more children than she can handle, a wicked boy kissing the girls and making them cry. And soon enough, from every sidewalk and public wall, spring the brutal images, symbols, and monosyllables that haunt every innocent soul's days until the end.

So what can you do? To begin with, you cannot solve problems by looking for ease and simplicity. They are just not there. If you value common sense – endorsed by most people as a good thing – then use enough of it to forget about the precinct of the simple, direct, straight-forward, natural expressions that have the substance of fairies and the shelf life of soap bubbles.

I could never adequately thank all those who have helped me with what is in this book, but I ought to name some whose presence has been an inspiration and an education. Some friends have died: Guy Owen, Norman Maclean, Cleanth Brooks, John Frederick Nims, Hugh Staples, A. R. Ammons, George Starbuck, Robert Kirkpatrick, Martin Gardner, George Hitchcock. I rejoice that others live on to receive my thanks: Robert Morgan, Jack Wheeler, Tom Daley, Ritchie Williams, Kathryn Starbuck, X. J. Kennedy, John Hollander, George T. Wright, Kathleen Norris, Frank Wall, Doug Stalker, Marly Youmans, George Lensing, George Core, Herb Leibowitz. With the preparation of this book in particular, I owe great debts to Emma Bennett, Ben Thatcher, and Frank Kearful.

Key to Symbols

⚒ = Basic tool, term, device, principle

📧 = Tip, advice, guidance

☠ = Warning, danger, hazard

BOLD CAPITALS = first appearance of a term included in the Glossary, or where this term is specifically defined and/or discussed.

1 The Arts of Story-Telling

Most poems belong in one of three categories: *narrative, dramatic, lyric*. Narrative poems, like many prose narratives, give an account of an action or incident. Insofar as they tell stories, poems and prose texts do not much differ. Since everybody enjoys hearing stories and almost everybody tells stories sooner or later, there is not much mystery about the arts of story-telling.

There is, however, a good deal of controversy about the technical terminology of story-telling, and a number of vexatious words have emerged since 1970. "Narratology," which first appeared in English in 1971, has caused some complaints because, among other offenses, it mixes Latin and Greek elements. But the same complaints were once prompted by "television," "homosexual," and even "bicycle" (some wanted "dicycle"!), but those words have long since joined the mainstream. Even so, narratology has remained an awkwardly technical-seeming term without very much technical material to justify it. Likewise, "prosaics" has been suggested as a complement to "poetics," on a rather shallow analogy: if poetry has poetics, prose ought to have "prosaics." And one can see titles like "The Prosaics of Ancient Romances." But *prosaic* has a well-established primary meaning of "mundane," "routine," "commonplace," "dull," and it seems unlikely that "prosaics" will ever gain much ground as a critical term for anything but mild condemnation. Turbulence in terminology may suggest chaos or confusion, but it may just as well suggest a productive ferment.

It is worth mentioning here that, as one progresses through the six main elements of a literary work – **PLOT, CHARACTER, MENTAL STATE, DICTION, SOUND EFFECTS, GRAPHIC EFFECTS** – one goes from almost unlimited regions of ill-defined concepts that merge helter-skelter

The Poetry Toolkit: For Readers and Writers, First Edition. William Harmon.
© 2012 William Harmon. Published 2012 by Blackwell Publishing Ltd.

into one another. Then, with diction, one reaches matters somewhat more definite, or at least less indefinite. If there are, say, a thousand considerations in the interdependent realms of plot, character, and inner state, the considerations of diction may number only in the hundreds, and those of sound and graphic effects only in the scores. With the later elements, one can suggest a certain amount of systematic analysis that just will not work with the earlier. It is a fact that an English syllable will contain no more than eight individual sounds (seven consonants and one vowel); it is not a fact that all plots can be reduced to eight basic patterns. Accordingly, these early chapters will seem more confused and less systematic than the later ones, but that is just the way things are.

Narrative poetry is much like narrative prose, in that it relates an orderly set of events involving characters in certain states of mind performing actions. If there is a coherent account with a beginning, middle, and end, it can be called a **STORY** with an **ACTION**. If the story is **EPISODIC** and therefore somewhat less coherent, then it is a story with *activity* but not necessarily an overall action.

The word "plot" is used for any plan, outline, or scheme. There are criminal plots and assassination plots and garden plots and graveyard plots. The overall story is a plot of action; there are also plots of character, thought, feeling, diction, sound, and layout. (In the theater, there are a lighting plot, a property plot, a makeup plot, and a costume plot, detailing what the technical crew needs to do at certain points in a show, demonstrating nightfall or daybreak, aging, growing, shrinking, promotion, demotion, and so forth. A member of a technical crew may be indifferent or oblivious to a play as such, concentrating only on a change of lighting, scenery, properties, sound effects, or costumes coming midway in the second act.)

In a sense, every sentence is a little story, with some kind of character as the **SUBJECT** and some kind of action as the **PREDICATE**. We may agree that a good story ought to be intelligible, interesting, and neither too long nor too short. We do not insist that a story be new or even novel, since many people – and not just children – enjoy hearing the same story over and over. Even so, one may not quite accept the argument of Robert Graves's "To Juan at the Winter Solstice": "There is one story and one story only/That will prove worth your telling." That may seem reductive and simplistic. (Note, however, that that sentiment does not have to be a universal generalization; it is part of a poem, after all, and may register the state of mind of a certain undefined character in certain undefined circumstances, possibly explained by the identity of "Juan" and the importance of the winter solstice; explanations can be found on the Internet.)

Over the years, thinkers have come up with some set number of basic plots – such as courtship, homecoming, discovery, comeuppance, or revenge – but there is no foolproof repository of formulas. We tell the stories that engage and amuse us.

A basic story begins "Once upon a time." It is in the past tense ("there was a child") and the third person ("child" – or the pronouns "he," "she," "it," "they"). Most narratives employ an identifiable point of view that governs how the story is managed. Point of view is a matter of pronoun person, verb tense, and other properties; typical points of view include past-tense third-person omniscient, past-tense third-person limited, past-tense first-person limited. (For good reasons, first-person omniscient is unlikely.)

The past-tense points of view can also be translated into present-tense points of view, and in many cases past and present are mixed. Second-person narration, again for understandable reasons, is unusual, although it is sometimes encountered, particularly in fiction since 1950.

English offers some idiomatic uses of "you" to mean people in general, but its presence gives a text an opportunity to seem to address the reader. In T. S. Eliot's *The Waste Land*, at or near the end of sections one, four, and five, this indefinite or unexplained pronoun seems to include a reader: "You! hypocrite lecteur! – mon semblable, – mon frère! ... Consider Phlebas, who was once handsome and tall as you. ... Why then Ile fit you." The first sentence of Ernest Hemingway's *To Have and Have Not* seems to ask "you" a question: "You know how it is there early in the morning in Havana with the bums still asleep against the walls of the buildings; before even the ice wagons come by with ice for the bars?" The first and last sentences of J. D. Salinger's *The Catcher in the Rye* both include such a second-person pronoun, along with an imperative form that implies "you" without stating it: "If you really want to hear about it, the first thing you'll probably want to know is where I was born, and what my lousy childhood was like, and how my parents were occupied and all before they had me, and all that *David Copperfield* kind of crap, but I don't feel like going into it, if you want to know the truth. ... Don't ever tell anybody anything. If you do, you start missing everybody."

In some cases, revision may come down to nothing more than a change of point of view. You may begin a story, "Very intelligently, I bought a car that turned out to be a classic, so that I multiplied my investment tenfold in a few years." That could, however, impress some as immodest, since the first-person speaker is claiming credit for much intelligence. In such cases having to do with great wisdom or talent, the third person may work better, since a seemingly objective witness is more convincing than a subjective participant. In stories that involve extraordinary powers or heroic exploits or supernatural phenomena, such as the familiar series of adventures of Sherlock Holmes, James Bond, Indiana Jones, or Harry Potter, the narrator is either an anonymous third-person teller or a first-person witness with little claim to extraordinary powers. Very rarely do such heroic personages tell their own stories.

Many popular accounts of charismatic characters – such as Heathcliff, Ahab, Holmes, Kurtz, Gatsby, Adrian Leverkühn, Willie Stark, Seymour Glass, Mozart, Randle Patrick McMurphy – are told by limited narrators or presented on the stage through limited viewers, such as Lockwood, Ishmael, Dr Watson, Marlow, Carraway, Buddy Glass, Salieri, Serenus Zeitblom, Jack Burden, "Chief" Bromden – who offer firsthand witnesses' accounts of extraordinary persons and events.

Such presence of a limited first-person narrator is more common in prose than in poetry. It is possible that poetry automatically confers a charismatic status on characters, so that no additional devices are required. But extreme charisma is difficult to manage, and heroic characters may belong more to poetry and to tragic drama than to prose, which tends toward the prosaic. With several of the charismatic characters listed above, identity itself remains mysterious, so that some – Heathcliff, Ahab, Kurtz – have only one name.

In narrative poetry, such as classical epics and modern adaptations thereof, the narrator is usually an anonymous all-knowing third-person figure with little but a voice and a style. In both prose and poetry, however, a hero very seldom tells of exploits in the first person. Mario Puzo, author of *The Godfather*, advised those aspiring to write best-sellers to avoid the first person. Film, a status to which many best-sellers aspire and progress, is mostly third person and achieves a semblance of a first-person viewpoint only by the use of such artificial techniques as voice-over and what is called a subjective camera. The most successful films, however, follow the formula of *Star Wars*: "A long time ago in a galaxy far, far away . . ." The audience never knows or cares who is talking.

Most of us prefer stories that have a coherent beginning, middle, and end – although those elements need not appear in that order – and we behave as though the ideal story involves change of some sort. The change can be slight or large, but we can say that as a rule favorite stories seem to involve maximal completed changes: from wretchedly single to happily married, from alive to dead, from ignorant to knowledgeable, from being at home to being away (and vice versa). Some taxonomists have devoted pages or websites to tables and charts of the twenty or hundred most popular plots, but the list could go on forever: Quest, Adventure, Pursuit, Rescue, Escape, Revenge, Metamorphosis, Maturation, Love, Discovery, Mystery, Decline, Fall, and so forth. Some appealing plots involve a combination of types. *Twin Peaks* (1990–1991), for example, is a murder mystery set in the Pacific Northwest with elements of supernatural quest, romance, demonic possession, satanic ritual, transvestitism, primitive magic, and jokes on names (brothers named Ben and Jerry, a lawman named Harry S. Truman, a character named Catherine Packard Martell, played by Piper Laurie, who had played a character named Sarah Packard in *The Hustler* thirty years earlier.) It is not necessary for writer or reader to be aware of everything that is going on. Many decisions and maneuvers remain unconscious, and many subjective responses cannot be understood rationally. Disturbances of the conventional time sequence, such as those which have been moving more and more into popular entertainment, are considered a feature of what is called "post-modern" literature, though they are not exactly new. The popular movies *Pulp Fiction* (1994) and *The Usual Suspects* (1995) involve gnarly complications of the time sequence, and the sequence of "actual" events in the former is still debated. *Memento* (2000) seems to unfold in reverse order, so that confused viewers have been advised to watch a DVD with the sequence of episodes reversed.

As a listener, one can entertain critical responses while a story is going on: "Get to the point!" "So what?" "You already said that . . ." Everybody has heard a storyteller pause and say something like "Did I mention that he was wearing a red apron?" It is better for a story to be too short than too long. The teller may not feel the pressure of responsibilities, but the success of a story depends on the teller's assessment of audience, material, context, and situation. Many stories involve technical details of a profession or region, and it is a challenge to size up the audience correctly.

Consider this poem:

"Cathy!!!"
"*Cindy.*"
"Cindy!!"

If you reject the proposition that this is a poem at all, think about why you should think so; and hold that thought.

It *is* a poem; at any rate it has been published as such in a respectable magazine and read aloud as such during public readings. With what you have been given, you can speculate that the three lines, consisting of three words (or two, with one of them repeated), represent speech: the quotation marks suggest that much. You cannot be sure how many people are speaking – one, two, or three. It seems unlikely that three separately quoted speeches represent the utterance of only one person, since that kind of speech would call for only one set of quotation marks around the whole thing. So, within reason, we can move on to the assumption that two or three people are talking, presumably in the same general area. One person exclaims "Cathy!!!" and that is probably addressed to another person. The person so addressed, however, is evidently not named Cathy, and so she (presumably) responds, with some emphasis, indicated by the italics, with the correct name: Cindy. So the first speaker corrects himself or herself, but with somewhat less emphasis, indicated by the two exclamation points instead of the original three. End of poem.

But not end of story. As a matter of fact, one element has been withheld: the title, which is "On Seeing an Old Girlfriend." Now things may become clearer. The word "old" suggests both that the girlfriend is not young and that she was someone's girlfriend long ago. With the passage of time and coming of age, the first speaker's memory has faded, and, although he or she remembers the girlfriend and is, furthermore, glad to see her, her name has slipped a bit from "Cindy" to "Cathy."

Now, consulting your personal experience, you may reflect that such things do happen. People often say, "The face is familiar, but . . ." The poem passes the tests of possibility and, beyond that, of probability. All we really know, tentatively, is that two people have encountered each other and one of them is named Cindy. Without much labor, one could reconstruct a plausible scenario. That is what everybody does every day when meeting with a situation that seems to call for explanation. In a way, we are all detectives and we are all story-tellers. Many things in life are not fully spelled out, and there are mysteries and even miracles that defy easy explanation. From childhood on, most people like puzzles and enjoy games that somehow parallel the struggles of life.

In our Mystery of the Forgotten Name, the solver of puzzles could go on at some length. "Once upon a time, in a small town, two young people knew each other. Some speculated that as adolescents they were sweethearts. But, as time passed and they grew up and went their separate ways, they gradually lost touch with each other. Then, after decades, they happened to see each other again, possibly at a reunion, but one of them, with the inevitable erosion of memory that comes with age, had forgotten the other's name, although an approximation suggested itself. He said, energetically and enthusiastically, "Cathy!!!" (In musical language, the first line could be *fortissimo*, the second *pianissimo*, the third *forte*.) Now, her name was not Cathy – a nickname possibly for Catherine or Kathleen – but Cynthia, and she was nicknamed Cindy; what is more, she did not like being called by the wrong name. Who does? We all like to be addressed in the correct form and by the correct name. We say things like "You can call me Samantha" or "My friends call me Roger" or "That's *Major* Fleming to you." In the case of our two people, Cynthia coolly and even sarcastically responds, with almost a hiss, "*Cindy*." (The initial sounds of the name may facilitate hissing: *Cindy*.) With his memory refreshed, and with his ardor slightly dampened, Cindy's old boyfriend can manage only a rather feeble and detectably less enthusiastic and energetic "Cindy!!" She then turned and walked away to join some old friends who did recall her name. Boy meets girl, boy woos and wins girl, boy and girl part, decades pass, boy encounters girl again but has forgotten her name, boy and girl part again. This is painfully slow and gradual, but it is probably the way we handle clues every day, progressing step by step until the materials make enough sense for us to go on. We lack the patience to subject every reading experience to such excruciating scrutiny, but a conscientious reader and writer may want to know how these things go.

Here is another story told in a short poem:

> Every morning
> I say, "Never again";
>   every night, "Again."

This seems to be the utterance of a single person who generalizes about his or her own experience. The statement, punctuated as a single sentence, is indeed a generalization, and nothing specifies any of the particulars of the situation. It is easy to imagine all sorts of reasons for saying "Never again" but then backsliding soon after. A. E. Housman captured a similar sentiment in a rather austere poem:

> How clear, how lovely bright,
> How beautiful to sight
>   Those beams of morning play,

How heaven laughs out with glee
Where, like a bird set free,
Up from the eastern sea
  Soars the delightful day.

To-day I shall be strong,
No more shall yield to wrong,
  Shall squander life no more;
Days lost, I know not how,
I shall retrieve them now;
Now I shall keep the vow
  I never kept before.

Ensanguining the skies
How heavily it dies
  Into the west away;
Past touch and sight and sound,
Not further to be found,
How hopeless under ground
  Falls the remorseful day.

(Incidentally, this poem furnished the punning title of "The Remorseful Day," the last episode of *Inspector Morse*, in which the inspector quotes a stanza of Housman's poem and then later dies.)

Remorse appears in a poem by Housman's American contemporary, George Ade; in fact, the poem (from a musical comedy) is called "R-E-M-O-R-S-E":

The cocktail is a pleasant drink,
It's mild and harmless, I don't think.
When you've had one, you call for two,
And then you don't care what you do.
. . . .
It is no time for mirth or laughter –
The cold, gray dawn of the morning after.

Let us return to the original poem:

  Every morning
I say, "Never again";
  every night, "Again."

In light of the familiar vernacular reference to "the morning after" and even "the morning after the night before," we may interpret the seventeen syllables as a reference to a hangover, when, by a revered tradition, one may say, "Never again." Without too much further experience, we may also reflect that the same people who say "Never again" in the morning feel well enough by evening to go right back to the same stupid behavior, and after one drink may say to a bartender, "Again." But the poem is not called "Hangover" or "The Morning After" or "Katzenjammer," so the reader must supply details. The same general pattern of "Never again" followed by "again" could apply to any sort of overindulgence – eating, drinking, spending, dancing, gambling, reading, scribbling, playing video games, staying up late – that can carry the punchline, "I'll never learn."

The poem in fact is called "**SENRYU**," the name of a Japanese comic or satiric form in seventeen syllables; the most common distribution of syllables is 5-7-5, as in haiku, but departures are freely permitted. Many of W. H. Auden's later poems are in seventeen syllables with a distribution of 5-6-6.

Both these short poems illustrate the possibilities of economy. They provide a minimum of material, so that the reader is left to work out plausible connections. That is a chore, but it is not hard work, and many readers prefer to get involved in things themselves. They resent having too much spelled out or explained, and they may feel insulted by a pedantic or preachy story that tells too much. There may be a kind of elegance in economy.

If a story is reasonably credible, it can be told in some straightforward way by first- or third-person narration in the past or present tense. Those variables account for most narrative poems. With some stories, however, a reader may feel skeptical about something not immediately plausible, and in such cases the story may need some shoring up. Sometimes an outer shell or frame sets off the inner material and gives some control. The outer poem has enough plausibility – a reasonable account of how a story is told – to confer contagious plausibility on the inner story. Samuel Taylor Coleridge's *Rime of the Ancient Mariner* presents just such an incredible story of a fantastic voyage among supernatural effects, but the presentation is not direct, that is, the poet does not tell the story straight. There is an outer story mostly in the present tense:

It is an ancient Mariner,
And he stoppeth one of three.

"By thy long grey beard and glittering eye,
Now wherefore stopp'st thou me?

The bridegroom's doors are opened wide,
And I am next of kin;
The guests are met, the feast is set:
Mayst hear the merry din."

He holds him with his skinny hand,
"There was a ship," quoth he.
"Hold off! unhand me, grey-beard loon!"
Eftsoons his hand dropped he.

With brilliant economy of means, the poet sets off on two stories at once. The outer story is much more mundane, but still under some pressure, since the "one of three" is on an important errand, to attend the wedding of a close kinsman. Despite this pressure, the guest pauses for quite a while to hear a detailed story from the "grey-beard loon." Some words are quoted without attribution, which requires the reader to figure out that the wedding guest addresses the mariner, providing details along the way about his beard and eye. The mariner, with no preliminaries, begins his past-tense story, "There was a ship." (The rare word "quoth" exists only in past-tense form with first- or third-person pronoun or noun, and it typically comes before the subject noun or pronoun, as here or in Poe's "Quoth the Raven ...")

We then may read with two impulses: to hear the mariner's story and to find out what happens to the poor wedding guest. In a few words, we have moved from "It is" to "There was." The fantastic story of a doomed voyage proceeds until the guest interrupts at the beginning of Part IV:

"I fear thee, ancient Mariner!
I fear thy skinny hand!
And thou art long, and lank, and brown,
As is the ribbed sea-sand.

I fear thee and thy glittering eye,
And thy skinny hand, so brown." –
"Fear not, fear not, thou Wedding-Guest!
This body dropped not down ...

And the story continues until it concludes by resuming the present tense for a few lines:

> The Mariner, whose eye is bright,
> Whose beard with age is hoar,
> Is gone; and now the Wedding-Guest
> Turned from the bridegroom's door.
>
> He went like one that hath been stunned,
> And is of sense forlorn:
> A sadder and a wiser man
> He rose the morrow morn.

It may seem strange that the Mariner's "eye *is* bright" but he "*Is* gone." Then, with the ambiguous transition of "and now" (suggesting a present past or a past present, really meaning "then" rather than "now"), the poem settles into a more normal past tense: the Guest "turned" and "went" and later "rose."

As that suggests, **FRAMING** is a structural device whereby an outer story contains an inner story. It is especially useful with an outlandish or farfetched narrative, so that the outer narrator is in a way absolved of responsibility: The speaker of a Housman poem says, "I tell the tale that I heard told . . .".

Percy Bysshe Shelley's "Ozymandias" uses the relatively compact form of the sonnet:

> I met a traveller from an antique land
> Who said: Two vast and trunkless legs of stone
> Stand in the desert. Near them, on the sand,
> Half sunk, a shattered visage lies, whose frown,
> And wrinkled lip, and sneer of cold command,
> Tell that its sculptor well those passions read
> Which yet survive, stamped on these lifeless things,
> The hand that mocked them and the heart that fed;
> And on the pedestal these words appear:
> "My name is Ozymandias, king of kings:
> Look on my works, ye Mighty, and despair!"
> Nothing beside remains. Round the decay
> Of that colossal wreck, boundless and bare
> The lone and level sands stretch far away.

There are two frames: the innermost text is the two-line inscription beginning "My name"; the intermediate text begins "Two vast and trunkless legs" and ends, probably, when the poem ends (the punctuation is somewhat confusing). We start in the past ("met," "said"), then shift to the present for the traveler's story ("stand," "lies," "tell," "appear"), then, further inside, the inscription is in a sort of monumental present ("is") along with an imperative ("Look," "despair"). From then to the end, we are back in the traveler's virtual present.

It is unlikely that such elaborate execution would be required for a story less fantastic than "The Rime of the Ancient Mariner" or "Ozymandias." For many narratives, the relative proportion of approaches, in descending order, is probably (1) third-person past-tense; (2) first-person past-tense; (3) third-person present-tense; (4) first-person present-tense.

One can experiment with various approaches. Thomas Hardy's "I Look into My Glass" is a first-person present-tense meditation, beginning

> I look into my glass,
>   And view my wasting skin,
> And say, "Would God it came to pass
>   My heart had shrunk as thin!"

(The poem could be an ironic response to Shakespeare's Sonnet III: "Look in thy glass, and tell the face thou viewest/Now is the time that face should form another," which concerns a young person.)

Hardy's stanza can be transformed into three other permutations:

> I looked into my glass,
>   And viewed my wasting skin,
> And said, "Would God it came to pass
>   My heart had shrunk as thin!"...

> He looks into his glass,
>   And views his wasting skin,
> And says, "Would God it came to pass
>   My heart had shrunk as thin!"...

> He looked into his glass,
>   And viewed his wasting skin,
> And said, "Would God it came to pass
>   My heart had shrunk as thin!"...

One can compare these versions in terms of immediacy, vividness, and drama. The poem may be more lyrical than narrative, since it presents only a moment in time, but it does have a plot, after all. In the original version, the remaining stanzas justify the first and then present a dramatic turn, signaled by "but":

I look into my glass,
    And view my wasting skin,
And say, "Would God it came to pass
    My heart had shrunk as thin!"

For then, I, undistrest
    By hearts grown cold to me,
Could lonely wait my endless rest
    With equanimity.

But Time, to make me grieve,
    Part steals, lets part abide
And shakes this fragile frame at eve
    With throbbings of noontide.

In Hardy's fiction, incidentally, the narration is almost exclusively past-tense third-person-omniscient.

During the nineteenth century, there seemed to be an explosion of excess in many things, and by about 1900 there was a hypertrophy of decoration, rhetoric, filigree, and sheer bulk. In the first decade of the twentieth century Thomas Hardy and Charles Montagu Doughty produced multi-volume poems combining epic, drama, history, legend, and speculation. Throughout the same period, however, there were also suggestions of brevity and economy. During the 1840s, Edgar Allan Poe had perfected the art of the short story in several styles: detection, science fiction, horror, and ciphers. He is also given some credit for encouraging symbolist and imagist poems that were usually short. In fact, Poe argued, "I hold that a long poem does not exist. I maintain that the phrase, 'a long poem,' is simply a flat contradiction in terms."

Some American Civil War personages are celebrated for brevity of utterance. Abraham Lincoln's "Gettysburg Address," at fewer than three hundred words, is notably short, especially in a period of bloated oratory. Ulysses S. Grant's "No terms except unconditional and immediate surrender" led to his being given the nickname "Unconditional Surrender" (which matched his own first two initials). When William Tecumseh Sherman was suggested as a Republican presidential candidate in 1884, he declined as unambiguously and emphatically as possible: "I will not accept if nominated and will not serve if elected." Those twelve words – or some permutation of the same idea – may have fitted into the cheapest class of telegram.

These figures' contemporary, Henry David Thoreau, feinted in the direction of economy, but the best he could do was "Simplicity, simplicity, simplicity!" Surely, if he had really meant that, he would have said simply "Simplicity!" His heart may have been in the right place, but his head hardly was. How you say something should not contradict what you say. Consider, "Don't use no double negatives; take pains to never split infinitives."

Since the middle of the twentieth century, Ezra Pound and some of his adherents have made a fuss about an equation drawn from a German–Italian dictionary: *dichten = condensare*. That is, "to compose poetry is to condense." That could be a laudable motto, although it ought to be augmented and elaborated, since some poetry depends on expansion, so that *dichten = ampliare*. And it may matter that there are two separate and distinct German verbs spelled *dichten*. The one that Pound had in mind is related to Latin *dictāre* "to dictate," but the one that means "to condense" is related to German roots meaning "thicken, tighten, seal, or caulk." Pound could be a playful or imaginative translator, or you might say creatively ignorant mistranslator. He could write some great poetry, but he could also be an untrustworthy role-model, arguing for renovation and renewal but at the same time reverting to archaic or pseudo-archaic forms (which one wag called "Old Ezraic"). He campaigned on behalf of brevity but also worked for six decades on an eight hundred-page poem noted for some unconscionable *longueurs*.

For most good stories, the outcome is not only possible but probable; in the best stories, the outcome seems to be inevitable, even though we like to have the inevitable combined with surprise. Laurence Sterne's Tristram Shandy says,

> . . . I set no small store by myself upon this very account, that my reader has never yet been able to guess at any thing. And in this, Sir, I am of so nice and singular a humour, that if I thought you was able to form the least judgment or probable conjecture to yourself, of what was to come in the next page, – I would tear it out of my book.
>
> (*Tristram Shandy*, I.xxv).

Along with change, another principle of good stories is vivid contrast (as can be seen on any television series involving an "odd couple" of some sort, such as *Steptoe and Son* or its American cousin *Sanford and Son*). A few basic patterns provide the foundation of a great many popular novels, movies, and television series. One recurrent setup involves three men and one woman, either in the form of a family with three sons and one daughter (*The Sound and the Fury, The Catcher in the Rye, The Godfather*) or a quartet of friends variously related (*Third Rock from the Sun, Seinfeld, Frasier*). Another pattern presents two women against their environment, with the darker-haired woman somewhat dominant (*Xena – Warrior Princess, Two Fat Ladies, Absolutely Fabulous, Star Trek: Voyager*). The storyteller need not repeat what has succeeded before, but it would be a good idea to think about how certain situations seem to appeal.

Samuel Johnson (1709–1784), making fun of the monotony of a common verse form found in ballads and songs, improvised a trivial story, one version of which says:

I put my hat upon my head
And went into the strand.
There I met another man
Whose hat was in his hand.

This first-person past-tense example shows that a trifling contrast – between having a hat on your head versus in your hand – hardly makes for interesting reading, except as a joke. Stories often provoke questions in listeners, but "So what?" should not be answered "So nothing." (Maybe one should reserve judgment, since where your hat is could be a code, but, with the information given in Johnson's four lines, the story generates little interest. The rhythm is likewise monotonous, and even the grammar is predictable, with a complete clause in practically every line. And the rhyming monosyllables at the end of every line are nouns. (By way of contrast, the rhyming pairs in Hardy's "I Look into My Glass" are all different parts of speech.)

Some nursery rhymes are small stories: "Mary had a little lamb"; "Humpty Dumpty sat on a wall"; "Little Jack Horner/Sat in a corner"; "Jack Sprat could eat no fat"; "Little Miss Muffet sat on a tuffet"; "Georgie Porgie, puddin' and pie, /Kissed the girls and made them cry"; "The itsy bitsy spider/Climbed up the water spout." These are common activities; three of them, in fact, involve sitting.

Some familiar narrative poems tell a third-person past-tense story, which may be completely imaginary or based on something actual, and then interpret the moral meaning of the story, just in case the reader has failed to pay attention. (The words *story* and *history* are related.) Felicia Hemans's most celebrated poem, "Casabianca," gives an account of an incident that happened on board a large French warship during the Battle of the Nile in 1798 involving a boy, possibly as young as ten, named Giocante Casabianca: first the dramatic nocturnal scene, gaining interest from the contrast of a child amid a violent military setting as well as the elementary contrast of fire and water:

The boy stood on the burning deck
Whence all but he had fled;
The flame that lit the battle's wreck
Shone round him o'er the dead.

Yet beautiful and bright he stood,
As born to rule the storm;
A creature of heroic blood,
A proud, though childlike form.

The flames rolled on – he would not go
Without his father's word;
That father, faint in death below,
His voice no longer heard.

He called aloud – "Say, father, say,
If yet my task is done?"
He knew not that the chieftain lay
Unconscious of his son.

"Speak, father!" once again he cried,
"If I may yet be gone!"
And but the booming shots replied,
And fast the flames rolled on.

Upon his brow he felt their breath,
And in his waving hair,
And looked from that lone post of death
In still, yet brave despair.

And shouted but once more aloud,
"My father! must I stay?"

While o'er him fast, through sail and shroud,
The wreathing fires made way.

They wrapt the ship in splendor wild,
They caught the flag on high,
And streamed above the gallant child,
Like banners in the sky.

There came a burst of thunder sound –
The boy – oh! where was he?
Ask of the winds that far around
With fragments strewed the sea! –

With mast, and helm, and pennon fair
That well had borne their part –
But the noblest thing that perished there
Was that young, faithful heart.

The advice in *Alice in Wonderland* – "Begin at the beginning and go on till you come to the end: then stop" – makes sense, but few shapely stories follow that sequence. Hemans's narrative begins almost at the end of an episode: the first verb is in the past tense ("stood") but the second is in the past perfect, which indicates an *earlier* past time ("had fled"). The sequence of incidents in the poem is not the same as the sequence in history, in which most of the sailors flee or die *before* the boy stands on the burning deck. A plain recital of the incident would begin in an indefinite past, leading up to the Battle of the Nile, then mention that the commander of the French ship instructs his young son to stay on deck, then describe the death of the commander and the fleeing of others, and only near the end of the account say, "The boy stood . . ." (Historically, the incident took place on August 1, 1798. Sunset at that latitude was about eight in the evening, and the ship exploded about two hours later.)

After the vivid introduction, Hemans's narrator provides interpretation:

Yet beautiful and bright he stood,
As born to rule the storm;
A creature of heroic blood,
A proud, though childlike form.

FABLES are narratives that come with an explicit moral message, often shamelessly spelled out as "the moral of this story..." Sophisticated modern readers may prefer not to be given such editorial matter with their news, but sometimes everybody needs guidance. Conceivably, given the extreme circumstances, the lesson of "Casabianca" could be something like "Don't take children along on warships during combat," "Don't just blindly obey orders," or "Change with changing conditions." The poem continues with more details about the boy's reason for staying on his post:

> The flames roll'd on ... he would not go
> Without his father's word;
> That father, faint in death below,
> His voice no longer heard.

At this point, as in many stories, the narrator discloses something that a character does not know:

> He call'd aloud ... "Say, father, say
> If yet my task is done!"
> He knew not that the chieftain lay
> Unconscious of his son ...

Then interpretation is added to the account of the final catastrophic explosion:

> But the noblest thing which perished there
> Was that young faithful heart.

Hemans's poem dates from 1826. Within fifty years, established as a favorite recitation piece, it appears in *Tom Sawyer* (1876), alongside Byron's "The Destruction of Sennacherib," which is likewise a third-person past-tense narrative about war in an exotic setting:

> The Assyrian came down like the wolf on the fold,
> And his cohorts were gleaming in purple and gold;
> And the sheen of their spears was like stars on the sea,
> When the blue wave rolls nightly on deep Galilee.

> Like the leaves of the forest when summer is green,
> That host with their banners at sunset were seen:
> Like the leaves of the forest when autumn hath blown,
> That host on the morrow lay withered and strown.

For the Angel of Death spread his wings on the blast,
And breathed in the face of the foe as he passed:
And the eyes of the sleepers waxed deadly and chill,
And their hearts but once heaved, and for ever grew still!

And there lay the steed with his nostrils all wide,
But through it there rolled not the breath of his pride:
And the foam of his gasping lay white on the turf,
And cold as the spray of the rock-beating surf.

And there lay the rider distorted and pale,
With the dew on his brow and the rust on his mail;
And the tents were all silent, the banners alone,
The lances unlifted, the trumpet unblown.

And the widows of Ashur are loud in their wail,
And the idols are broke in the temple of Baal;
And the might of the Gentile, unsmote by the sword,
Hath melted like snow in the glance of the Lord!

(After a past-tense account of the historical episode that II Kings recounts in a few sentences, Byron ends with a present and perfect perfect scene: "are . . . are . . . hath melted." The poem remained familiar enough to be slightly misquoted at the beginning of Tom Clancy's *The Sum of All Fears* (1991): "'Like a wolf on the fold.' In recounting the Syrian attack on the Israeli-held Golan Heights at 1400 local time on Saturday, October 6th, 1973, most commentators automatically recalled Lord Byron's famous line.")

Hemans's combination of the past and the past perfect is common in stories ("I *sat* in the waiting room; I *had been* there for two hours"). Ordinary speech routinely thus combines past and past perfect, as well as present and present perfect ("The UK *uses* a decimal currency; it *has done* so since 1971"). One rarely sees the future and future perfect, but it is grammatical. ("I *will shop* on Thursday, because by then I *will have run* out of groceries.) Poems, usually more compact than prose, can change tenses with relative freedom, especially between simple past and simple present.

Sir Walter Scott's lines from the narrative poem *Marmion* begin in the present or present perfect and shift to the past:

Oh, young Lochinvar *is come* out of the west,
Through all the wide Border his steed *was* the best . . .

("Is come" may be an archaic version of "has come," the present perfect tense.) Another well-known narrative from Scott combines the past perfect with the simple past:

> The stag at eve *had drunk* his fill,
> Where *danced* the moon on Monan's rill,
> And deep his midnight lair *had made*
> In lone Glenartney's hazel shade;
> But when the sun his beacon red
> *Had kindled* on Benvoirlich's head,
> The deep-mouthed bloodhound's heavy bay
> *Resounded* up the rocky way . . .
>
> (*The Lady of the Lake*, Canto First)

Except for the occasional formulaic "I sing" or "sing me," familiar classic **EPICS**, such as Homer's *Iliad* and *Odyssey* and Virgil's *Aeneid*, almost exclusively use a third-person past-tense format for large stories that have to do with important events in history or myth (Ezra Pound called epic "a poem containing history"). In imitation of certain features of such epics, Henry Wadsworth Longfellow produced long narrative poems concerning events in America in the seventeenth and eighteenth centuries. *The Courtship of Miles Standish* begins in the past and stays there:

> In the Old Colony days, in Plymouth the land of the Pilgrims
> To and fro in a room of his simple and primitive dwelling,
> Clad in doublet and hose, and boots of Cordovan leather,
> *Strode*, with a martial air, Miles Standish the Puritan Captain.

Evangeline begins with a short present-tense prologue ("This *is* the forest primeval") but soon launches its story proper in the past tense:

> In the Acadian land, on the shores of the Basin of Minas,
> Distant, secluded, still, the little village of Grand-Pré
> *Lay* in the fruitful valley. Vast meadows *stretched* to the eastward,
> Giving the village its name, and pasture to flocks without number.

The present tense, usually more vivid and immediate than the past, may work well for short spells, but most stories, as self-conscious accounts of something that has already happened, are better off in the past tense. The present tense may strain credibility, and it wears out its welcome pretty fast. Thayer's "Casey at the Bat" uses the conventional third-person past-tense approach for forty-four of its fifty-two lines (beginning "The outlook *was*n't brilliant...") but shifts to the present in the final eight lines: "He *pounds* with cruel violence his bat upon the plate..." This is sometimes called the "historical present," as in summaries that say things like "Napoleon meets his final defeat at Waterloo in June of 1815..."

Gerard Manley Hopkins's "The Windhover" begins in the past ("I caught") but moves to the present ("the fire that breaks"); complementarily, William Butler Yeats's "Leda and the Swan" begins in the present ("He holds") but moves to the past ("Did she put on his Knowledge...?"):

I caught this morning morning's minion,
    kingdom of daylight's dauphin,
    dapple-dáwn-drawn Falcon, in his riding
Of the rólling level úndernéath him steady
    áir, and stríding
High there, how he rung upon the rein of
    a wimpling wing

In his ecstasy! then off, off forth on a swing,
    As a skate's heel sweeps smooth on a bow-
    bend: the hurl and gliding
Rebuffed the big wind. My heart in hiding
Stirred for a bird, – the achieve of, the
    mastery of the thing!

Brute beauty and valour and act, oh, air,
    pride, plume, here
    Buckle! AND the fire that breaks from
    thee then, a billion
Times told lovelier, more dangerous,
    O my chevalier!
    No wónder of it: shéer plód makes plóugh
    down sillion
Shine, and blue-bleak embers, ah my dear,
    Fall, gáll themsélves, and gásh góld-
    vermílion.

A sudden blow: the great wings beating still
Above the staggering girl, her thighs caressed
By the dark webs, her nape caught in his bill,
He holds her helpless breast upon his breast.

How can those terrified vague fingers push
The feathered glory from her loosening
    thighs?
And how can body, laid in that white rush,
But feel the strange heart beating where it
    lies?

A shudder in the loins engenders there
The broken wall, the burning roof and tower
And Agamemnon dead.
                                Being so caught up,
So mastered by the brute blood of the air,
Did she put on his knowledge with his power
Before the indifferent beak could let her drop?

Both poems are **SONNETS** – Italian and **ANGLO–ITALIAN** – and both concern a god and a bird. The fluctuating tenses emphasize the extreme drama, with one poem reverting to exclamations, the other to questions. Yeats's present-tense beginning puts the reader inside the painting, with the extreme action going on *now*. The questions in the second quatrain are also in the present, as though actively seeking an answer. The questions, however, are rhetorical that is, the answer is negative. *No*, the fingers *cannot* push, and body *cannot* help feeling the strange heart. The question at the end of the poem is in the past, and it is not clear that it is rhetorical. It may be, instead, a genuine question to which we still seek an answer. And we care, because Leda represents humanity, caught in a violent struggle between the divine and the animal.

The three stanzas of Thomas Hardy's "Drummer Hodge" cover all the main tenses, beginning with the present ("They throw"), moving to the past ("Young Hodge the Drummer never knew"), and ending in the future ("Yet portion of that unknown plain/Will Hodge forever be").

> They throw in Drummer Hodge, to rest
>   Uncoffined – just as found:
> His landmark is a kopje-crest
>   That breaks the veldt around;
> And foreign constellations west
>   Each night above his mound.
>
> Young Hodge the Drummer never knew –
>   Fresh from his Wessex home –
> The meaning of the broad Karoo,
>   The Bush, the dusty loam,
> And why uprose to nightly view
>   Strange stars amid the gloam.
>
> Yet portion of that unknown plain
>   Will Hodge forever be;
> His homely Northern breast and brain
>   Grow to some Southern tree,
> And strange-eyed constellation reign
>   His stars eternally.

As with the "But" that begins the last of three stanzas of "I Look into My Glass," the "Yet" that begins the last stanza here signals the kind of reversal or contrast that adds excitement and interest to a work. (In both Italian and English sonnets, a common feature is the **VOLTA**, which marks the pivot or turning point – usually in the ninth line of the Italian and the ninth or thirteenth of the English – and in many cases the volta can be spotted by a "but" or "yet." In many of Petrarch's sonnets in Italian, the ninth line begins *ma*, "yet.")

Hardy's "At Castle Boterel" presents a chaotic arrangement of tenses: beginning in an anecdotal present ("As I drive"), then presenting a recollected past scene but in the present tense ("We climb the road"), then unaccountably moving to the past perfect ("We had just alighted"), and then a jumble of past, present, and future:

> As I drive to the junction of lane and highway,
>   And the drizzle bedrenches the waggonette,
> I look behind at the fading byway,
>   And see on its slope, now glistening wet,
>   Distinctly yet
>
> Myself and a girlish form benighted
>   In dry March weather. We climb the road
> Beside a chaise. We had just alighted
>   To ease the sturdy pony's load
>   When he sighed and slowed.
>
> What we did as we climbed, and what we talked of
>   Matters not much, nor to what it led,
> Something that life will not be balked of
>   Without rude reason till hope is dead,
>   And feeling fled.
>
> It filled but a minute. But was there ever
>   A time of such quality, since or before,
> In that hill's story? To one mind never,
>   Though it has been climbed, foot-swift, foot-sore,
>   By thousands more.
>
> Primaeval rocks form the road's steep border,
>   And much have they faced there, first and last,
> Of the transitory in Earth's long order;
>   But what they record in colour and cast
>   Is – that we two passed.
>
> And to me, though Time's unflinching rigour,
>   In mindless rote, has ruled from sight
> The substance now, one phantom figure
>   Remains on the slope, as when that night
>   Saw us alight.

I look and see it there, shrinking, shrinking,
  I look back at it amid the rain
For the very last time; for my sand is sinking,
  And I shall traverse old love's domain
    Never again.

(Here the "but" seems buried around the mid-point, in stanza four.)

This poem is in a set of twenty-one, all in different verse forms, called *Poems of 1912–13*, which Hardy wrote just after the death of his first wife, Emma, toward the end of 1912. Their marriage had long been troubled, and there seems to have been profound bitterness on both sides. But all the trouble and bitterness fell away as soon as she had died, and Hardy's memories went back forty years to their original meeting in Boscastle, on the coast of Cornwall. (The Cornish name is Kastell Boterel.) Travel was impossible in the winter season after her death, but Hardy made a pilgrimage back to Boscastle in the spring of 1913.

The poem begins in a conventional present, "As I drive . . ." The speaker says, "I . . . see," which represents an act of visualizing, after which *what* he sees is also in the present tense: "We climb the road . . ." Looking back forty years, he imagines that what happened is still somehow present, so that the poem offers what might be called a "past present" along with a "present present." Here the poem makes a peculiar jump to the past perfect tense ("We had just alighted") and then abruptly to a simple past ("When he sighed and slowed . . ."). Then, in a single sentence, comes a succession of past ("we did"), present ("Matters"), and future ("will not be balked of"), even touching a sort of "future present" ("till hope is dead"). Such turbulence is a reminder that "emotion" contains "motion," and that the roots of "emotion," according to the *Oxford English Dictionary*, include "civil unrest, public commotion . . . agitation of mind, excited mental state . . . movement, disturbance . . . strong feelings, passion." From the viewpoint of the management of tenses, "At Castle Boterel" must hold a record for complication.

Much of Keats's "The Eve of Saint Agnes," a fanciful medieval romance set hundreds of years before the poet's own time, sticks only sporadically to the third-person past-tense pattern that one may expect. But the poem also veers into a moment of first-person plural that seems to include writer and reader ("These let *us* wish away") and a moment of second-person imperative in which the narrator talks to a character ("Now prepare, /Young Porphyro, for gazing on that bed") in the manner of Homer who, although normally an omniscient narrator, would occasionally directly address Patroclus or another character, with a peculiarly intimate effect. Throughout "The Eve of Saint Agnes," the tenses fluctuate dizzily between past and present in ways that may suggest a moving camera changing position and focal length for variety, such as that between close-ups and long shots. It seems difficult, however, to justify these changes on the basis of striving for vividness, since some gorgeous passages are in the past tense; the management of point of view is lively but inconsistent. Some such fluctuations may have the effect of involving the reader in the texture of the poem.

The first three Spenserian stanzas illustrate such fluctuation:

I.

ST. AGNES' Eve – Ah, bitter chill it was!
The owl, for all his feathers, was a-cold;
The hare limp'd trembling through the frozen grass,
And silent was the flock in woolly fold:
Numb were the Beadsman's fingers, while he told
His rosary, and while his frosted breath,
Like pious incense from a censer old,
Seem'd taking flight for heaven, without a death,
Past the sweet Virgin's picture, while his prayer he saith.

II.

His prayer he saith, this patient, holy man;
Then takes his lamp, and riseth from his knees,
And back returneth, meagre, barefoot, wan,
Along the chapel aisle by slow degrees:
The sculptur'd dead, on each side, seem to freeze,
Emprison'd in black, purgatorial rails:
Knights, ladies, praying in dumb orat'ries,
He passeth by; and his weak spirit fails
To think how they may ache in icy hoods and mails.

III.

Northward he turneth through a little door,
And scarce three steps, ere Music's golden tongue
Flatter'd to tears this aged man and poor;

> But no – already had his deathbell rung;
> The joys of all his life were said and sung:
> His was harsh penance on St. Agnes' Eve:
> Another way he went, and soon among
> Rough ashes sat he for his soul's reprieve,
> And all night kept awake, for sinners' sake to grieve.

(The –*th* forms, such as "saith" and "turneth," are archaic present-tense verbs, but the poem also offers the standard form "fails." The third stanza mixes such present forms with simple past ("flatter'd," "was," "sat," "kept") and past perfect ("had... rung").

Charles Montagu Doughty's *The Dawn in Britain* is worth looking at for its peculiar diction and punctuation; some readers affirm that the style can be affecting:

> Esla is priestess, of the moon, in Sena;
> And daughter to a king of Gaul's mainland.
> Her garments, long, up-gathered, of white lawn;
> Now, on this shore, sweet maiden, she paced down:
> So skips, from stone, on her white feet, to stone... (Book IX)

The frequent commas make the utterance seem breathless, and the fluctuations of tense almost suggest that time does not matter. We are taken along from present ("is") through an elliptical passage ("Her garments, long, up-gathered, of white lawn") to a past form ("paced") before returning to a brilliantly executed present activity ("So skips, from stone, on her white feet, to stone"), in which the interruption of "on her white feet" mimics the iambic rhythm of skipping. Here, as elsewhere, Doughty uses "now" with a past-tense form, meaning "at this time" past or present, not just the usual meaning of "at this present time." (One subsidiary meaning of "now" given by *The Oxford English Dictionary* is "At this time; at the time spoken of or referred to; then, next, by that time; at this point. Also more generally: over or during the period under discussion.")

Doughty (1843–1926) belonged to a generation that witnessed much turbulence in the world of affairs and even a good deal of turbulence in English language and literature. Doughty's notable contemporaries in-clude Wilfrid Scawen Blunt (1840–1922), Thomas Hardy (1840–1928), Robert Bridges (1844–1930), and Gerard Manley Hopkins (1844–1889).

Somewhat like Hardy, Doughty is known for prose written mostly in the nineteenth century and poetry written mostly in the twentieth. In Doughty's case, the prose work is *Travels in Arabia Deserta* (1888); in Hardy's, the prose work consists of about fifty stories and fourteen novels, at least five of which rank as masterpieces. During the first decade of the twentieth century, Hardy and Doughty both worked on ambitious historical poems of epic scope: Hardy's *The Dynasts* (1904–1908) and Doughty's *The Dawn in Britain* (1906). Doughty was not the only member of his generation to be known for peculiarities of spelling, punctuation, diction, and versification, but his case is extreme, especially in the erratic-seeming management of tenses, as shown in a further passage:

> Lighted one Tertius, servant to the quæstor,
> (His *tabellarius*) mongst the Gaulish horse;)
> One, whom had raging spear of Antethrigus
> Hurt. Weary after battle; he, with few,
> Which, scaped to horse, had all that night ridden forth,
> Towards rising stars. He lights, by the brook Maran;
> To rest, and wash his angry wound and bind.
> But feeling come, with trembling, the cold death;
> Rent Tertius, hastily, roll of his account:
> And part, (on Jovis Vindex, calling !) binds
> He, round light scabbard of his horseman's glaive;
> And wrote, *Ex clade Romanorum, VER.*
> So cast, in Maran's stream, his dying hand! (Book XVII)

The tenses move from past ("Lighted") to the past perfect ("had . . . Hurt" and "had . . . ridden"), then suddenly to the present ("lights"), then to fluctuating tenses in one sentence ("Rent," "binds," "wrote," "cast"). Whatever the tense, most of the verbs describe physical action; the mixing of tenses almost suggests that tense itself does not much matter, and that the "time" of the poem is indifferent to shallow concepts of past and present. (If one takes the time to follow the maze of tenses, incidental puzzles seem to matter less. Ver and Maran are rivers in Hertfordshire; "quæstor" = "paymaster"; *tabellarius* = "letter-carrier"; Antethrigus = ruler of an Iron Age tribe; "Jovis Vindex" = "Jove the Protector"; "glaive" = "sword"; *Ex clade Romanorum* = "out of the destruction of the Romans.")

Didactic poems openly teach a lesson, either moral or intellectual or both. The children's verse "One, two, /Buckle your shoe" teaches intellectual lessons (how to count) in its odd-numbered lines and moral lessons (how to be tidy) in its even-numbered lines. Such lessons need to be memorable, and they ought to be true. "Thirty days hath September" is a good didactic poem; "Thirty days hath December" is not. (Although it may be a perfectly good poem about somebody with limited intelligence or faulty memory.) Often such poems present a vivid example of some human truth and then discuss the situation or problem. Robert Frost's "Provide, Provide" can be interpreted as a poem of character disguised as a didactic poem teaching a moral lesson. It has some imperative moments ("Make the whole stock exchange your own!"), which resemble sentiments in William Butler Yeats's "Vacillation" ("Get all the gold and silver that you can"). Frost's poem provides a memorable example:

> The witch that came (the withered hag)
> To wash the steps with pail and rag,
> Was once the beauty Abishag...

Then draws a tentative conclusion:

> Too many fall from great and good
> For you to doubt the likelihood.

The poem ceases to be a straight didactic lesson, since it moves on to an injunction – "Die early" – that will seem objectionable to many, in a way that "Thirty days hath September" would not be objectionable. At this point, the texture of the poem changes, although the rhythm, meter, and rhyme scheme stay the same. The heavily end-stopped lines give way to fluent enjambments, and the heavy reliance on rhyming nouns gives way to a good deal of variation, with rhyme words forming the patterns verb-adjective-pronoun, verb-noun-adjective, and verb (past participle)-noun-verb (imperative):

> Better to go down dignified
> With boughten friendship at your side
> Than none at all. Provide, provide!

What begins as a single-celled narrative telling the story of an interesting fall from a high to a low position becomes a meditation on what anyone might do to thwart fate. The poem keeps its distance, even so, never introducing an overtly first-person voice to do the meditating. Instead of a didactic poem, "Provide, Provide" offers an account of the state of mind of someone seeking order amid decline and chaos. One tipoff to an extreme state may be the archaic "boughten," not something anyone would say in normal circumstances.

The standard Latin versions of Aesop's fables carried the formula: "Haec Fabula Docet." "This story teaches." The American writer Ambrose Bierce produced a poem with the title "Haec Fabula Docet":

A rat who'd gorged a box of bane
And suffered an internal pain,
Came from his hole to die (the label
Required it if the rat were able)
And found outside his habitat
A limpid stream. Of bane and rat
'Twas all unconscious; in the sun
It ran and prattled just for fun.
Keen to allay his inward throes,
The beast immersed his filthy nose
And drank – then, bloated by the stream,
And filled with superheated steam,
Exploded with a rascal smell,
Remarking, as his fragments fell
Astonished in the brook: "I'm thinking
This water's damned unwholesome drinking!"

Robert Frost, who was about thirty years younger than Bierce, also titled a poem "Haec Fabula Docet." It ends,

All those who try to go it sole alone,
Too proud to be beholden for relief,
Are absolutely sure to come to grief.

The design or plot of such didactic poems may involve a past element ("The witch that *came*") along with a present generalization ("Too many *fall*"). The didactic also relies fairly often on the imperative ("Provide!" "Buckle your shoe").

Such overtly educational texts might have grown in popularity in response to the spread of public education throughout the English-speaking world during the nineteenth century. By 1830 or so, a number of general-appeal magazines appeared, with stories, poems, puzzles, and features dealing with self-improvement. The new generations of literates were hungry for entertainment and for instruction, and evidently for entertainment that also instructed. At about the same time, a group of writers reached maturity, and they were employed as teachers (as was Longfellow), preachers, lecturers, journalists, and other sorts of entertainer–instructor. Some of them – known sometimes as "Schoolroom Poets" – were unembarrassed about teaching. Longfellow taught lessons about interesting personages and episodes in American history, such as the Pilgrims, the Acadians, the Native Americans, and Revolutionary War heroes; one of his best-known portraits gives a melodramatic present-tense account of a familiar figure in many towns throughout the nineteenth century:

> Under a spreading chestnut tree
>   The village smithy stands;
> The smith, a mighty man is he,
>   With large and sinewy hands;
> And the muscles of his brawny arms
>   Are strong as iron bands.
>
> His hair is crisp, and black, and long,
>   His face is like the tan;
> His brow is wet with honest sweat,
>   He earns whate'er he can,
> And looks the whole world in the face,
>   For he owes not any man.

Longfellow felt free to include his reader in the second person:

> Week in, week out, from morn till night,
>   You can hear his bellows blow;
> You can hear him swing his heavy sledge
>   With measured beat and slow,
> Like a sexton ringing the village bell,
>   When the evening sun is low.

And children coming home from school
  Look in at the open door;
They love to see the flaming forge,
  And hear the bellows roar,
And watch the burning sparks that fly
  Like chaff from a threshing-floor.

He goes on Sunday to the church,
  And sits among his boys;
He hears the parson pray and preach,
  He hears his daughter's voice,
Singing in the village choir,
  And it makes his heart rejoice.

It sounds to him like her mother's voice,
  Singing in Paradise!
He needs must think of her once more,
  How in the grave she lies;
And with his hard, rough hand he wipes
  A tear out of his eyes.

Toiling, – rejoicing, – sorrowing,
  Onward through life he goes;
Each morning sees some task begin,
  Each evening sees it close;
Something attempted, something done,
  Has earned a night's repose.

Then, at the end, in another second-person maneuver, the poet addresses the smith himself with the archaic singular "thou" and openly thanks him for the lesson, even including a first-person presence ("my"):

Thanks, thanks to thee, my worthy friend,
  For the lesson thou hast taught!
Thus at the flaming forge of life
  Our fortunes must be wrought;
Thus on its sounding anvil shaped
  Each burning deed and thought!

Obeying a similar good-hearted impulse, John Greenleaf Whittier (who was born in 1807, as was Longfellow) could in "Maud Muller" narrate a rather rough-hewn story and shamelessly draw a moral:

> Maud Muller, on a summer's day,
> Raked the meadows sweet with hay.
>
> Beneath her torn hat glowed the wealth
> Of simple beauty and rustic health.
>
> Singing, she wrought, and her merry glee
> The mock-bird echoed from his tree.
>
> But, when she glanced to the far-off town,
> White from its hill-slope looking down,
>
> The sweet song died, and a vague unrest
> And a nameless longing filled her breast –
>
> A wish, that she hardly dared to own,
> For something better than she had known.
>
> The Judge rode slowly down the lane,
> Smoothing his horse's chestnut mane.
>
> He drew his bridle in the shade
> Of the apple-trees, to greet the maid,
>
> And ask a draught from the spring that flowed
> Through the meadow across the road.
>
> She stooped where the cool spring bubbled up,
> And filled for him her small tin cup,
>
> And blushed as she gave it, looking down
> On her feet so bare, and her tattered gown.
>
> "Thanks!" said the Judge, "a sweeter draught
> From a fairer hand was never quaffed."
>
> He spoke of the grass and flowers and trees,
> Of the singing birds and the humming bees;
>
> Then talked of the haying, and wondered whether
> The cloud in the west would bring foul weather.

And Maud forgot her briar-torn gown,
And her graceful ankles bare and brown;

And listened, while a pleasant surprise
Looked from her long-lashed hazel eyes.

At last, like one who for delay
Seeks a vain excuse, he rode away,

Maud Muller looked and sighed: "Ah, me!
That I the Judge's bride might be!

"He would dress me up in silks so fine,
And praise and toast me at his wine.

"My father should wear a broadcloth coat;
My brother should sail a painted boat.

"I'd dress my mother so grand and gay,
And the baby should have a new toy each day.

"And I'd feed the hungry and clothe the poor,
And all should bless me who left our door."

The Judge looked back as he climbed the hill,
And saw Maud Muller standing still.

"A form more fair, a face more sweet,
Ne'er hath it been my lot to meet.

"And her modest answer and graceful air
Show her wise and good as she is fair.

"Would she were mine, and I to-day,
Like her, a harvester of hay:

"No doubtful balance of rights and wrongs,
Nor weary lawyers with endless tongues,

"But low of cattle, and song of birds,
And health, and quiet, and loving words."

But he thought of his sisters, proud and cold,
And his mother, vain of her rank and gold.

So, closing his heart, the Judge rode on,
And Maud was left in the field alone.

But the lawyers smiled that afternoon,
When he hummed in court an old love-tune;

And the young girl mused beside the well,
Till the rain on the unraked clover fell.

He wedded a wife of richest dower,
Who lived for fashion, as he for power.

Yet oft, in his marble hearth's bright glow,
He watched a picture come and go:

And sweet Maud Muller's hazel eyes
Looked out in their innocent surprise.

Oft when the wine in his glass was red,
He longed for the wayside well instead;

And closed his eyes on his garnished rooms,
To dream of meadows and clover-blooms.

And the proud man sighed, with a secret pain,
"Ah, that I were free again!

"Free as when I rode that day,
Where the barefoot maiden raked her hay."

She wedded a man unlearned and poor,
And many children played round her door.

But care and sorrow, and child-birth pain,
Left their traces on heart and brain.

And oft, when the summer sun shone hot
On the new-mown hay in the meadow lot,

And she heard the little spring brook fall
Over the roadside, through the wall,

In the shade of the apple-tree again
She saw a rider draw his rein,

And, gazing down with timid grace,
She felt his pleased eyes read her face.

Sometimes her narrow kitchen walls
Stretched away into stately halls;

The weary wheel to a spinnet turned,
The tallow candle an astral burned;

And for him who sat by the chimney lug,
Dozing and grumbling o'er pipe and mug,

A manly form at her side she saw,
And joy was duty and love was law.

Then she took up her burden of life again,
Saying only, "It might have been."

Alas for maiden, alas for Judge,
For rich repiner and household drudge!

God pity them both! and pity us all,
Who vainly the dreams of youth recall;

For of all sad words of tongue or pen,
The saddest are these: "It might have been!"

Ah, well! for us all some sweet hope lies
Deeply buried from human eyes;

And, in the hereafter, angels may
Roll the stone from its grave away!

(A spinnet or spinet is a small keyboard instrument; an astral is a kind of star-shaped oil lamp; lug is the cheek or side of a fireplace.) Most of the narration is in the simple past tense, with an occasional past perfect to fill in the earlier past ("had known"). Maud's fantasies are also in a simple past tense, as when she imagines her spinning wheel and tallow candle being replaced by a household musical instrument and a fancier oil-burning fixture. At the end, the poet introduces a present-tense generalization ("are these"), the first-person plural "us," and the subjunctive modals "might" and "may" to widen the scope of the simple narrative.

The one writer who resisted the temptation to teach and preach was Edgar Allan Poe, who was two years younger than Longfellow and Whittier. Poe labored brilliantly in the service of one idea: that the aim of poetry was the creation of beauty, and that it had nothing to do with the good and the true.

The narratives of the poor village blacksmith and the poor country girl are linear, in a way that may earn the label "sentimental" or "melodramatic." The contrasts are offered without much nuance, subtlety, irony, complication, or depth (though one may justifiably feel that Whittier's has a little more than Longfellow's). Such stories, as with most beast fables like Aesop's, lend themselves to easy moralizing. As Bierce demonstrated, however, there is room for humor, as in the free-verse "The Fatal Glass Of Beer," made famous in a short film by W. C. Fields in 1933:

There was once a poor boy
And he left his country home
And he came to the city to look for work.

He promised his ma and pa
He would lead a civilized life
And always shun the fatal curse of drink.

Once in the city
He got a situation in a quarry
And there he made the acquaintance of some college students.

He little thought they were demons
For they wore the best of clothes
But the clothes do not always make the gentleman.

They tempted him to drink
And they said he was a coward
And at last he took the fatal glass of beer.

When he seen what he had did
He dashed the glass upon the floor
And staggered through the door with delirium tremens.

Once upon the sidewalk
He met a Salvation Army girl
And with one kick he broke her tambourine

When she seen what he had did
She placed a mark upon his brow
With a kick she'd learned before she was converted

Now, as a moral to young men
Who come down to the city
Don't drink that fatal glass of beer

And don't go around breaking other people's tambourines.

It may be unfair to leave Longfellow as the simple-hearted adherent of
low-level moralizing, since he was a very learned and very original poet,
with impressive technical mastery and a wide range of foreign languages.
And he was interested in complex stories with twists and turns, such as
the Salem witchcraft trials in his *Giles Corey*, in which he developed a
dramatic version of New England speech that may prefigure Robert
Frost's diction. One of the *Tales of a Wayside Inn* involves a gruesome
irony:

The Spanish Jew's Tale: Azrael

King Solomon, before his palace gate
At evening, on the pavement tessellate
Was walking with a stranger from the East,
Arrayed in rich attire as for a feast,
The mighty Runjeet-Sing, a learned man,
And Rajah of the realms of Hindostan.
And as they walked the guest became aware
Of a white figure in the twilight air,
Gazing intent, as one who with surprise
His form and features seemed to recognize;
And in a whisper to the king he said:
"What is yon shape, that, pallid as the dead,
Is watching me, as if he sought to trace
In the dim light the features of my face?"
The king looked, and replied: "I know him well;
It is the Angel men call Azrael,
'Tis the Death Angel; what hast thou to fear?"
And the guest answered: "Lest he should come near,
And speak to me, and take away my breath!
Save me from Azrael, save me from death!
O king, that hast dominion o'er the wind,
Bid it arise and bear me hence to Ind."

The king gazed upward at the cloudless sky,
Whispered a word, and raised his hand on high,
And lo! the signet-ring of chrysoprase
On his uplifted finger seemed to blaze
With hidden fire, and rushing from the west
There came a mighty wind, and seized the guest
And lifted him from earth, and on they passed,
His shining garments streaming in the blast,
A silken banner o'er the walls upreared,
A purple cloud, that gleamed and disappeared.
Then said the Angel, smiling: "If this man
Be Rajah Runjeet-Sing of Hindostan,
Thou hast done well in listening to his prayer;
I was upon my way to seek him there."

This story has Talmudic antecedents:

There were two Cushites that attended on King Solomon, Elichoreph and Achiyah, sons of Shisha, who were scribes of Solomon.

One day, Solomon noticed that the Angel of Death looked sad. Solomon asked him: Why are you sad? He replied: Because they have demanded from me the two Cushites that dwell here. Solomon had demons take them to the city of Luz [a legendary city where no one dies]. However, as soon as they reached the gates of Luz, they died. The next day, Solomon noticed that the Angel of Death was happy. He asked him: Why are you so happy? He replied: Because you sent them to the very place where they were supposed to die. (Sukkah 53a)

A similar twist occurs in a tale recounted in a play by Somerset Maugham:

There was a merchant in Bagdad who sent his servant to market to buy provisions and in a little while the servant came back, white and trembling, and said, Master, just now when I was in the marketplace I was jostled by a woman in the crowd and when I turned I saw it was Death that jostled me. She looked at me and made a threatening gesture, now, lend me your horse, and I will ride away from this city and avoid my fate. I will go to Samarra and there Death will not find me. The merchant lent him his horse, and the servant mounted it, and he dug his spurs in its flanks and as fast as the horse could gallop he went.

Then the merchant went down to the marketplace and he saw me standing in the crowd and he came to me and said, Why did you make a threating gesture to my servant when you saw him this morning? That was not a threatening gesture, I said, it was only a start of surprise. I was astonished to see him in Bagdad, for I had an appointment with him tonight in Samarra.

This version, in turn, explains the title of John O'Hara's first novel, *Appointment in Samarra*.

There was a reaction against the Schoolroom Poets even when they were alive in the nineteenth century, but we have never satisfactorily solved the problem of how to tell a story without somehow also suggesting a moral lesson. If we have learned anything, it is that explicit moral explanations are unnecessary. Leave the reader something to do; let the reader be active and not passive.

2 The Arts of Character

Although the foregoing chapter concentrated on plots of action, we could hardly avoid meeting characters: Giocante Casabianca standing on a burning deck, young Lochinvar coming out of the west, Miles Standish striding militarily, mighty Casey striking out, Drummer Hodge in his humble grave, Young Porphyro preparing to gaze, Esla the priestess of the moon skipping, Ozymandias bragging, an Ancient Mariner stopping one of three, a village blacksmith setting a good example, Maud Muller raking hay, the Judge she does not marry, a Salvation Army girl with some knowledge of martial arts to complement her tambourine, a poor boy with *delirium tremens*, and Runjeet-Sing trying to flee death. **Plot and character are interconnected in so many ways that we might as well consider them inextricable.** As we saw, a basic plot is a sentence in which the character is the subject and the action is the predicate. As a work unfolds, one confronts a plot of action and also a plot of character. Characters so do things that their fortune improves or deteriorates, and as the characters follow this change of action their nature also changes. Both actions and characters are subject to turnabouts. Plots of vengeance, say, become plots of reconciliation and forgiveness; the foolish become wise, say, and the poor become rich.

Usually, the first questions with a story are "*What* happened?" and "*What* happened next?" **That suggests that action is primary, with character – the general matter of *who* did what to *whom* – somewhat less important.** Many titles attract us by some engaging action or activity – Return, Revenge, Adventure, Battle, Education, Rise and Fall, and so forth.

Even so, it is impossible to separate action from character precisely and neatly. As Henry James said, "People often talk of these things" –

The Poetry Toolkit: For Readers and Writers, First Edition. William Harmon.
© 2012 William Harmon. Published 2012 by Blackwell Publishing Ltd.

description and dialogue, incident and description – "as if they had a kind of internecine distinctness, instead of melting into each other at every breath and being intimately associated parts of one general effort of expression." An idle viewer may flip through television channels and form some impression of things going on – car chase, kiss, mountain climbing, bullfight – without knowing who is involved. Since moving pictures *move*, after all, the movement probably attracts more attention than who or what is doing the moving. But it would be silly to try to isolate the action of "kissing," say, as though it did not involve kissers and kissees. The significance of such an action may have some fundamental inherent interest, but the interest may increase many times over when we find out who the kissing partners are: strangers, siblings, parents and children, people who are engaged or married, perfect strangers, enemies, same sex or different, same species or not, and so on.

⌂ **A writer has to take care of the characters and the actions with almost equal care. Action without character is activity at best, chaos at worst; character without action is stasis.**

"The boy stood on the burning deck" – the abiding interest of that story shows the power of both the subject and the predicate: the only character physically present is Casabianca, "the boy," about whom we know little (his age is uncertain), and the immediate action, lasting no more than a few minutes, consists of his standing on the deck of a large burning ship until it blows up and kills him

"The boy stood on the burning deck" – there we see a very common subject and a very uncommon predicate. ⌂ **Since there are more potential subjects than predicates – since billions of people go through the same handful of basic experiences – character may be more complicated than action.** In life and literature alike, we encounter almost unlimited ranges of individual characters and character types, most of them human but also some animals, machines, and supernatural figures of various sorts, but, relatively speaking, fewer types of action. Many actions in life do not demand or deserve much attention. A small number of actions make it into the newspapers, and typical headlines represent the sort of thing that interests most readers. According to legend, a savvy journalist once said, "When a dog bites a man, that is not news, because it happens so often. But if a man bites a dog, that is news." And it may also be literature. Similarly, when a mad dog bites a man and then dies, as in Goldsmith's "An Elegy on the Death of a Mad Dog," another set of tables get turned:

Good people all, of every sort,
Give ear unto my song;
And if you find it wondrous short,
It cannot hold you long.

In Islington there was a man,
Of whom the world might say
That still a godly race he ran,
Whene'er he went to pray.

A kind and gentle heart he had,
To comfort friends and foes;
The naked every day he clad,
When he put on his clothes.

And in that town a dog was found,
As many dogs there be,
Both mongrel, puppy, whelp and hound,
And curs of low degree.

This dog and man at first were friends;
But when a pique began,
The dog, to gain some private ends,
Went mad and bit the man.

Around from all the neighbouring streets
The wondering neighbours ran,
And swore the dog had lost his wits,
To bite so good a man.

The wound it seemed both sore and sad
To every Christian eye;
And while they swore the dog was mad,
They swore the man would die.

But soon a wonder came to light,
That showed the rogues they lied:
The man recovered of the bite,
The dog it was that died.

The young Giocante Casabianca standing alone on the burning deck gets our attention much more than a boy standing on a beach or even an adult sailor on a warship dying during battle. Such a compelling combination of child and fire shows up in many places: Saint Robert Southwell's poem "The Burning Babe" (1595); the line "Now burn, new born to the world" in Gerard Manley Hopkins's "The Wreck of the Deutschland" (1876); Dylan Thomas's poem "A Refusal to Mourn the Death, by Fire, of a Child in London" (1945); and Stephen King's story *Firestarter* (1981). The dramatic scene in "Casabianca" depends on the child-fire dynamic and also on the water-fire dynamic, here made even more dramatic by the nocturnal setting. The title of the poem, which is the last name of the boy as well as his father, may suggest that in this case character is foremost.

Literary art calls for a complementary mastery of both character and action. As with action, character demands a combination of originality, probability, contrast, and surprise. A boy should be a boy – that much is expected – but there is art in making him also a hero, victim, and martyr. Much the same principle applies to Hardy's "Drummer Hodge," which concerns another boy who dies in a distant war, at the other end of Africa, a hundred years after the Battle of the Nile. The poem is worth another look:

> They throw in Drummer Hodge, to rest
> > Uncoffined – just as found:
> His landmark is a kopje-crest
> > That breaks the veldt around:
> And foreign constellations west
> > Each night above his mound.
>
> Young Hodge the drummer never knew –
> > Fresh from his Wessex home –
> The meaning of the broad Karoo,
> > The Bush, the dusty loam,
> And why uprose to nightly view
> > Strange stars amid the gloom.
>
> Yet portion of that unknown plain
> > Will Hodge for ever be;
> His homely Northern breast and brain
> > Grow to some Southern tree,
> And strange-eyed constellations reign
> > His stars eternally.

Any sitcom on radio or television will be populated by characters who seem to belong to a familiar type but with a difference, and sometimes the difference offers great contrast, as when poor hillbillies become wealthy citizens of Beverly Hills or, conversely, when wealthy city-dwellers move to a rundown farm. Similar contrasts animate the stories of John Clayton III, Viscount Greystoke, also known as Tarzan the Ape-Man (beginning in 1912). Another John, aka "John the Savage," is a central character in Aldous Huxley's *Brave New World* (1932). Both Johns are of a familiar type called the Noble Savage.

We size up literary characters in about the same way we size up people in daily life: as we get to know them, we make judgments based on our perceptions and appraisals of their physical, intellectual, and moral qualities. Our judgments may be guided by reason and experience, but for many people there is an element of prejudice and stereotyping. In many cases, we rely on classification and anticipation, and we fall almost inevitably into conventional types. We customarily expect old people to act differently from young, and so forth. Some of these judgments amount to kinds of prejudicial profiling, social evils that may also amount to aesthetic flaws.

⌂ **The creation of credible characters depends on familiarity with convention but also willingness to experiment with invention.** Often, the creation of an interesting character calls for a combination of disparate elements, as can be seen in such titles as *The Royal Slave, Il Re Pastore* (*The Shepherd King*), *The Gypsy Baron, The Student Prince, The Barefoot Contessa,* and even *Mighty Mouse.* ⌂ **Our response to these titles depends on what we expect from certain types of character, types that go back thousands of years to sets of "STOCK CHARACTERS."** From folktales going back into prehistory, from Greek Old Comedy, from Roman comedy, from medieval drama, from highly evolved Spanish plays of the Renaissance, from the *commedia dell'arte,* from the puppet and marionette theatre, from nursery rhymes and fairy tales, all the way to twenty-first-century sitcoms, one can witness several familiar varieties of stock characters about whom, for better or worse, most people form stock responses and of whom most people expect certain sorts of language and behavior. And most people delight in dramatic combinations and contrasts. The gallery of types includes the giddy ingénue, the boastful soldier (Latin *miles gloriosus*), the conceited cook, the braggart (Greek *alazon*), the snide ironic understater (Greek *eiron*), the hick or redneck (Greek *Agroikia*), the glutton (Latin *Bucco*), the miser, the young cavalier (Spanish *galán*), the anarchic hunchback (English Punch, Italian *Pulcinella*, Russian *Petrushka*), the gentleman (Spanish *caballero*), the lady's maid (Spanish *criada*), the courtesan (Latin *meretrix*), the clown or buffoon (Greek *bomolochos*, Spanish *gracioso*), the old man (Greek *geron*, *gerontion*, or *pappos*; Latin *pappus*, *senex*, or *senecio*; Spanish *barba*), the wild man of the woods (English *woodwose*), the quack, the dandy, the shrew or termagant, the boozer, the milquetoast, the femme fatale, to a more recent gallery of disgruntled postal employees, couch potatoes, hippies, boomers, bikers, surfers, goths, nerds, dorks, Sloane rangers, and valley girls. Even the reality shows of various sorts have produced their own stock types, which seem to have less to do with real reality than with the purest fiction. (These include the despicable dude or backstabber, the slut and her nemesis, the good girl, the bitch, the angry woman, the beauty-obsessed waif, the showoff, and the bully.)

Two notable twentieth-century poets wrote poems of which the title is a common character type, T. S. Eliot's "Gerontion" ("little old man") and Ted Hughes's "Wodwo" (a variant of "woodwose"). "Gerontion" begins,

> Here I am, an old man in a dry month,
> Being read to by a boy, waiting for rain.
> I was neither at the hot gates
> Nor fought in the warm rain
> Nor knee deep in the salt marsh, heaving a cutlass,
> Bitten by flies, fought.

Similarly, "Wodwo" begins with a probing of the "am" of identity:

> What am I? Nosing here, turning leaves over
> Following a faint stain on the air to the river's edge
> I enter water. Who am I to split
> The glassy grain of water looking upward I see the bed
> Of the river above me upside down very clear
> What am I doing here in mid-air? Why do I find
> this frog so interesting as I inspect its most secret
> interior and make it my own?

Among the basic types – apart from the usual categories of age, race, gender, occupation, nationality – are characters who can be called "overstated" or "understated," often found in volatile combination. In certain classic pairings, such as Stan Laurel and Oliver Hardy or "Ralph Kramden" and "Ed Norton" (played by Jackie Gleason and Art Carney), one member is large and loud, the other smaller and quieter. More recently, Albert Finney and Tom Courtenay have made a similar pair in both *The Dresser* and *A Rather English Marriage*. A very familiar *overstated* character is the braggart, especially in the form of the boastful and profane soldier. An equally familiar *understated* character is the ingénue, usually an innocent teenaged girl. George Bernard Shaw brilliantly combined these two seemingly antithetical types in the character of Saint Joan, who is, on the one hand, an innocent illiterate rustic virgin who dies at nineteen, but also a bold military leader who even uses profane language. (Although she is innocent of its meaning, she calls English soldiers "goddams." When asked, "Do you know why they are called goddams?" she can only reply, "No. Everyone calls them goddams." Authentic historical records from 1431 attest that she and others among the French called the English "goddems." The use of profanity by military braggarts continued into *Patton*, *Full Metal Jacket*, and after. Though profane, General Patton seems to have been also pious, sensitive, and even poetic.)

🕮 **Literary characters may be distinctively rendered by means of language, both that used in describing them and in that used by them in speech and writing.** Often, we receive mixed signals, as when an old character sounds young, or vice versa.

In fanciful stories, a single personage can contain antithetical or complementary character types: Clark Kent is a mild-mannered bespectacled understated gentleman who is also a superhero; Diana Prince is a normal modest bespectacled boutique owner who is also a superheroine; among *The Usual Suspects* is Roger "Verbal" Kint, a cripple called "stupid" who is revealed (*spoiler alert!*) as also the supervillain Keyser Söze. Billy Batson is a modest understated adolescent who is another superhero; Bruce Wayne is a nonchalant wealthy playboy who is yet another. Most superheroes have such a human host or alter ego. For some, the change is voluntary. For others, such as David Banner and the Incredible Hulk, the change is involuntary.

Many comedies and dramas on broadcast media involve an ensemble of types gathered in a dwelling or workplace, such as a hospital, school, bar, radio station, television station, firehouse, or police station, with unlimited possibilities for combinations, permutations, and exchanges. Theatrical companies have long consisted of a set of performers who can adapt to a large range of plays and roles: male and female leads, old men and women, young men and women, comedians, servants, assistants, and so forth. Many performers find themselves placed in the same roles over and over, since they have become "type cast" as gangsters, detectives, pick-pockets, aristocrats, or military officers. ⌕ **The artist's challenge is to create characters who are believable in their roles but with some surprise along the way. What reversal is to plot, contradiction is to character.**

⌕ **Action and character are intertwined so intimately that we cannot neatly isolate a poem of action as against a poem of character.** There are no action-adventure films without characters of some sort to perform the actions and have the adventures. Even so, there are matters of degree and of treatment, so that character may become the most important element. In Shakespeare's *Measure for Measure*, for example, the character Mariana is one part of the overall plot, and accordingly we judge her as a subordinate contributor to that general action. But she becomes the speaker and focal character in Tennyson's "Mariana," which has to do with her sad life during parts of the play before she appears on stage. In Shakespeare's *The Tempest* (1610), likewise, the brutish character Caliban is one element in the overall plot, and we judge him as a subordinate figure in that general action. With uncouth manners, as well as a name that sounds like an anagram of *cannibal*, Caliban represents either a primitive member of the human species or the offspring of a witch and a devil. In Robert Browning's "Caliban upon Setebos" (1864), on the other hand, we have little but a single sustained speech of Caliban's, made more interesting by its operation as a beastly creature's meditation on theology. He imagines Setebos, the god worshipped by his mother, the witch Sycorax:

> 'Thinketh, it came of being ill at ease:
> He hated that He cannot change His cold,
> Nor cure its ache. 'Hath spied an icy fish
> That longed to 'scape the rock-stream where she lived,
> And thaw herself within the lukewarm brine
> O' the lazy sea her stream thrusts far amid,
> A crystal spike 'twixt two warm walls of wave;
> Only, she ever sickened, found repulse
> At the other kind of water, not her life,
> (Green-dense and dim-delicious, bred o' the sun)
> Flounced back from bliss she was not born to breathe,
> And in her old bounds buried her despair,
> Hating and loving warmth alike: so He.

In crude self-protection, Caliban speaks of himself in a truncated third-person form, as though to say "He thinks it came from being ill at ease" and "He has spied . . ." The capitalized "He" is Setebos. Incidentally, some of the submarine imagery resembles that in "Wodwo."

Even more unlikely is the Caliban in W. H. Auden's *The Sea and the Mirror: A Commentary on Shakespeare's* The Tempest, whose address to the audience is an exercise in the exceedingly refined late prose style of Henry James. ("Our native Muse, heaven knows and heaven be praised, is not exclusive. Whether out of the innocence of a childlike heart to whom all things are pure, or with the serenity of a status so majestic that the mere keeping up of tone and appearances, the suburban wonder as to what the strait-laced Unities might possibly think, or sad sour Probability possibly say. . . .")

But there is little action to speak of in Browning's poem spoken by Caliban or in Tennyson's spoken by Mariana, and none at all in Auden's prose poem. Much the same effect can be observed in differences between the character of Peter Quince in Shakespeare's *A Midsummer Night's Dream* and Wallace Stevens's "Peter Quince at the Clavier." ⏏ **In a complete drama a character is mostly a means to an end, a cause of an effect; in a poem devoted exclusively to character, however, character is mostly an end in itself.** In many poems of character, the central personage exists before the poem, in other works, or in myth, or in real life. For the creator of a poem of character, the character has probably already been created. The challenge is to find a character to render, and to make the handling novel and convincing. During the nineteenth century, when the novel dominated the field of narrative and narrative poetry itself declined, poets tended to pass over the element of story and to concentrate on character itself. Robert Browning and Charles Dickens, both born in 1812, imagined vivid characters, but Browning, although he wrote some dramas and narrative poems, excelled in a kind of poem known as "dramatic monologue." ⚔ **A DRAMATIC MONOLOGUE is interpreted as the single sustained utterance of a character under some pressure to reveal his or her character, in a speech addressed to an identifiable interlocutor.** With only the character's voice as guidance, the background has to be imagined by the reader. Few speakers of dramatic monologues are pure inventions. Rather, they are real people (like Lucretius, Fra Lippo Lippi, and Andrea del Sarto), pre-existing personages from myth and legend (Tithonus, Ulysses), familiar characters from earlier literature (Mariana, Caliban), or a stock character ("Gerontion," a "little old man" like the little old man named "Lilloman" in Mel Brooks's *High Anxiety*, as well as "Wodwo"). Richard Howard's "The Giant on Giant-Killing" is represented as the speech of Goliath after being slain by David as realized in Donatello's bronze *David* of around 1430, in which the giant-killer is shown as a rather sensual nude boy, younger, prettier, and much less muscular than Michelangelo's *David*. Michelangelo shows nothing of Goliath; Donatello shows him reduced to a gigantic helmeted head at David's feet. In Howard's poem, the giant is slain not by the boy's sling but by his physical beauty.

A similar modern poem is Elder Olson's "Childe Roland, Etc.," which refers to a giant-slaying poem by Robert Browning called "Childe Roland to the Dark Tower Came," which is in turn a quotation from a mad speech in Shakespeare's *King Lear*. Olson's Childe Roland seems to be a modern man, and the giant (or Elf-King) a much misunderstood person. The giant opens the door of his castle:

I think I have never met a more charming person.
True, he was ugly, and – large; but he had a manner.
You know how personality makes up for so much! . . .

Later, with coffee and brandy, I had the facts.
Land and cattle were his; the people were squatters.
He did not resent the trespassing and depredation,
But thought it a pity they felt so possessive.
He ready me his poems, humbly took my suggestions,
Played some things of Chopin's rather well.
I left quite late, rather reluctantly . . . .

Later, "he had eaten six men"; that very day
I had a little note from him – half invitation,
Half begging the name of a competent lawyer . . . .

These representations of a giant or monster resemble Peter Boyle's inter-pretation of the creature at the end of *Young Frankenstein* – a gentleman of culture and refinement. One could also cite John Gardner's novel *Grendel* as a variation on the same revisionist theme. In all the foregoing cases, a pre-existing character or model is renovated, reinterpreted, and repre-sented, as it were, in modern dress. Other complex giants, who might even be benevolent and gentle, include Rubeus Hagrid in the Harry Potter series, Fezzik in *The Princess Bride*, and Shrek.

⌐ **The dramatic monologue acts as though it were a single sustained speech in a drama of which nothing else is provided. The reader usually has enough information to figure out who the speaker is, to whom the speaker is talking, and in what circumstances.** Fra Lippo Lippi has been caught off-limits after curfew and must talk his way out of a jam. Accordingly, he butters up the constabulary and presents himself as a normal man with feelings and desires like his captors. The Bishop who orders his tomb at Saint Praxed's church is on his deathbed with his sons in attendance – a Catholic bishop should not have sons, but this churchman combines religion, art, and sensuality in a heady kaleidoscopic mixture that betrays his confused mind as well as his complicated life. Andrea del Sarto is talking to his wife, Lucrezia, who is about to leave him.

Robert Browning wrote other character-centered poems that do not exactly qualify as dramatic monologues. **✗ A SOLILOQUY is a single sustained speech that represents the inner thoughts of a character as though overheard by an audience or reader; it is assumed that what is said in a soliloquy is true.** The words *soliloquy* and *monologue* mean about the same thing – "speaking alone" – and the terms have been loosely used as interchangeable. It remains useful, however, to distinguish *soliloquy* as the true outward utterance of inward thoughts and feelings not spoken to another character but only overheard by an audience, and *monologue* as something spoken aloud in a single sustained utterance to an identifiable interlocutor. Robert Browning's monologues and **EPISTLES** are mostly in blank verse; his soliloquies, on the other hand, are mostly in rhymed stanzas. The best known are "The Soliloquy of the Spanish Cloister" and a matched pair together titled "Madhouse Cells": "Porphyria's Lover" and "Johannes Agricola in Meditation." Most of the soliloquies involve a measure of derangement. **✗ An epistle or letter is also a single sustained utterance, but it is presented as though written from one person to another or to others.** In its literary uses, the epistle is written in circumstances that may put some pressure on the writer to reveal inner thoughts and feelings. The epistle, like an ordinary letter, tends to follow a formulaic structure for beginning and ending but to wander easily from topic to topic in the middle. Many books of the New Testament are epistolary, the most famous being those of Saint Paul to various churches in the Roman world. Horace wrote **VERSE EPISTLES**; what is called his *Ars Poetica* or *De Arte Poetica* is actually a verse epistle to some friends, the Pisos. Epistolary literature enjoyed a resurgence during the eighteenth century, with many distinguished epistolary novels, including all of Samuel Richardson's, and many distinguished epistolary poems, most notably those of Alexander Pope. Robert Browning's best-known epistolary poems are "An Epistle Containing the Strange Medical Experience of Karshish, the Arab Physician" and "Cleon." Both have to do with early responses by fictional educated pagans – an Arab and a Greek – to the presence of Christ. Karshish in his wanderings has come to Jericho and met Lazarus, who was brought back from the dead. He is tempted to diagnose Lazarus as insane, but he remains awestruck by possibilities. His letter to his teacher, Abib, also a physician, ends on a note of wonderment:

> The very God! think, Abib; dost thou think?
> So, the All-Great, were the All-Loving too –
> So, through the thunder comes a human voice
> Saying, "O heart I made, a heart beats here!
> Face, my hands fashioned, see it in myself!
> Thou hast no power nor mayst conceive of mine,
> But love I gave thee, with myself to love,
> And thou must love me who have died for thee!"
> The madman saith He said so: it is strange.

Cleon writes to a bountiful king named Protus to thank him for gifts and answer his questions about Cleon's many talents in all arts and philosophy. He goes on at great length about his own achievements and ideas, and only at the end turns to something other than himself. Protus, who seems to have an inquiring mind, has also dispatched a letter intended for Saint Paul and evidently asked the messenger to try to find him. Cleon concludes:

> Live long and happy, and in that thought die:
> Glad for what was! Farewell. And for the rest,
> I cannot tell thy messenger aright
> Where to deliver what he bears of thine
> To one called Paulus; we have heard his fame
> Indeed, if Christus be not one with him –
> I know not, nor am troubled much to know.
> Thou canst not think a mere barbarian Jew,
> As Paulus proves to be, one circumcised,
> Hath access to a secret shut from us?
> Thou wrongest our philosophy, O king,
> In stooping to inquire of such an one,

As if his answer could impose at all!
He writeth, doth he? well, and he may write,
Oh, the Jew findeth scholars! certain slaves
Who touched on this same isle, preached him and Christ;
And (as I gathered from a bystander)
Their doctrine could be held by no sane man.

In both of these poems that mention Christ, the modern reader may know and believe something not shared by the pagan letter-writers. But, if the modern reader is not a Christian, then the impact of the poems will probably change. Many poems require at least acquiescence in a belief system that the reader may not share. You do not have to be a Medieval Italian Catholic to understand Dante, or a seventeenth-century English Puritan to understand Milton, or a twentieth-century Anglo-Catholic to understand Eliot. In fact, it may be easier if your aesthetic perceptions and judgments are severed from contingent philosophical or theological opinions.

Some of Pope's epistles share a feature with some of Horace's: they change from an epistolary to a dramatic form and assign certain speeches to the addressee, as though to suggest "I can imagine you saying at this point . . ." (It is worth noting that Pope's epistle is written to a physician friend, as is Browning's "An Epistle Containing the Strange Medical Experience of Karshish, the Arab Physician." Both of these letters enjoy the privileged status of one's communication with a physician, to whom one might say things not told to any others. And the reader may feel a certain thrill of eavesdropping to see what someone says to his or her physician.) The impact of an epistle may depend on the addressee as much as the writer. Yet another literary work involving a letter to a physician is Hemingway's five hundred-word story "One Reader Writes," which describes a perplexed woman and quotes a marginally literate letter she writes to a newspaper physician, asking for advice about her husband who has come home after three years of military service.

Now here is the situation – I married a man in U. S. service in 1929 and that same year he was sent to China, Shanghai – he staid three years – and came home – he was discharged from the service some few months ago and went to his mother's home in Helena, Arkansas. He wrote for me to come home. I went, and found he is taking a course of injections and I naturally ask, and found he is being treated for I don't know how to spell the word but it sound like this 'sifilus.'

Pope's "Epistle to Dr. Arbuthnot" combines the epistolary format with narrative and dramatic manners. It begins, "Shut, shut the door, good John! fatigu'd, I said" – referring to a servant – and goes on to describe the writer's suffering a plague of poets seeking advice and help. He then turns to Arbuthnot directly:

> Friend to my life! (which did not you prolong,
> The world had wanted many an idle song)
> What drop or nostrum can this plague remove? ...

Eventually the doctor seems to interrupt:

> "Good friend, forbear! you deal in dang'rous things.
> I'd never name queens, ministers, or kings;
> Keep close to ears, and those let asses prick;
> 'Tis nothing" –

Then Pope himself re-interrupts in mid-line:

>   – Nothing? if they bite and kick? ...

Later a similar exchange occurs:

> "Hold! for God-sake – you'll offend:
> No names! – be calm! – learn prudence of a friend!
> I too could write, and I am twice as tall;
> But foes like these!" One flatt'rer's worse than all.
> Of all mad creatures, if the learn'd are right,
> It is the slaver kills, and not the bite ....

At times, Arbuthnot himself becomes the satirist:

> Let Sporus tremble – "What? that thing of silk,
> Sporus, that mere white curd of ass's milk?
> Satire or sense, alas! can Sporus feel?
> Who breaks a butterfly upon a wheel?"
> Yet let me flap this bug with gilded wings,
> This painted child of dirt that stinks and stings ....

Most of Pope's epistles are written in the first person as though in his own voice, or as though spoken by a character named "Pope." An exception is "Eloisa to Abelard," which resembles some of the epistles in Ovid's *Heroides* offered as "letters of heroines" from classical legend or myth, mostly involving heroic women who are separated from their lovers or husbands for some reason: Dido, Medea, Penelope, Oenone, Deïanira, and so forth. Browning's Christological epistles are by imaginary but typical letter-writers: an Arab physician and a conceited Greek poet, possibly suggested by a text in Acts 17:28 cited by Browning in the epigraph, "For in him we live, and move, and have our being; as certain also of your own poets have said, For we are also his offspring."

Epistolary literature of whatever sort holds out the strong temptation to take a peek at other people's mail. For monologues and soliloquies, the reader acts as hearer of something spoken outwardly or inwardly, and we judge by what can be heard or overheard. But with epistles the reader acts as one who gets to know the character by the style of writing and even spelling (such as Hemingway's woman's "sifilus"). Karshish and Cleon seem to be professionals who write as part of their occupation, even though we can imagine hearing their voices speak, as maybe in dictating their letters. **One of the deadliest hazards for a poet is to fall into the lamentable habit of writing everything in his or her own voice in the first person. One way out of the hazard is to objectify matters by writing in the second or third person in the voice of another. Instead of frontally expressing nothing but "I" and "me," try writing a letter by one of your characters.**

With Tennyson's "Ulysses," we can see how a dramatic monologue can be shaped by technical concerns. That poem seems to move from uncertainty to assurance by certain lexical and prosodic means. The first sentence suggests that "an idle king" is the subject of a clause:

> It little profits that an idle king,
> By this still hearth, among these barren crags,
> Match'd with an aged wife, I mete and dole
> Unequal laws unto a savage race,
> That hoard, and sleep, and feed, and know not me.
> . . .

but it turns out that the absence of punctuation deceives the reader. A modern writer would probably insert a comma after "that," since "king" is in apposition to the real subject, "I." Grammatical uncertainty is abetted by the lack of coincidence between word units and rhythmic units. We will get to these matters in later chapters, but now they demonstrate how the realms of character, diction, and prosody freely overlap and interact. Of the five iambic feet in the first line, none contains discrete words; each foot begins or ends with a fraction:

It lit | tle prof | its that | an id | le king....

The last line changes all that: every foot is also a discrete lexical unit with no fractions:

To strive, | to seek, | to find, | and not | to yield.

One could also notice that the rhetoric of the poem is pervaded by what is known as **LITOTES**, the statement of a positive by means of two negatives. Sometimes we say things like "not unlikely" to mean "possible" or "somewhat likely." Ulysses says, "Myself not least," meaning "among the greatest." He says his son is "decent not to fail" meaning "likely to succeed." His "Not unbecoming" means "totally becoming." This is the rhetoric of Ulysses the trickster, the master of the ambiguous negative, who told the Cyclops Polyphemus that his name was "Nobody," so that eventually Polyphemus was to cry to his brothers, "Nobody has hurt me." The Trojan Horse was his idea. For that deceptive stratagem, for tricking Achilles into joining the Greek expedition, and for despoiling the sacred shrine of Athena, Dante placed Ulysses far down in the Inferno. But Tennyson's Ulysses is neither Homer's nor Dante's, and certainly not Joyce's. Browning's most popular dramatic monologue may also be his least typical:

My Last Duchess
(Ferrara)

That's my last duchess painted on the wall,
Looking as if she were alive. I call
That piece a wonder, now; Frà Pandolf's hands
Worked busily a day, and there she stands.
Will't please you sit and look at her? I said
"Frà Pandolf" by design, for never read
Strangers like you that pictured countenance,

That depth and passion of its earnest glance,
But to myself they turned (since none puts by
The curtain drawn for you, but I)
And seemed as they would ask me, if they durst,
How such a glance came there; so not the first
Are you to turn and ask thus. Sir, 't was not
Her husband's presence only, called that spot
Of joy into the Duchess' cheek: perhaps
Frà Pandolf chanced to say "Her mantle laps
Over my lady's wrist too much" or "Paint
Must never hope to reproduce the faint
Half-flush that dies along her throat:" such stuff
Was courtesy, she thought, and cause enough
For calling up that spot of joy. She had
A heart – how shall I say? – too soon made glad,
Too easily impressed: she liked whate'er
She looked on, and her looks went everywhere.
Sir, 't was all one! My favour at her breast,
The dropping of the daylight in the West,
The bough of cherries some officious fool
Broke in the orchard for her, the white mule
She rode with round the terrace – all and each
Would draw from her alike the approving speech,
Or blush, at least. She thanked men – good! but thanked
Somehow – I know not how – as if she ranked
My gift of a nine-hundred-years-old name
With anybody's gift. Who'd stoop to blame
This sort of trifling? Even had you skill
In speech – (which I have not) – to make your will
Quite clear to such an one, and say, "Just this
Or that in you disgusts me; here you miss
Or there exceed the mark" – and if she let
Herself be lessoned so, nor plainly set
Her wits to yours, forsooth, and made excuse
– E'en then would be some stooping; and I choose
Never to stoop. Oh sir, she smiled, no doubt,
Whene'er I passed her; but who passed without
Much the same smile? This grew; I gave commands;
Then all smiles stopped together. There she stands

As if alive. Will 't please you rise? We'll meet
The company below, then. I repeat,
The Count your master's known munificence
Is ample warrant that no just pretence
Of mine for dowry will be disallowed;
Though his fair daughter's self, as I avowed
At starting is my object. Nay, we'll go
Together down, sir. Notice Neptune, though,
Taming a sea-horse, thought a rarity,
Which Claus of Innsbruck cast in bronze for me.

Chapters 3, 4, and 5 will go into much more detail about rhetoric, diction, and sound, but, as was shown with "Ulysses," all these elements are interconnected and cannot be separated neatly into boxes. What we readers see on the page influences what we hear, what we hear determines how we interpret language, language so interpreted tips us off about ideas and feelings, which in turn make up the complex fabric of character, which has a part in an overall plot of action. In a dramatic monologue, there is almost no explicit plot of action but mostly a plot of character, as progressively revealed in a speaker's own words. Readers are free to deduce a context for the single speech that constitutes a monologue, and most such poems provide some clues. Here we have a duke, since duchesses are the wives of dukes, and we know he is from Ferrara. He spends a good deal of time describing a portrait of his late wife and discussing the circumstances that gave rise to her expression in the painting. It seems further that he has been involved in prenuptial negotiations with the envoy of a count. Dukes are two or three notches above counts in most schemes, but both are noble and probably aristocratic. It is up to the reader to try to figure out why the duke goes on at such length and in such and such a way, since there seems to be no good reason for much of his ostensibly irrelevant talk. Readers have been debating the fine points of this poem ever since it first appeared in 1842, and it does not seem that a final answer to every question will ever be found. But there are a few details worth noting.

First, from beginning to end, the poem moves from "My" to "me." That much may suggest an unusual concentration on self, so that it is possible that we are hearing the voice of an egotist. We may notice that most other monologues, soliloquies, and epistles by Browning have titles that seem outside the poem: "Fra Lippo Lippi," "Andrea del Sarto," "Cleon," "Porphyria's Lover," "Caliban upon Setebos," and so forth seem provided by the poet or some other third party (and the same is true of Tennyson's "Ulysses," "Tithonus," "Lucretius," and so forth). But "My Last Duchess" has a title drawn from the monologue itself: this duke is overweeningly present from the first word to the last. He has the first word and the last, and both are first-person singular pronouns.

Three matters of wording warrant some examination: "but I," "a nine-hundred-years-old name," and "such an one." All three have been attested before and after Browning's poem, but for most speakers the likelier locutions are "but *me*," "a nine-hundred-*year*-old name," and "such *a* one." In constructions like this "but I" and Felicia Hemans's "whence all but he had fled," "but" is construed not as a preposition (as it was in Old English and as it remains in colloquial English today), so that there may be something rather stiff and formal in the speaker's attitude. The preservation of the plural in "nine-hundred-years-old" may be defensible on literal grounds – "nine hundred" is a plural, after all – but idiomatically we say "five-foot-tall basketball player" and "three-year contract" and not "five-feet-tall basketball player" and "three-years contract." "Such an one" is found also in Browning's "Cleon," but it remains unusual, as though the speaker were unaware that the first sound in "one" is a consonant and is therefore preceded by "a." All three of these choices suggest that the speaker is over-correcting, being too anxiously careful to say the right thing. (This happens commonly when people say things like "to Michelle and I," even though they would not say "to I.") Our duke may sound self-centered but he is lacking in confidence and experience as a speaker.

Most of the dramatic monologues of Tennyson and Browning are in blank verse. "My Last Duchess," though short, looks like all the others, but on closer inspection turns out to involve rhymed couplets. But they are not the crisply **END-STOPPED COUPLETS** of Dryden, Pope, and Johnson. Of the fifty-six lines in Browning's poem, thirty-seven end with no punctuation; they are ✘ **RUN-ON LINES, which do not pause at the end of the line. (⌕ This is also called ENJAMBMENT.)** The effect is handled so subtly that many readers, though conscientious, have been unaware that there was rhyme at all. For one fairly long uninterrupted stretch, no line ends with a comma, period, or other punctuation:

> She thanked men – good! but thanked
> Somehow – I know not how – as if she ranked
> My gift of a nine-hundred-years-old name
> With anybody's gift. Who'd stoop to blame

This sort of trifling? Even had you skill
In speech – (which I have not) – to make your will
Quite clear to such an one, and say, "Just this
Or that in you disgusts me; here you miss
Or there exceed the mark" – and if she let
Herself be lessoned so, nor plainly set
Her wits to yours, forsooth, and made excuse
– E'en then would be some stooping; and I choose
Never to stoop. Oh sir, she smiled, no doubt,
Whene'er I passed her; but who passed without
Much the same smile? This grew; I gave commands;...

That is, after a rough, breathless, uneven rehearsal of what the Duke imagines the Duchess's flaws to be, there comes a slight pause after "doubt" and then a bigger pause after the sinister "commands." At this point he may catch his breath.

In standard end-stopped couplets and **QUATRAINS** of the eighteenth century, rhyming words tended to be accented monosyllables or else unambiguously accented final syllables in longer words. In "My Last Duchess" there are such rhyming pairs as "wall/call," "hands/stands," and so forth. But there are also rhymes of another sort. The rhyme between "eye" and "symmetry" (Blake), "lie" and "eternity" (Marvell), and "me" and "equanimity" (Hardy) involves one fully accented monosyllable and a matching word of three or more syllables that normally ends as a dactyl: /∪∪. ✖ **In the rhymes in question, a conventional or courtesy accent is applied to the final syllable of the longer word, so that the scansion becomes an AMPHIMACER (/∪/). This process is called "PROMOTION."** By this familiar practice, "sýmmĕtrў" becomes "sýmmĕtrý." Along with this change of accent, the vowel quality changes, so that the muted sound at the end of "symmetry" becomes some thing closer to "tree" or "try." ⌖ **In most such cases, the fully accented monosyllable precedes the promoted accent in the longer word, as though for guidance.** Without such guidance, a reader will not know whether "vanity," say, is going to rhyme with "sanity" (triple rhyme), "sea," or "sigh."

As it happens, there are three such rhymes in "My Last Duchess," and in every one of them the promoted form precedes the fully stressed form: "countenance/glance," "munificence/pretence," and "rarity/me." In such suspended rhymes, the reader is left in doubt for a few seconds, and the speaker's imagined accent is ambiguous. Will "rarity" find a match with "charity"? No: it rhymes by promotion with the keyword "me."

One more acoustic matter: the last line contains an instance of multiple alliteration: "Which **Cl**aus of Inns**br**uck **c**ast in **br**onze for me." The ornate pattern of **c/br/c/br** works to isolate the first eight syllables, so that the unambiguously iambic "for me" is underscored.

> Which Claus of Innsbruck cast in bronze
>   for me

(All these considerations of rhetoric, diction, and prosody will be discussed at length in Chapters 3, 4, and 5.)

Typical monologues present a character in his or her own voice, and it is possible, as some critics suggest, that hearing someone's voice, however wicked or obnoxious, may make us more sympathetic. If they are taking the time to reveal themselves to us in some way, we can take the time to listen without necessarily judging. With no plot of action to serve as context for the speech, we are under no pressure to judge the speaker as good or bad. That suspension of judgment may be what causes so many monologues to concern rather disagreeable people at unpleasant but revealing moments.

In some cases, a character so presented will be so interesting that we naturally wonder what caused a situation to develop and what happened later. **PREQUELS** and **SEQUELS** are common enough in popular entertainment. "My Last Duchess" leaves several questions unanswered and several problems unsolved. Did he really have his wife killed? When he says "my *last* duchess" does he mean "my *most recent* duchess" (presumably in an indefinite series) or "my *final* duchess" (since nothing can conceal the fact that I am a murderer who is unable to conceal his crime). Some of these questions are addressed in Richard Howard's "Nikolaus Mardruz to his Master Ferdinand, Count of Tyrol, 1565," written supposedly as a report by the envoy to whom "My Last Duchess" is addressed. The envoy is not very impressed by the aging grandiloquent duke, his castle, or his art collection.

♫ **One of the oldest functions of poetry is to bless or CURSE.** Some vivid and entertaining curses come from Celtic traditions, which credited poets and poetry with extraordinary powers. Modern versions of older curses from Welsh and Irish poetry turn up in James Stephens's

"The Glass of Beer" (from a seventeenth-century original by David
O'Bruadair):

> The lanky hank of a she in the inn over there
> Nearly killed me for asking the loan of a glass of beer:
> May the devil grip the whey-faced slut by the hair
> And beat bad manners out of her skin for a year.
> That parboiled imp, with the hardest jaw you will ever see
> On virtue's path, and a voice that would rasp the dead,
> Came roaring and raging the minute she looked at me,
> And threw me out of the house on the back of my head.
>
> If I asked her master he'd give me a cask a day;
> But she with the beer at hand, not a gill would arrange!
> May she marry a ghost and bear him a kitten and may
> The High King of Glory permit her to get the mange.*

A similar poem is Robert Graves's "The Travellers' Curse after Mis-
direction" (from the Welsh).

In the other direction, poems of character that bless and praise are also
abundant, if less entertaining than curses. An elementary poem of praise is
the **EPITAPH** that begins "Here lies..," along with a brief summary of the
life. A once-popular variation is the poem spoken as though from the grave
by a dead person. Many poems of this sort turn up in the miscellany known
as *The Greek Anthology*. Here is a modern adaptation of one such poem,
called "A Thief":

> Look at my corpse washed up in this bad place.
>
> Endless and endlessly evil Sea, you killed me easily
> with such gentlemanly smooth unthinking grace –
> all in a day's work, perfunctorily drowning another sailor.
> But even the endlessly malicious Sea
> could suffer an access of decent embarrassment
> enough to leave me at least a modest something with which

---

*James Stephens: "A Glass of Beer" from *Collected Poems*, Macmillan Publishing Co., Inc.
Permission to reprint granted by the Society of Authors as the Literary Representative of the
Estate of James Stephens.

to cover myself; it took another human being, a brother
and fellow-citizen of the solid continent
to help himself to – to *steal* – my last stitch.

And look at my body, beached in this bad place,
aground-awash, aground-awash, robbed naked by a man:
God sink that bastard like a plumb bob to hell's bottom pit –
let Judas and Hitler take time out to look at him there
running around in nothing but a dead man's underwear.

An anonymous Greek epitaph is sometimes called "On an Unhappy Man": "I Dionysius of Tarsus lie here at sixty, having never married; and would that my father had not." Thomas Hardy's adaptation is called "Epitaph on a Pessimist":

I'm Smith of Stoke, aged sixty-odd,
    I've lived without a dame
From youth-time on; and would to God
    My dad had done the same.

Edgar Lee Masters's *Spoon River Anthology* collects scores of such epitaphs updated to the American Midwest of a century ago. In all such poems the emphasis is on the revelation and exploration of character as such, without much attention to an overall plot. In a pair of poems in this collection, an implicit plot is subtly unveiled:

Elsa Wertman

I was a peasant girl from Germany,
Blue-eyed, rosy, happy and strong.
And the first place I worked was at Thomas Greene's.
On a summer's day when she was away
He stole into the kitchen and took me
Right in his arms and kissed me on my throat,
I turning my head. Then neither of us
Seemed to know what happened.
And I cried for what would become of me.
And cried and cried as my secret began to show.

One day Mrs. Greene said she understood,
And would make no trouble for me,
And, being childless, would adopt it.
(He had given her a farm to be still.)
So she hid in the house and sent out rumors,
As if it were going to happen to her.
And all went well and the child was born – They were so kind to me.
Later I married Gus Wertman, and years passed.
But – at political rallies when sitters-by thought I was crying
At the eloquence of Hamilton Greene –
That was not it.
No! I wanted to say:
That's my son! That's my son!

And then the next in the series:

Hamilton Greene

I was the only child of Frances Harris of Virginia
And Thomas Greene of Kentucky,
Of valiant and honorable blood both.
To them I owe all that I became,
Judge, member of Congress, leader in the State.
From my mother I inherited
Vivacity, fancy, language;
From my father will, judgment, logic.
All honor to them
For what service I was to the people!**

There is a story here that connects the two epitaphs, but the only outright plot is that of a graveyard with funeral plots. ⏸ **It is not necessary that every detail of a story be spelled out, and it is shrewd to leave the reader something to do.** Since these two poems are together in *The Spoon River Anthology*, it is no great chore to figure out the connections, but the poet gives the people a chance to speak in their own voices, even if one is deeply wrong about himself.

**Edgar Lee Masters: "Hamilton Greene" from *The Spoon River Anthology*,
© 1916 Macmillan Publishing Co., Inc. Permission to reprint granted by Hilary Masters.

As we progressed through these monologues and other poems of character, we had to include some discussion of diction and prosody, and in these excursions we could not avoid mentioning the thoughts and feelings that make up so much of character, and this would be a good point to move on to such elements of the literary work.

3 The Arts of Sentiment: States of Mind and Feeling

"The boy stood on the burning deck" – the subject "boy" is the character, the predicate "stood on the burning deck" is the action; and those contrasting two elements make a compelling start, a most effective hook for the reader's attention, prompting the request "Tell me more." "More" could involve further details of character and action, but sooner or later the reader will ask, "*Why* did the boy stand on the burning deck?" With that, a third important element is added to the plot of action and the plot of character: states of mind and feeling that might explain both character and action. Action can be physical and visible: it is often unambiguous. One can see a deck burning and a boy standing.

One can see a human figure, but that perception is not always distinct, made questionable by distance, fog, darkness, obstacles, defective vision. We may not be able to say whether someone is male or female, old or young, dapper or shabby. But we can see and hear *something*. Beyond that, what goes on inside a character is always invisible and indefinite.

𝄢 **The vague term "sentiment" will have to do to cover internal states, mental and emotional, that make up a total of sensibility.** Short-lived feelings add up to longer-lasting emotions, and emotions in turn add up to the dispositions that constitute a sensibility. Any given state of mind is a mishmash of facts and feelings, and for most people feelings far outnumber facts. The bare information in "We are approaching Springfield," say, could stir up many feelings in many people, from blank indifference (in those who know and feel nothing about the place) to intense excitement (in those returning to their beloved Springfield home after a long absence) to fear (in condemned criminals being transported to Springfield, site of the prison that houses death row). In the artful delivery

---

The Poetry Toolkit: For Readers and Writers, First Edition. William Harmon.
© 2012 William Harmon. Published 2012 by Blackwell Publishing Ltd.

of an aesthetic experience, our inner states are manipulated to handle facts, images, ideas, and feelings in extremely complex configurations, so that we may never figure out exactly what we have gone through. That is one reason for valid disagreement about every aspect of an artwork.

✗ A LYRIC POEM conveys a state or mind of feeling, possibly without much presentation of action or character. There may be a first-person speaker whose identity and situation are only sketchily provided. The main elements are mental perceptions and emotional responses to a given set of circumstances. A poem called, say, "Delight in Disorder" presents a more or less objective quality – Disorder – along with a more or less subjective reaction – Delight. That combination already generates interest, since, for many, disorder may not necessarily create delight (if, say, they have been subjected to such injunctions as "pick up sticks," "lay them straight," "wipe your nose," "tie your shoes"). The unspecified speaker of Robert Herrick's poem elaborates:

> A sweet disorder in the dress
> Kindles in clothes a wantonness:
> A lawn about the shoulders thrown
> Into a fine distraction:
> An erring lace which here and there
> Enthrals the crimson stomacher:
> A cuff neglectful, and thereby
> Ribbons to flow confusedly:
> A winning wave (deserving note)
> In the tempestuous petticoat:
> A careless shoe-string, in whose tie
> I see a wild civility:
> Do more bewitch me than when art
> Is too precise in every part.

That is not a narrative poem: there is no action and no narrator. And it is not a dramatic poem of any sort that we have looked at: soliloquy, monologue, epistle. The only element of character is an opinion, which could be entertained by anybody. We do not know who is talking, or to whom, or in what circumstances. We would not even be justified in calling the speaker "Herrick," because all we know of Robert Herrick's state of mind is that he wanted to write a poem, and that is a pretty vague impulse. ☠ It is hazardous to try to identify the speaker of a lyric poem as the

actual poet, since poets sometimes express themselves in rather oblique and devious ways. T. S. Eliot's "The Love Song of J. Alfred Prufrock" contains the line "I grow old . . . I grow old . . ." but the poet who wrote that was no more than twenty; ten years later, at thirty, Eliot began "Gerontion" (the title means "little old man") with "Here I am, an old man . . ." Even later, in "Little Gidding," when Eliot went on about "the gifts reserved for age," he was not yet fifty-five, with many years left to live.

Tennyson, likewise, spoke "Tithonus" in the voice of a man who has the gift of immortality but not the gift of eternal youth, so that he just grows older and older, like the Struldbrugs in *Gulliver's Travels*. Tennyson wrote "Tithonus" when he was about twenty-five; a few years later, giving a voice to Ulysses, he could argue that "Old age hath yet his honour and his toil."

Herrick's "Delight in Disorder" is typical of much lyric poetry that the reader confronts: (1) something objective along with (2) a measure of subjective feeling. There is no particular action or activity, other than beholding and reflecting, and of the character we can only say that he or she delights in disorder, especially in women's clothing. The speaker, whose character is here sketchily exhibited, has only a ghostly presence, found in one "I" and one "me" with no more specificity than that. A modern version of what sounds like the same basic idea is in Wallace Stevens's "Connoisseur of Chaos," but with exaggerated thinking and muted feeling.

Speaking of Wallace Stevens, he wrote a poem called "Sunday Morning," and so, according to a reliable index, did several others, including Ted Kooser, W. H. Auden, L. A. G. Strong, David Ray, Donald Davie, and Louis MacNeice. With slight elaboration, there are Robert Lowell's "Waking Sunday Morning" and Kris Kristofferson's "Sunday Morning Coming Down." All of that suggests a more or less objective setting, to which the poem is likely to add an emotion response of some sort. One can assume, conditionally, a modern Western setting, since that is the home of all of those English-speaking poets; but in many parts of the world Sunday morning may have no such special meaning. Such assumptions are normal enough, but it is prudent to keep certain considerations in mind. June, for example, is a spring and summer month in half the world, but it is an autumn and winter month in the other half.

✖ **Many lyric poems have titles that furnish the objective setting or occasion along with a subjective sentiment.** Dylan Thomas's title "A Refusal to Mourn the Death, by Fire, of a Child in London" challenges a reader's sensibility, since for most people the objective "death, by fire, of a child" would hardly cause a subjective *refusal* to mourn. One reads the poem to get an explanation of a paradoxical situation. ⏻ **It is a good idea to provide a poem with a title that can generate interest but not deal all the cards face up.** Robert Frost's "The Road Not Taken" is not about the road not taken, nor is his "Come In" about coming in – on the contrary.

Many poems of sentiment, bypassing intricate problems of plot and character, explicitly offer themselves as thoughts in a given situation, customarily an occasion or place. An index of titles shows hundreds of "thoughts": Night Thoughts, Lenten Thoughts, Forest Thoughts, Autumn Thoughts, Bitter Summer Thoughts, . . . Thoughts: *of* a Briton on the Subjugation of Switzerland, *to* a Concerto of Telemann, *from* a Bar Stool, *after* a Bridge Party, *from* a Bottle. Many poets begin their career with such a poem of reflection on some meaningful occasion. Some poems, tailored for an occasion, are classified therefore as "**OCCASIONAL POEMS.**" And one unfortunate lyric, now mostly notorious but once respected, begins, "I think that I shall never see . . . " A poem that bears the title "Thoughts . . . " or begins "I think" is obliged to display a measure of thinking, but not many do. ⏻ **The most interesting poems contain a measure of surprise, or at least of something unexpected.** The well-mannered reader may have been brought up to avoid disorder, so that "Delight in Disorder" contains a sentiment that does not necessarily fit the subject. A more predictable sentiment may be something like "Disgust with Disorder," along these lines:

> A slight disorder in the dress
> Is more than slightly just a mess.
> Hair or makeup out of place
> Does nothing to enhance a face.
> Let every cuff and every pleat
> Be even, smooth, and very neat . . .

That may tally with what many dutiful pupils would like to think they think, but it makes a very dull poem.

⚒ **RHETORIC, conditionally defined as the purposeful relation of statement to meaning,** is discussed here in connection with lyric poetry, although it is obviously important in all other kinds of discourse as well. But, since emotion is particularly the province of lyric, rhetoric fits in here as well as anywhere. It is also more conspicuous because most lyric poems, with no story to tell and no character to develop, are relatively short and foreground the sorts of subjectivity and emotion that may call out for rhetorical handling. A lyric poem, accordingly, can be quite short, since the only plot is a plot of feeling, which can be adequately expressed in a few seconds. Among words traditionally associated with lyric poetry, "O!" and "Oh!" and "Ah!" must rank high.

The Roman poet Martial produced a famous **EPIGRAM** that registers only a familiar feeling:

> Non amo te, Sabidi, nec possum dicere quare;
> Hoc tantum possum dicere, non amo te.

["I do not love you, Sabidius; I cannot say why; /I *can* say only this: I do not love you."]

The poem is best known in a seventeenth-century adaptation by Thomas Brown when he was a student at Oxford, disciplined by a dean named John Fell, who had threatened to expel Brown for misconduct unless he could produce a translation of Martial's poem, with this result:

> I do not love thee Dr. Fell
> The reason why I cannot tell;
> But this I know and know full well,
> I do not love thee Dr. Fell.

One can inquire into the particulars of Martial's Sabidius and Brown's Dr Fell, but the poem survives as is, without embellishment. (Both Brown and Fell went on to distinguished careers, Brown as a satirist and playwright, Fell as a bishop.)

� We have first (1) a "PLAIN" statement, in which the verbal utterance and conceptual meaning coincide; then (2) OVERSTATEMENT, in which the statement exceeds the meaning; and (3) UNDERSTATEMENT, in which the statement undershoots the meaning. We also have (4) an IRONY or reversal in which the statement contradicts the surface meaning. One may, for example, make a plain statement, "I am hungry." For effect, one may overstate: "I'm so hungry I could eat a horse." (Or, as Al Bundy says, "a vegetable.") One may understate: "Well, I may be just a little hungry . . . I could nibble half a bite." Or one may indulge in irony: "Hungry? No, I'm not a bit hungry. Why should I be hungry? I ate two days ago, didn't I?" 🗂 **In all these cases, the meaning of a statement can be abetted by gestures, tone of voice, facial expression, and other such devices.** Overstatement is often delivered in a loud tone of voice, understatement the reverse. Irony comes with its own brand of exaggeration: "Hungry? 'Hungry'? Oh *no-o-o-o-o*, not a bit."

"Why should I be hungry?" – asked in a situation in which the answer is obvious – in this case is a **RHETORICAL QUESTION**. ✗ **A rhetorical question is a question in form only, since it is really a way of making a statement.** If you ask me whether I'm hungry, and I'm very hungry, then I may say "Yes!" I may also ask a rhetorical question: "Is the Pope a Catholic?" In a majority of instances, rhetorical questions are a way of saying something negative. With a certain intonation, "Who knows?" and "Who cares?" mean "Nobody knows" and "Nobody cares." "Why not?" almost always means "No reason why not." A question seems to invite some response, and the rhetorical question offers a way to avoid being too direct. A rhetorical question, however elementary, has the effect of involving the interlocutor.

William Blake's "The Tiger" consists exclusively of questions – a dozen of them:

Tyger, Tyger, burning bright
In the forests of the night,
What immortal hand or eye
Could frame thy fearful symmetry?

In what distant deeps or skies
Burnt the fire of thine eyes?
On what wings dare he aspire?
What the hand dare seize the fire?

And what shoulder, & what art,
Could twist the sinews of thy heart?
And when thy heart began to beat,
What dread hand? & what dread feet?

What the hammer? what the chain?
In what furnace was thy brain?
What the anvil? what dread grasp
Dare its deadly terrors clasp?

When the stars threw down their spears
And water'd heaven with their tears,
Did he smile his work to see?
Did he who made the Lamb make thee?

Tyger, Tyger, burning bright
In the forests of the night,
What immortal hand or eye
Dare frame thy fearful symmetry?

(These are authentic questions, although some may also be rhetorical.) Francis Scott Key's "In Defense of Fort McHenry" ("The Star-Spangled Banner") begins with a series of questions: "O say can you see...?" etc. W. B. Yeats's "On Hearing that the Students of Our New University Have Joined the Agitation Against Immoral Literature" consists of nothing but one rhetorical question:

Where, where but here have Pride and Truth,
That long to give themselves for wage,
To shake their wicked sides at youth
Restraining reckless middle-age? [*nowhere*]

Likewise, Yeats's "No Second Troy" offers four complex rhetorical questions:

Why should I blame her that she filled my days
With misery, or that she would of late
Have taught to ignorant men most violent ways,
Or hurled the little streets upon the great,
Had they but courage equal to desire? [*no reason*]
What could have made her peaceful with a mind
That nobleness made simple as a fire,
With beauty like a tightened bow, a kind
That is not natural in an age like this,
Being high and solitary and most stern? [*nothing*]
Why, what could she have done being what she is? [*nothing*]
Was there another Troy for her to burn? [*no*]

The implied answers are, as suggested, all negative.

☠ **Beware: rhetorical questions can backfire if the answer is not generally obvious.** Imagine an innocent person asking, "Who would not place his country's interest above his own?" The answer may be, "Plenty of people." J. G. Frazer's *The Golden Bough* (1890) begins with a rhetorical question that works for very few readers in the twenty-first century: "Who does not know Turner's picture of the Golden Bough?" Who can compute the number of dismayed readers who have given up at that point?

⚒ **Another feature of rhetoric is figurative language, sometimes called "the colors of rhetoric."** Here, a literal meaning is expressed by translation or transformation into non-literal terms. In Herrick's "A sweet disorder in the dress/Kindles in clothes a wantonness," the literal meaning is something like "Disorder in dress/Suggests wantonness." The modest redundancy of "in the dress" and "in clothes" could be a primitive rhetorical device: repeating for emphasis. "Sweet" applies a common sensual quality, originally a matter of taste, to an abstract entity ("disorder"), in much the same way as "kindles" uses a physical activity (igniting a fire) in place of an abstract process (suggesting a quality).

Such figurative language, found everywhere in daily life, is by no means exclusive or peculiar to literature in general or to poetry in particular. Many times every day we wittingly or unwittingly employ a tangible concrete term instead of an intangible abstraction. For example, Latin *currere*, literally "to run," leads to *curriculum*, "a racecourse," later adapted to mean a course of study. (The same prolific ancestor yields *corridor*, *courier*, *currency*, *current*, *cursive*, *car*, *cargo*, *chariot*, *carry*, and quite a few others.)

Ralph Waldo Emerson, in characteristic exaggeration, stated the case:

> The poets made all the words, and therefore language is the archives of history, and, if we must say it, a sort of tomb of the muses. For, though the origin of most of our words is forgotten, each word was at first a stroke of genius, and obtained currency, because for the moment it symbolizes the world to the first speaker and to the hearer. The etymologist finds the deadest word to have been once a brilliant picture. Language is fossil poetry.

Daisy is "day's eye"; *dandelion* is "lion's tooth." Almost every abstraction can be traced to a specific physical term: *aviation* means "being a bird." But, since these are fossils, they are dead to most speakers. Nobody has time to think about the "star" once shining in the primary root of "consider" and "desire," "aster" and likewise "disaster." Just as the implicit metaphorical content of many words is dead, many explicit figures can wear out and die. The first time you hear that something went over "like a lead balloon," you may be impressed; by the fiftieth time, however, such figures, abundant as the sands of the desert, pack no punch whatever. They may even diminish a speaker's reputation for originality. When you hear "last ditch stand" and "eleventh-hour decision," the cliché may breed indifference. The speaker has not taken the time to be direct or to be creatively indirect.

For extreme literalists, implicit metaphors can raise a red flag. Since the root of *dilapidate* is Latin *lapis*, "stone," such critics complain that a wooden structure cannot really be dilapidated. (Unless, that is, *dilapidate* means "to scatter like stones.") *Decimate* means to execute every tenth soldier, so that a force reduced by half cannot be called "decimated." Such problems may belong to people with too much time on their hands. We freely mix up metaphors without losing sense. Someone known for quick wit may be called "a sharp cookie," even though "sharp" and "cookie" move in different directions. Thomas Gray's "Elegy Written in a Country Churchyard" mentions "Some heart once pregnant with celestial fire," in which the figures maneuver in three or four directions at once, some of them almost surreal. But even a thoroughly ordinary phrase like "full of holes" can become paradoxical or surreal.

✸ **A SIMILE is a figure in which comparison is explicitly stated by means of a word such as *as*, *like*, or even *compare* itself.** One of William Shakespeare's sonnets asks, "Shall I compare thee to a summer's day?" William Carlos Williams's "The Young Housewife" is similar:

. . .
Then again she comes to the curb
to call the ice-man, fish-man, and stands
shy, uncorseted, tucking in
stray ends of hair, and I compare her
to a fallen leaf.

(✒ **A point of style: these *unilateral* comparisons are comparing *to*. Another kind of *bilateral* comparison is a comparing *with*, as when one compares Poland with Latvia or beer with cider.**)

✸ **In formal METAPHOR, the comparison is expressed without an explicit "as" or "like" being stated, so that, for example, instead of "Love is like a garden" one says "Love is a garden."** A further step, in which all abstractions are subdued, involves a statement that seems literal – "We are in a garden" – but is handled with such passion that the possibility of metaphoric interpretation is clear. ✸ **Such a process is sometimes described by the term SYMBOLISM.** Since this kind of discourse avoids overt and explicit statement of the essential meaning, the surface meaning will probably be indefinite or indistinct, an affair more of suggestion than of demonstration. In a poem, some of the emotional accompaniment may be achieved by rhythm and other sound effects. Throughout T. S. Eliot's *Four Quartets*, for example, roses appear with a strong emotional charge, much in excess of what most people expect from a horticultural enthusiasm. The first quartet, "Burnt Norton," meditates on what has happened but also on what has not happened:

> Footfalls echo in the memory
> Down the passage which we did not take
> Towards the door we never opened
> Into the rose-garden. My words echo
> Thus, in your mind.
>   But to what purpose
> Disturbing the dust on a bowl of rose-leaves
> I do not know.

It may be that two people have been discussing what they did not do and speculating on what might have happened. Roses and gardens recur throughout the poem, too mysteriously to be equated flatly with "love" of some sort. (The words "footfalls echo" occurred earlier in a translation from the Chinese by H. A. Giles – "No footfalls echo on the floor" – which Ezra Pound adapted as "There is no sound of foot-fall." Eliot also used the word in *Murder in the Cathedral* (1935): "Puss-purr of leopard, footfall of padding bear.") We can find out that Burnt Norton is a manor located in Gloucestershire that Eliot visited with Emily Hale during 1934. (An earlier great house was burnt during the eighteenth century.) She had been his college sweetheart before he left for Europe in 1914; he married someone else in 1915, but was separated from his wife from the early 1930s until her death in 1947. Even after their time at Burnt Norton, Eliot stayed in close correspondence with Emily Hale, and it seems that the only importance of Burnt Norton for them is that its rose garden furnished the site of an intense discussion of what had been and what might have been. They remained in communication until his second marriage in 1957. In terms of symbolism, it is possible that their failure to do anything about their feelings is represented by

> the passage which we did not take
> Towards the door we never opened
> Into the rose-garden.

Feelings are so complicated in everybody that their full and honest expression is almost impossible. It is very hard even to answer a primitive question like "How do you feel?" According to some thinkers, human life is driven by conflicting urges: as living creatures, we want to preserve, enhance, and maybe reproduce life; but, as physical objects, we want to be at rest. So the life force of biology and the death wish of physics are in constant tension, from which arises a desire for understanding and expression. A common sentiment in classical antiquity is registered as a paradox in many poems, the best known probably being Catullus's:

> Odi et amo. Quare id faciam fortasse requiris.
> Nescio, sed fieri sentio, et excrucior.

"I hate and I love. You may ask why I do so. /I don't know, but I feel it happening and am tormented." Catullus, who lived decades before Martial, found the ideal expressive form in two lines.

Eventually, the lyric expression of such paradoxes found answerable outlets in various verse forms that somehow register or enact conflict and possibly resolution. ✖ **For more than six hundred years, the sonnet has been the fundamental lyric form to express powerful feelings that move in many directions, life and death, love and hate, yes and no, all at the same time.** For most of its long career, the sonnet has served as a working model for mental and emotional combat, especially in the service of secular or sacred love.

⌂ **By this point it has become impossible to keep action, character, sentiment, diction, prosody, and layout in neat compartments. For normal expression, all exist at once, and almost any approach may seem incomplete or incoherent.** It matters most that all of the important elements are considered, not the order in which they are taken up. It is clear, however, that in most lyric poems the elements of action and character are subdued. The only action may be somebody talking, and the only character is the unidentified person doing that talking. What is prominent in lyric is the state of mind and feeling.

✖ **The classic model of the sonnet is a fourteen-lined poem divided into an octave (eight lines) and a sestet (six).** Ideally, each subset is further divided into matching halves that repeat a rhyme scheme, but seldom exceed a total of five rhyme sounds overall. The first eight lines rhyme *abbaabba*. In many cases the grammatical pauses do not fall at the same place as rhyme boundaries, so that the plot of sense is something like ab | ba | ab | ba. With the octave, one has established one sort of mastery, and there is no need to go beyond that. The sestet ought to present different rhymes in a different arrangement, ideally *cde cde*, again with matching subdivisions. ✗ **As noted earlier, in many of the early Italian examples, the beginning of the ninth line marks a turning point or volta.** This hinge or pivot may appear as Italian *ma*, "but." Grossly summarized, the first four lines present a condition, the next four a continuation, confirmation, variation, or consequence. Then the ninth line turns in the opposite direction and offers another sequence of condition and continuation. Thomas Hardy's "Hap" departs from the classic *abbaabba cdecde* rhyme scheme, but it preserves the logical structure with extreme clarity:

> If but some vengeful god would call to me
> From up the sky, and laugh: "Thou suffering thing,
> Know that thy sorrow is my ecstasy,
> That thy love's loss is my hate's profiting!"
>
> Then would I bear, and clench myself, and die,
> Steeled by the sense of ire unmerited;
> Half-eased, too, that a Powerfuller than I
> Had willed and meted me the tears I shed.
>
> But not so. How arrives it joy lies slain,
> And why unblooms the best hope ever sown?
> – Crass Casualty obstructs the sun and rain,
> And dicing Time for gladness casts a moan...
> These purblind Doomsters had as readily strown
> Blisses about my pilgrimage as pain.

The division into units of four, four, and six lines is graphically clear, and the logical design is impossible to miss:"If" for four lines, "Then" for four more, "But not so" introducing the rest. In symbolic logic the "if-then" sequence is called "**ANTECEDENT-CONSEQUENT**." The negation of the antecedent ("But not so") implies the negation of the consequent, which leads in turn to baffled questions: "How arrives it...?" and "why unblooms...?" The conceptual contrast between octave and sestet is made even sharper by a sudden quantitative shift in diction: after elaborate sentences of thirty-three and thirty-two words in the octave, the sestet opens with a fragment of three abrupt monosyllables: "But not so." (Hardy, trained as an architect, understood design and structure.)

The sonnet design, whether in the Italian (eight-six), English (four-four-four-two), or Anglo-Italian (like "Hap," four-four-six), is neatly adapted to the expression of mixed feelings. In the English sonnet, the volta may be delayed until the thirteenth line, which commonly begins "but" or "yet." (Of Shakespeare's 154 sonnets, about fifteen have "but" or "yet" near the beginning of the thirteenth line.)

The paradoxical extremes of the secular sonnet also make the form suitable for religious sentiments, nowhere more conspicuous than in Donne's Holy Sonnets, which adhere to a modified Italian or Anglo-Italian format (*abbaabba cdcdee*) with a volta at line 9 or 10:

Holy Sonnet	Line	Beginning
IV	9	**Yet** grace, if thou repent
V	10	**But** oh it must be burnt
VII	9	**But** let them sleep,
IX	9	**But** who am I
XIII	9	No, no; **but**
XIV	9	**Yet** dearly I love you
XVI	9	**Yet** such are thy laws
XVII	9	**But** why should I beg more love

[The numbering of Donne's sonnets has been a matter of dispute, but this is one acknowledged scheme.]

Narrative poems typically tell the story of some external conflict or contest; dramatic poems typically dramatize some internal conflicts or contradictions within a character; lyric poems, while they may involve some of the common elements of the narrative and the dramatic, concentrate on the conflicts and contradictions among a set of thoughts and feelings. There can also be contradictions or paradoxes between the levels, so that what may look like a speech by an epic hero like Ulysses turns out to be an exploration of a complex state of mind and feeling.

A lyric poem as such does not have a narrator. If the speaker of the poem can be identified, he or she may be described as a "persona," which is a mask through which the poet speaks. Even if you encounter frustrating difficulties in trying to express *your* self, you can rest easy in the assurance that you can create *a* self that can be expressed by the means you have available. Anybody's genuine personal self is locked and hidden away from any treatment available to art or language.

What T. S. Eliot's J. Alfred Prufrock exclaims – "It is impossible to say just what I mean!" – is true of everybody. But, in creating the complex character of Prufrock, Eliot has created a type; according to the *Oxford English Dictionary*, "Prufrockian" means "Resembling or characteristic of the timid, passive Prufrock or his world of middle-class conformity and unfulfilled aspirations." It is unlikely that Eliot set out to express himself through the means of an invented character who then turned into a type. It is much likelier that he set out to create a character who inevitably shares some of his own personality but who also does *not* share some of his own personality. F. Scott Fitzgerald created Jay Gatsby as a character (who also became a type), but he did not set out to be autobiographical, or only autobiographical. Fitzgerald said, "Begin with an individual, and before you know it you find that you have created a type; begin with a type, and you find that you have created nothing." In some ways you cannot *not* express yourself in everything you do, but such expression is not the primary purpose of art and is not something a serious artist worries much about. Ezra Pound often cited a Chinese saying that your character is evident in every one of your brushstrokes.

It is unwise, then, to identify speakers or narrators as autobiographical projections of an author. A disclaimer at the beginning of Evelyn Waugh's *Brideshead Revisited* (1945) asserts, "I am not I; thou art not he or she; they are not they." The Preface to Arnold Bennett's *Old Wives' Tale* (1908) is cautionary:

> It has been asserted that unless I had actually been present at a public execution, I could not have written the chapter in which Sophia was at the Auxerre solemnity. I have not been present at a public execution, as the whole of my information about public executions was derived from a series of articles on them which I read in the *Paris Matin*. Mr. Frank Harris, discussing my book in "Vanity Fair," said it was clear that I had not seen an execution (or words to that effect), and he proceeded to give his own description of an execution. It was a brief but terribly convincing bit of writing, quite characteristic and quite worthy of the author of "Montes the Matador" and of a man who has been almost everywhere and seen almost everything. I comprehended how far short I had fallen of the truth! I wrote to Mr. Frank Harris, regretting that his description had not been printed before I wrote mine, as I should assuredly have

utilized it, and, of course, I admitted that I had never witnessed an execution. He simply replied: "Neither have I." This detail is worth preserving, for it is a reproof to that large body of readers, who, when a novelist has really carried conviction to them, assert off hand: "O, that must be autobiography!"

Around the middle of the twentieth century, a number of influential critics recognized that much poetry involved contradictions and conflicts. In 1930, William Empson, himself an accomplished versifier, published *Seven Types of Ambiguity*, concerning the typical language of poetry (mostly lyric). In 1947 Cleanth Brooks, a teacher and editor but not a poet, published *The Well Wrought Urn: Studies in the Structure of Poetry*, arguing that paradox is at the heart of lyric and dramatic poetry. In the years following Empson's and Brooks's influential books, many other critics have examined paradox, contradiction, ambiguity, tension, undecidability, and the general failure of language to match the world or anything outside itself. (This is not the place to join the rather stale debate over what Jacques Derrida meant by "il n'y a pas de hors-texte" – "there is no outside-text" or "there is nothing outside the text.") All such critical maneuvers have met with resistance, and poetry itself has survived with its customary vivacity, doing whatever it does and always has done, even though we cannot say precisely what that is.

⌂ **Obscure poetry tends to be of the lyric sort, since inner states are themselves murkier than actions and characters.** A lyric can represent an effort to register what feeling feels like, and that is hard to do. W. H. Auden's suggestion, "Poetry might be described as the clear expression of mixed feelings," certainly applies to lyric poems, and clarity of expression can be as baffling as mixed feelings themselves.

We may now be better situated to approach more systematically a given text, such as that most famous of soliloquies – that in *Hamlet* beginning "To be or not to be." The overall plot of *Hamlet* involves a complex act of revenge, a favorite action in Renaissance drama and still very popular. A revenge plot involves an offense, which is detected and confirmed, and an offender, who is identified and found. The acts of detection, confirmation, identification, and location can all take time and are all subject to obstacles and delays, and in many cases the offender resists detection, identification, and so forth. In *Hamlet* the offender is Claudius, who has killed his own brother, King Hamlet, the father of Prince Hamlet. The murder seems to have been prompted by Claudius's ambition to be king himself and compounded by his lust for Queen Gertrude, Hamlet's mother, whom he marries soon after the death of the former king. Delays come in many forms, including uncertainty about the reliability of certain supernatural visions of the ghost of Hamlet's father. Much of the action of the play consists in a protracted effort to confirm what the ghost has told Hamlet, as well as Hamlet's own occasional reluctance to act. Much that happens in the play can be seen as delaying tactics that stretch out the action and intensify the satisfaction of the eventual revenge itself. The design of the plot orchestrates a set of characters who themselves act in various ways to retard the forward motion of the revenge plot.

In Act III, after much has gone on and the audience has confirmed, by an aside, that Claudius is guilty, Hamlet almost comes to a dead stop and considers suicide – that is the substance of this soliloquy, which is devoted to explaining yet more delay. Toward its conclusion, Hamlet says:

> Thus conscience does make cowards of us all;
> And thus the native hue of resolution
> Is sicklied o'er with the pale cast of thought,
> And enterprises of great pith and moment
> With this regard their currents turn awry,
> And lose the name of action.

He has begun to feign madness, as an act of self-concealment, and is about to set in motion another scheme to confirm Claudius's guilt, by watching his reaction to a play with an action close to that of the murder that Hamlet suspects.

The substance of the soliloquy, then, is not a general meditation on life, death, and suicide, although it may be detached and treated as an independent utterance. In the immediate context of the play, the speech expresses the inward thoughts of a character, and, as noted earlier, it is assumed that what someone says in a soliloquy is accepted as true, as least as far as that character can know the truth. The thoughts and feelings expressed in the soliloquy contribute to our understanding of a character, and that understanding in turn contributes to our comprehension of the plot, which is a complex arc of revenge. The weight (and, one might add, the brilliance) of the soliloquy can be appreciated as a function of how well it suits the character and how well that character suits the plot. That speech, those thoughts, and that character cannot be deposited just anywhere – they belong in a certain part of a certain play. In another play or with another character, the same speech may have other functions, but here its chief significance is how it credibly contributes to a delay. As Julius Caesar (from another play) might remark of Hamlet, "He thinks too much." In any event, we have now seen enough to appreciate the relative values and interactions of plot, character, and sentiment, and it is time to look more into the arts of diction.

4 The Arts of Diction

When you sit down to write something new, you could start with anything. You may have a story to tell; you may want to explore a character; you may be interested only in a state of mind or a feeling. Some have testified that they start with a word or even a rhythm, and then build from that beginning. There are no directions that tell a writer to start with any particular thing, and you can even start with nothing special in mind except spending some time seeing what happens. Even so, for the sake of organizing what is known about writing and reading, it may help to try to be systematic.

So far, wanting to write something, you could have taken care of devising a plot of action, creating suitable characters to carry out the action, and imagining plausible states of mind and feeling to account for what those characters do and say. You could do all that in your head and yet never write a word or even think of one.

The three foregoing chapters have dealt with elements – story, character, states of mind and feeling – that can be found indiscriminately in the prose and poetry of any literature, regardless of language or writing system, if any. Those are the elements that can survive translation, because we recognize that a knife, say, is a knife, regardless of what you call it. Now, however, with diction, we come to an element that so changes from language to language that it probably will not survive translation without some loss of nuance. (Robert Frost said, "Poetry is what is lost in translation" – which probably refers to effects of diction and sound peculiar to a given kind of English.) English *autumn* and *fall* as the name of a season mean about the same thing, but Frost's line "And comes that other fall we name the fall" would not be exactly the same in translation, since the two meanings of

The Poetry Toolkit: For Readers and Writers, First Edition. William Harmon.
© 2012 William Harmon. Published 2012 by Blackwell Publishing Ltd.

"fall" will probably not carry over into another language. The same principle applies to Gerard Manley Hopkins's poem "Spring and Fall," which depends on such actions as springing and falling as well as the names of seasons. Currently, *autumn* is more common in Britain than in America, although both forms can easily be heard in both places.

✗ **Such a choice belongs in the realm of diction, which can conveniently be subdivided into VOCABULARY (words one at a time) and SYNTAX (word order).** Children acquire units of vocabulary before they acquire patterns of syntax, but soon enough, within two or three years, any speaker can find ways to express all sorts of meaning. Speakers speak by (1) choosing individual units from a menu of possibilities and then (2) combining the units in patterns that deliver meaning. Both processes may involve a degree of conscious choice, but to a native speaker the whole thing comes to seem natural and automatic. To a careful writer, however, the processes may become rather more deliberate and are subject to much more revision.

Of the thousands of ways to classify English words, the commonest would have to include short and long, old and new, plain and fancy, formal and casual, Latinate and Germanic, direct and indirect, abstract and concrete, native and foreign. For many common activities, the speaker can choose something ordinary (*die*), something elevated (*go to one's reward*), something **EUPHEMISTIC** (*pass away*), or something crude (*croak*). The choice depends on many variables and considerations, but the usual standards call for appropriateness and economy. ᗡ **It is usually best to choose the commonest, shortest, most familiar decent word.** Winston Churchill, among others, is given credit for stating, "Short words are best and the old words when short are best of all." (Some words are even classified by old-fashioned dictionaries as "poetic," which probably means that they are ornate and archaic. Indeed, some amateurs begin writing poetry by saying "Eftsoons forsooth methinks . . .". That's not such a good idea, unless the amateur wants to present somebody as an idiot, and that seems unkind. In a juvenile poem, Robert Frost could say "Wide fields of asphodel fore'er," but he soon matured into the monosyllabic plainness of "Whose woods these are I think I know," "Here come real stars," and "Back out of all this now too much for us." Only rarely does any modern poet need to reach back to archaisms like "thee" and "thou" to make a point; there are almost always better means of achieving elevation. ☠ **Anybody who thinks that "I am desirous of obtaining a beverage" is ever better than "I want a drink" needs to think again.** A poet's time could hardly be better spent than in the study of words. James Joyce wrote in *Stephen Hero* that Stephen, around 1899, "read Skeat's *Etymological Dictionary* by the hour." As Ford Madox Ford said, according to Ezra Pound: "Get a dictionary and learn the meaning of words." Since 1858, the great dictionary of English has been the *Oxford English Dictionary*, earlier titled the *New English Dictionary*. (W. W. Skeat, whose *Etymological Dictionary* first appeared in 1888, was part of the project.) There have been two principal print editions and several versions online or on CD-ROM. Between 1884 and 1928 the dictionary appeared in fascicles (constituent volumes), to which one could subscribe; Thomas Hardy did so.

It is reported that Robert Graves "sold all that he had and bought the full set of the *Oxford English Dictionary*," probably either the successive fascicles or the print edition of 1928. Laura (Riding) Jackson and her husband Schuyler Jackson owned a copy that he probably purchased during the 1930s. W. H. Auden described the contents of his "cave of making," including "dictionaries (the very/best money can buy)." In fact, the dictionary was not dauntingly expensive. In the United Kingdom during the 1960s one could buy a copy for £65 ($182) – not cheap but not exorbitant either, for thirteen heavy volumes.

The first comprehensive print edition was published in twelve volumes in 1928; a supplement with additions and corrections, constituting the thirteenth volume, was added in 1933. The second comprehensive print edition in twenty volumes was published in 1989. Since then, a number of versions of the CD-ROM have appeared, and an online version is updated continuously.

Here's an example: In 1928, "Neptune" was defined as "the outermost planet." By 1933, Neptune was the "second most remote planet of the solar system, discovered by Galle in 1846, and lying beyond Uranus." A parenthesis notes that "a more distant planet, Pluto, was discovered in 1930." Then, in 1989, Pluto had become "a small planet of the solar system lying beyond the orbit of Neptune, discovered only in 1930 by C. W. Tombaugh." By the twenty-first century, Pluto was "a small planetary body orbiting the sun, mostly beyond the orbit of Neptune." A note muses: "... From the time of its discovery it was regarded as the ninth (outermost) planet of the solar system, but in the 1990s its unusual characteristics led astronomers to question its planetary nature. In August 2006 the International Astronomical Union formally declared Pluto to be a dwarf planet rather than a planet proper . . . ." That has been the fate of one word over an eighty-year span, and it seems typical of what one can find on almost every page of the dictionary. For the serious writer, a decent dictionary is the only such resource of any value. One does not need a thesaurus: nobody knows too few words. Most know too many, and they ought to submit to vocabulary-reduction exercises, shedding excrescences such as "orientate," "obligate," "utilize," "preventative," and "technicological." Any writer ought to be able to get by with the vocabulary he or she already has. Depending on a thesaurus to suggest synonyms probably means that one repeats too much. Once is enough. Undue emphasis on vocabulary building has been a favorite campaign of some educators, but it does not have much to do with writing well.

Thomas Hardy, at about age twenty-five, bought himself a pronouncing dictionary and a rhyming dictionary, which seem to have formed part of his ingenuous and laborious self-education. Twenty-first-century media ensure that everybody knows how words sound, so that pronouncing dictionaries may be of value only to broadcasters. Rhyming dictionaries seem to be of even more limited use. Again, a writer with ears knows enough sounds and can find rhymes without suggestions from a book. One who chooses a word just because it fills out a rhyme is probably not very inspired.

♫ **One most important feature of a word's meaning is its "part of speech" – that is, whether it functions as a noun, pronoun, verb, adjective, adverb, or whatnot.** (The way a word *functions* determines its category, since many words, such as "spring" and "walk," function as nouns and verbs.) The heart of language has two main chambers: nouns (and pronouns) and verbs, and you can tell a whole story with just those: "People lied."

Many adjectives are derived from nouns (*miraculous* from *miracle*, say), and many adverbs in turn are derived from adjectives (*miraculously* from *miraculous*, say). Such successive derivations have the effect of drawing writing away from its center toward a periphery, where it can become bloated. Another source of bloat is lack of confidence in what a word can do. Why say "give this serious consideration"? All consideration is serious; and the verb "consider" says in one word what the phrase "give consideration" says in two. "Consider this" halves the wordage of "give this serious consideration" (even worse is "give serious consideration to this") and gains in clarity as well as impact. Many people waste time on overweight locutions like "free gift," "heartfelt thanks," "cordial welcome," and "consensus of opinion." If there is really no need to say something, there is no need to say "Needless to say." If something goes without saying, let it. Why say "It goes without saying?" Instead of saying "To cut a long story short," just do so.

A poem may follow a "plot of diction." Thomas Hardy's "I Found Her Out There," for example, begins and ends with ordinary monosyllables:

> I found her out there
> On a slope few see ...
> And joy in its throbs
> With the heart of a child.

Between those extremes, however, the vocabulary shifts to the exotic and far-fetched: Dundagel's famed head," "Lyonnesse," and "domiciled" (rhyming with "child"). The general design of the diction of the poem is a departure and return, plain-fancy-plain:

> I found her out there
> On a slope few see,
> That falls westwardly
> To the salt-edged air,
> Where the ocean breaks
> On the purple strand,
> And the hurricane shakes
> The solid land.
>
> I brought her here,
> And have laid her to rest
> In a noiseless nest
> No sea beats near.
> She will never be stirred
> In her loamy cell
> By the waves long heard
> And loved so well.
>
> So she does not sleep
> By those haunted heights
> The Atlantic smites
> And the blind gales sweep,
> Whence she often would gaze
> At Dundagel's famed head,
> While the dipping blaze
> Dyed her face fire-red;

And would sigh at the tale
Of sunk Lyonnesse,
While a wind-tugged tress
Flapped her cheek like a flail;
Or listen at whiles
With a thought-bound brow
To the murmuring miles
She is far from now.

Yet her shade, maybe,
Will glide underground
Till it catch the sound
Of that western sea
As it swells and sobs
Where she once domiciled,
And joy in its throbs
With the heart of a child.

Thanks to its uniquely mixed heritage, English can call on down-to-earth monosyllables as a sort of ground bass, and some poems consist of little else. Chidiock Tichborne's "Elegy," written shortly before his execution for treason in 1586, is eighteen lines of iambic pentameter. In most versions, every one of the 180 words is a monosyllable:

My prime of youth is but a frost of cares,
My feast of joy is but a dish of pain,
My crop of corn is but a field of tares,
And all my good is but vain hope of gain.
The day is gone and I yet I saw no sun,
And now I live, and now my life is done.

The spring is past, and yet it hath not sprung,
The fruit is dead, and yet the leaves are green,
My youth is gone, and yet I am but young,
I saw the world, and yet I was not seen,
My thread is cut, and yet it was not spun,
And now I live, and now my life is done.

I sought my death and found it in my womb,
I look't for life and saw it was a shade,
I trode the earth and knew it was my tomb,
And now I die, and now I am but made.
The glass is full, and now the glass is run,
And now I live, and now my life is done.

Tichborne's age is not known for certain. It is possible that the eighteen lines of his poem memorialize his having lived for only eighteen years. (The life expectancy in 1586 was less than forty years.) He was executed within a week of the autumnal equinox of 1586, so that his "prime" may ironically allude to the spring season (prime, primavera=early spring): in the springtime of his life he comes to an autumnal end. The way the poem repeats "now" exploits the ambiguity of that word, meaning both a time in the past and a time in the present, as though to say "One minute you're alive, the next, not."

A similar contrast occurs in Shakespeare's Sonnet XCVII: "The teeming autumn, big with rich increase, /Bearing the wanton burden of the prime" and Milton's Sonnet IX: "Lady that in the prime of earliest youth, /Wisely hath shun'd the broad way and the green."

By the last quarter of the sixteenth century English was losing so many of its sounded inflections that monosyllables became more abundant. Even today, a few words can be pronounced with either one or two syllables: *aged, learned, striped, crooked*. Beginning around 1575, English poetry could revel in hard-hitting lines like "And if I did what then?" (George Gascoigne) and "Since there's no help, come, let us kiss and part" (Michael Drayton). Some words that vary in their scansion can count as one or two syllables. "Heaven," for example, sometimes scans as monosyllabic "heav'n," as in Campion's line "Heav'n is music." (Also in the line "And Heaven and nature sing.") Robert Bridges noticed that early Milton may scan words like "power" as two rather leisurely syllables – "Whose power hath a true consent" in "Il Penseroso" – but that by the mature years of *Paradise Lost* they had become compressed into one:

His utmost pow'r with adverse pow'r opposed –

which sounds, well, more powerful.

English words coming from the south of Europe (Italic, Hellenic) routinely consist of many short uniform syllables, on the pattern of *veracity*, in which each of the four syllables consists of a single **CONSONANT** sound followed by a single **VOWEL** sound: *ve ra ci ty*. The counterpart from the north of Europe (Germanic, Celtic) would be *truth* or *truthfulness*, in which the syllables are longer and bulkier, all with one or more consonant sounds before and after each vowel. A speaker using a word like *veracity* may raise the pitch of the voice (and sometimes the eyebrows too), creating a music more varied and complex than what is available in more consistent languages. Try speaking this from Herrick:

When as in silks my *Julia* goes,
Then, then (me thinks) how sweetly flows
That liquefaction of her clothes.

Next, when I cast mine eyes and see
That brave Vibration each way free;
O how that glittering taketh me!

The first fifteen words are easy and familiar enough, but it is likely that you have never before spoken "liquefaction" or possibly even seen or heard the word before. It is almost always a technical or "inkhorn" term, in alchemy, meteorology, biology, and even – a special sense – theology. Herrick, a resourceful clergyman, brilliantly appropriates it to render the physical effect of moving silk. It is difficult to keep the voice and eyebrows from going up when you pronounce it. "Vibration," although similar in history and structure, is a commoner word. Again, however, voice and eyebrows may be elevated. The impact of the passage could be enhanced also by the repeated consonant and vowel sounds in "brave Vibration." "Brave" here, as in Miranda's "brave new world" in *The Tempest*, does not mean "courageous" so much as "fine, splendid, excellent, capital," and in Herrick's time in the early seventeenth century could even specifically mean "Finely-dressed . . . splendid, showy, grand, fine, handsome" (*Oxford English Dictionary*).

    The interplay of common and uncommon words is one of the great resources of English, exploited in different ways by different poets. John Donne keeps his idiom at a pretty high level, seldom sounding like anything anyone would actually say, as in this passage from "The Ecstasy":

When love with one another so
   Interinanimates two souls,
That abler soul, which thence doth flow,
   Defects of loneliness controls.

There is no record that "interinanimate" had ever been used before this poem, which dates from 1631. (Some manuscript versions read "interanimates," which is a possible reading, although it may be rhythmically deficient. Donne used "inanimate" in a sermon, meaning "to animate, give a soul to." His coined verb "interinanimate" means "mutually animate or inanimate.")

Almost three hundred years later, as we saw earlier, "I Look into My Glass," the last poem in Thomas Hardy's first book of verse, *Wessex Poems* (1898), shows that vocabulary had grown plainer and syntax less contorted, but that drama was still available in the contrast of common and uncommon words:

I look into my glass,
   And view my wasting skin,
And say, "Would God it came to pass
   My heart had shrunk as thin!"

For then, I, undistrest
   By hearts grown cold to me,
Could lonely wait my endless rest
   With equanimity.

But Time, to make me grieve,
   Part steals, lets part abide
And shakes this fragile frame at eve
   With throbbings of noontide.

And, as noted earlier, the six rhyming pairs all represent different parts of speech: noun–verb, noun–adjective, verb (participle)–noun, pronoun––noun, verb–noun, verb–noun. In many English poems, rhyming pairs tend to be the same part of speech, and, in about half of those cases, the words are nouns. Early in Frost's "Provide, Provide," most of the rhyming words are nouns: hag–rag–Abishag, Hollywood–good (noun)–likelihood. By the end of the poem, however, the monotony is dispelled:

Some have relied on what they knew;	*verb*
Others on simply being true.	*adjective*
What worked for them might work for you.	*pronoun*
No memory of having starred	*verb (participle)*
Atones for later disregard,	*noun*
Or keeps the end from being hard.	*adjective*
Better to go down dignified	*verb (participle)*
With boughten friendship at your side	*noun*
Than none at all. Provide, provide!	*verb*

It is impossible to write the way you talk. A speaker, who normally has no written record, may need to repeat a great deal. Despite that limitation, speech usually has the advantage of living contact and a broad range of vocal resources, including pace, pitch, volume, accent, and personal style. You can recognize the way somebody talks long before you can spot a style of writing. The advantages of living speech are offset, however, by certain restrictions: as a rule, you can talk only to people within the sound of your unamplified voice. Writing has the advantage of clarity and durability, so that the writer needs to say something only once. A reader enjoys the privilege of skipping, while a listener has to pay attention continuously (or pretend to do so).

Repetition, the chief difference between talking and writing, comes in three basic forms: (1) brute repetition ("This *book* is a good *book*"); (2) repetition by synonym ("This *novel* is a good *book*"); and repetition by pronoun ("*This* is a good *book*; I enjoyed *it*"). All can be trouble. The first is plainly unnecessary. A heedless speaker may say, "This one is one of the ones which . . ." but no writer should ever do so. ⌂ **As a rule, what needs a hundred words in speaking can be said in fifty words of writing.** For most writers, a first draft of fifty words can easily be reduced to twenty-five, with no loss of meaning. Consider this, from a book that seems to have been dictated:

There is considerable irony in the fact that, though Cole Porter was the most thoroughly trained musician of all the writers discussed in this book, he is better known and more highly considered for his lyrics than his music.

> – Alec Wilder, with James T. Maher, *American Popular Song: The Great Innovators, 1900–1950.*

One could forgive a speaker for talking like that, but no serious writer would write "There is considerable irony in the fact that" – eight words that can easily be reduced to one: "Ironically." With no loss of substance, one could write that sentence as this: "Ironically, though Cole Porter was the most thoroughly trained musician of all those discussed here, he is better known for his lyrics than for his music." We go from thirty-nine words to twenty-six, a reduction of one-third.

If you could write the way you talk, you would write poetry. A great deal of written poetry falls back on some of the devices that animate speech: pulse, variety, repetition of rhythms, meters, consonants, and vowels. When something is written, whether in prose or poetry, the reading of it aloud can be problematic. Not many people are very good at reading poetry aloud, and some fine poets are quite terrible as readers, even with their own verse. A trained theatrical performer may do better, but the job is hard for anyone. It is as though poetry insists on honoring its birth in writing. The "virtual" pulses and repetitions of written poetry project the *illusion* of speech, but, for many, reading or even reciting a poem out loud is redundant, adding real sound effects to the artificial sound effects of rhythm, meter, rhyme, **ALLITERATION**, and so forth. It is almost as though poetry did not exist until writing came along and made it necessary. Until you have writing, speech alone is all the poetry you need. You could confirm this by listening to the speech of illiterate adults or pre-school children. Their speech can sound quite musical.

Written poetry could be called "3G": a Third Generation use of language. The first is ordinary speech, with all its repetitions and variations. The second is writing, which does without the repetitions and variations. The third is written poetry, which restores repetitions and variations in order to suggest the qualities of living speech. Since written poetry already has its own "music," it does not need to be read aloud or set to music. That would be redundant. Paul Valéry said, "Having verse set to music is like looking at a painting through a stained-glass window." For most memorable vocal music, the words – confusingly called "lyrics" – do not need to be very distinguished. Those who specialize in writing words for songs are usually less well known than those who specialize in music. (Cole Porter, mentioned earlier in an example of dilatory prose, wrote words for his own music, as did Irving Berlin.) Ira Gershwin, the lyricist, is much less famous than his composer younger brother George. The same thing goes for obscure lyricists Yip Harburg and Otto Harbach, who wrote clever or touching lyrics to music by composers such as Jerome Kern, who remain famous. For that matter, millions know compositions by G. F. Handel and J. S. Bach but who can name those who composed or assembled the texts of oratorios and cantatas? Start with Charles Jennens and Salomo Franck – but the point is clear. Words as words probably don't need music. On the other hand, words written to be set to music do not need to be very distinguished. Among opera composers, very few set their own words. Richard Wagner is the most prominent exception, since he wrote words and music for all his important music dramas. Other such instances are rare: Arrigo Boito wrote libretto and music for *Mefistofele*, and Nikolai Rimsky-Korsakov did the same for *The Snow Maiden: A Spring Fairy Tale*.

More people attend poetry readings than buy books of poetry, but both audiences are relatively small in the overall environment of live performance and printed text. Most reciters of poetry either overdo the pulsation and division into lines or else ignore these qualities, so that what they read just sounds like peculiar prose.

If you have to deliver a piece of prose writing aloud, you face a similar predicament, since what constitutes good writing on paper may flop when read out loud. Hence the rarity nowadays of good speakers of prose and good reciters of poetry. ♫ **In both prose and poetry, however, economy is almost always a virtue.** What you write to be read silently, whether prose or poetry, follows certain rules having to do with its "virtual" status as something heard or overheard. With something written to be delivered aloud, whether a paper or a poem to be read, you need to take some pains to imagine how it will sound when realized out loud. It is hard to reproduce the effect of speech in a written paper, but the process may be aided by attention to selective repetitions, pauses, and changes of pace.

It is interesting to compare a work that exists as prose fiction, drama, and film, since each medium has its own peculiar emphasis and pace. It is entertaining to read a novel such as *The Caine Mutiny*, then to read or watch the stage version, and then to compare both with the film version. It has been argued that in the migration from medium to medium the work so changes that there is a different focal character in each manifestation.

Some have noticed that memorable oratory, while usually a species of prose, may share certain qualities of poetry. Abraham Lincoln's Gettysburg Address (1863) relies on parallel constructions, antithesis, alliteration, and rhyme as well as repetition of words and rhythms:

> But, in a larger sense, we cannot dedicate . . . we cannot consecrate . . . we cannot hallow this ground. The brave men, living and dead, who

struggled here have consecrated it, far above our poor power to add or detract. The world will little note, nor long remember, what we say here, but it can never forget what they did here.

Lincoln's Second Inaugural Address (1865) shares many of the same qualities:

Fondly do we hope – fervently do we pray – that this mighty scourge of war may speedily pass away. Yet, if God wills that it continue, until all the wealth piled by the bond-men's two hundred and fifty years of unrequited toil shall be sunk, and until every drop of blood drawn with the lash, shall be paid by another drawn by the sword . . . .

Winston Churchill's speeches are likewise memorable, and for many of the same reasons. Here is a passage from a speech in June 1940:

We shall go on to the end, we shall fight in France,
we shall fight on the seas and oceans,
we shall fight with growing confidence and growing strength in the air,
we shall defend our Island, whatever the cost may be,
we shall fight on the beaches,
we shall fight on the landing grounds,
we shall fight in the fields and in the streets,
we shall fight in the hills;
we shall never surrender . . . .

And, again, the same sort of poetic repetition may be heard in Martin Luther King's celebrated "I Have a Dream" speech from 1963:

Let freedom ring from Stone Mountain of Georgia.
Let freedom ring from Lookout Mountain of Tennessee.
Let freedom ring from every hill and molehill of Mississippi.
From every mountainside, let freedom ring . . . .

For most normal speakers, sentences are relatively short and grammatically uncomplicated. ꄃ **The usual order of parts in an English DECLARATIVE sentence is subject-verb-object: "Children like dessert."** Flexibility results in part from the placement of adjectival and adverbial matter. In most cases, adjectives precede nouns: "a blue jacket." In certain formal or archaic locutions traceable to a Romance language nouns *precede* adjectives: "court martial," "knight errant," "Table Round," "House Beautiful." Articles always precede nouns, and almost all prepositions, true to their name, are *pre-positioned*, that is, they come before their object. In a few cases, however, such as *whereof* and *thereon*, the preposition follows. Ezra Pound roundly ridiculed the style of Sir Henry Newbolt, whose "Ballad of John Nicholson" includes some inexcusable inversions:

> The Captains passed in silence forth
> And stood the door behind;
> To go before the game was played
> Be sure they had no mind.

In an experiment in archaism, Robert Creeley's "Kore" playfully displaces a preposition:

> As I was walking
> I came upon
> chance walking
> the same road upon.

Thomas Hardy's "The House of Hospitalities" pushes inversion to a nearly grotesque extreme:

> . . . . .
> Yet at midnight if here walking,
> When the moon sheets wall and tree,
> I see forms of old time talking,
> Who smile on me.

For most speakers, the normal form of the first line would be "Yet if walking here at midnight," and the relocation of the conjunction "if" may seem particularly jarring. One of A. E. Housman's poems begins "Here dead lie we" – a sequence of adverb, adjective, verb, pronoun (subject). Given all possible permutations, there are twenty-four ways ($4 \times 3 \times 2 \times 1$) in which to arrange those four words, and almost all seem grammatical enough, probably starting with "We lie here dead."

♫ **The versatility and flexibility of adverbs also determines much of syntactic variation. Many fairly long utterances in prose and poetry**

**begin with adverbs, adverb phrases, or adverb clauses, any of which can
function to modify verbs, adjectives, or other adverbs.**

Since nominative and accusative forms of nouns are not inflected in
English as they are in many other languages, subjects and objects can
sometimes change places. A familiar line in Thomas Gray's "Elegy Written
in a Country Church-yard" shows such reversibility: "And all the air a
solemn stillness holds," by displacing the verb to the end, could mean both
"And all the air holds a solemn stillness" and "A solemn stillness holds all
the air." Something similar but more complex occurs in a hallucination in
Tennyson's "Lucretius":

> The mountain quickens into Nymph and Faun,
> And here an Oread – how the sun delights
> To glance and shift about her slippery sides,
> And rosy knees and supple roundedness,
> And budded bosom-peaks – who this way runs
> Before the rest! – a satyr, a satyr, see,
> Follows . . . .

The postponement of the verb "follows" permits the oread to follow the
satyr while the satyr follows the oread, as if they are running around a tree,
each following the other.

Longfellow's "Snow-flakes" demonstrates the meaningful flexibility of
English word order:

> Out of the bosom of the Air,
> 　Out of the cloud-folds of her garments shaken,
> Over the woodlands brown and bare,
> 　Over the harvest-fields forsaken,
> 　　Silent, and soft, and slow
> 　　Descends the snow.

Those thirty-three words come down to a simple sentence of three words
– "The snow descends" – amplified by six adverb phrases and three
alliterated adjectives. The syntactic reversal of verb and subject, delayed
to the very last word, may suggest the suspension of time and freezing of
space. A similar effect of displacement can be seen in the first stanza
of Thomas Hardy's "The Convergence of the Twain" (Lines on the loss of
the *Titanic*):

In a solitude of the sea
Deep from human vanity,
And the Pride of Life that planned her, stilly couches she.

Walt Whitman could say something simple amounting to "I sing a reminiscence" in a very complex-seeming way, although it remains a simple sentence with a prodigious amount of adverbial preliminaries:

Out of the cradle endlessly rocking,
Out of the mocking-bird's throat, the musical shuttle,
Out of the Ninth-month midnight,
Over the sterile sands, and the fields beyond, where the child, leaving his
  bed, wander'd alone, bare-headed, barefoot,
Down from the shower'd halo,
Up from the mystic play of shadows, twining and twisting as if they were
  alive,
Out from the patches of briers and blackberries,
From the memories of the bird that chanted to me,
From your memories, sad brother – from the fitful risings and fallings I
  heard,
From under that yellow half-moon, late-risen, and swollen as if with
  tears,
From those beginning notes of sickness and love, there in the trans-
parent mist,
From the thousand responses of my heart, never to cease,
From the myriad thence-arous'd words,
From the word stronger and more delicious than any,
From such, as now they start, the scene revisiting,
As a flock, twittering, rising, or overhead passing,
Borne hither – ere all eludes me, hurriedly,
A man – yet by these tears a little boy again,
Throwing myself on the sand, confronting the waves,
I, chanter of pains and joys, uniter of here and hereafter,
Taking all hints to use them – but swiftly leaping beyond them,
A reminiscence sing.

Up until about 1950, for reasons not completely understood, English poetry could experiment with word order freely, placing adverbial matter at any place in a sentence, reversing subject and object, and playing with syntax in fascinating patterns. In Book X of his autobiographical poem *The Prelude*, William Wordsworth recalls his time in France at the beginning of the Revolution:

> Bliss was it in that dawn to be alive,
> But to be young was very heaven! . . .

The normal wording of that would be: "To be alive in that dawn was bliss, but to be young was very heaven." That is, the order of the first clause has been somewhat disturbed while the second is normal. The concept puts two ideas in a parallel form, but the wording in the poem reverses the parts of the sentence, so that we see predicate-subject-subject-predicate arranged around pivotal uses of "was." The first line represents a departure, the second a return. ✖ **This general pattern of *abba* is called a CHIASMUS.** A similar pattern occurs in a witty line from Keats's *Eve of St. Agnes*: "Out went the taper as she hurried in." The line is bracketed by two antithetical adverbs, "out" and "in." The basic wording would be something like "The taper went out as she hurried in," but the departure-and-return chiasmus makes a much more interesting pattern.

A century later, Yeats could say, "How can I, that girl standing there/My attention fix . . ." Eliot could say, "To Carthage then I came." Pound could say, "Stands genius a deathless adornment"; "Shines/in the mind of heaven God/who made it . . ."; "Came Neptunus . . ." But it became increasingly difficult for later poets to do much disturbance of word order. ☘ **Now and then, someone desperate to complete a design of rhyme or rhythm will rearrange the parts of a sentence, but that usually seems awkward and amateurish.** Points from the career of W. H. Auden illustrate one poet's evolution from rather strained and mannered verse to something much closer to an ordinary idiom. The early poem "The Wanderer" includes a prayer:

> Save him from hostile capture,
> From sudden tiger's leap at corner;
> Protect his house,
> His anxious house where days are counted
> From thunderbolt protect . . . .

All articles have been omitted, giving an abrupt and alien effect. We might expect "From the sudden tiger's leap at a corner" or "From a sudden tiger's leap at a corner" and "where the days are counted." And

we might note the peculiar echoic chiasmus of "Protect his house...."
His anxious house...protect." Within about twenty-five years, Auden
had worked through to clarity, with articles restored and syntax
straightforward:

> A ragged urchin, aimless and alone,
>   Loitered about that vacancy; a bird
> Flew up to safety from his well-aimed stone:
>   That girls are raped, that two boys knife a third,
>   Were axioms to him, who'd never heard
> Of any world where promises were kept,
> Or one could weep because another wept.
>   ("The Shield of Achilles")

At about the same time, Dylan Thomas, although his life was short, had
time to evolve in somewhat the same way, from contortion to clarity:

> Never until the mankind making
> Bird beast and flower
> Fathering and all humbling darkness
> Tells with silence the last light breaking
> And the still hour
> Is come of the sea tumbling in harness
>
> And I must enter again the round
> Zion of the water bead
> And the synagogue of the ear of corn
> Shall I let pray the shadow of a sound
> Or sow my salt seed
> In the least valley of sackcloth to mourn
>
> The majesty and burning of the child's death.

(A single 83-word sentence beginning with 53 words of adverbial matter,
draped without punctuation over thirteen rhymed lines) – "A Refusal to
Mourn, the Death by Fire of a Child in London."

> Do not go gentle into that good night,
> Old age should burn and rave at close of day;
> Rage, rage against the dying of the light.

(Twenty-six words, mostly monosyllables, in three complete independent clauses with much punctuation.) It is as though the ordinary were extraordinarily difficult for a poet to achieve. Similar patterns can be seen in early and late poems by Robert Frost, T. S. Eliot, and Ezra Pound. ⚒
PARATAXIS means "equal arrangement" of parts: "The snow comes down; my temperature goes up" or "The snow comes down, and my temperature goes up." The Latin counterpart of Greek *parataxis* is *coordination*, and parataxis involves the relatively simple functions of *and*, *but*, *or*, *for*, *nor*, *so*, and *yet* (you seldom need *and/or*). Parataxis often joins **POLYSYNDETON** (repeated conjunctions, usually "and") in a protracted **CATALOG**, which may be further enhanced by **ANAPHORA** (the repetition of the beginnings of successive units), as in Shakespeare's Sonnet 66:

> Tired with all these, for restful death I cry,
> As, to behold desert a beggar born,
> And needy nothing trimmed in jollity,
> And purest faith unhappily forsworn,
> And gilded honour shamefully misplaced,
> And maiden virtue rudely trumpeted,
> And right perfection wrongfully disgraced,
> And strength by limping sway disabled,
> And art made tongue-tied by authority,
> And folly doctor-like controlling skill,
> And simple truth miscalled simplicity,
> And captive good attending captain ill:
>   Tired with all these, from these would I be gone,   [*chiasmus*]
>   Save that, to die, I leave my love alone.

Other sophisticated features of syntax turn up more often in writing than in speech, probably because they require some untangling, with which a written record helps. The eighteenth century seems to have been the heyday of such labyrinths. Alexander Pope's "Epistle to Dr. Arbuthnot" (1735), already examined in Chapter II, bitingly surveys the pains and pitfalls of the literary life, and deploys a prismatic style to ridicule those who have no style at all:

> What walls can guard me, or what shades can hide?
> They pierce my thickets, through my grot they glide;
> By land, by water, they renew the charge;
> They stop the chariot, and they board the barge.

The full form of the first line would be "What walls can guard me, or what shades can hide me?" The omission of the second "me" is an example of ✂ **ELLIPSIS, the deliberate omission of part of a phrase or clause that is parallel to another.** Later in the "Epistle," the poet asks more questions:

> Whom have I hurt? has poet yet, or peer,
> Lost the arch'd eye-brow, or Parnassian sneer?
> And has not *Colly* still his Lord, and Whore?
> His butchers *Henley*, his Free-masons *Moor*?

The full form of the second couplet would look something like this: "And has not Colly his Lord, and Whore still? And has not *Henley* his butchers still? And has not *Moor* his Free-masons still?" Two changes, one **LEXICAL** and one syntactic, have influenced the final form: ellipsis of "has not... still" from the second and third clauses, and chiasmus of the two later clauses. That is, the subject-object order of "*Colly*...Lord and Whore" is upended in the object-subject order of "butchers *Henley*" and "Free-masons *Moor*." It is unlikely that a speaker would spontaneously generate such elaborations, but writing makes it somewhat easier.

Similar devices are on display in a stanza from Thomas Hardy's "The Darkling Thrush" (1902):

> The land's sharp features seemed to be
> The Century's corpse outleant,
> His crypt the cloudy canopy,
> The wind his death-lament.

The original full form of all that would be something like "The land's sharp features seemed to be the Century's corpse outleant, the cloudy canopy seemed to be his crypt, the wind seemed to be his death-lament"; rather like Pope, Hardy has gained in elaboration by a combination of **ASYNDETON**, ellipsis, and chiasmus.

CONJUNCTIONS operate in one ordinary mode and two extraordinary modes. The ordinary mode uses a conjunction like *and* or *but* to join two things: "He was tired and hungry"; "He was tired but eager." For more than two, one conjunction will suffice before the last item: "red, blue, and yellow." ⊟ **Polysyndeton is a surplus of conjunctions: "red and blue and yellow." Asyndeton is the opposite: a shortage of conjunctions: "red, blue, yellow." Polysyndeton may seem expansive,**

asyndeton congested. Hardy's "The Convergence of the Twain" provides examples of both:

> Over the mirrors meant
> To glass the opulent
> The sea-worm crawls – grotesque, slimed, dumb, indifferent . . . .
>
> Jewels in joy designed
> To ravish the sensuous mind
> Lie lightless, all their sparkles bleared and black and blind.

So we have "bleared and black and blind" (showing polysyndeton, where the repetition is reinforced by alliteration); and "grotesque, slimed, dumb, indifferent" (showing asyndeton).

A passage in Gerard Manley Hopkins's "The Windhover" seems to undulate with airy polysyndeton and then, immediately, excited asyndeton: "Brute beauty and valour and act, oh, air, pride, plume, here/Buckle!" Most instances of polysyndeton involve coordinating conjunctions, usually "and." Ernest Hemingway's *A Moveable Feast*, however, offers a remarkable sentence, with a moment of second-person narration, with ordinary repetition of "and" but ending with polysyndeton involving the same *subordinating* conjunction three times:

> All of the sadness of the city came suddenly with the first cold rains of winter, *and* there were no more tops to the high white houses as you walked but only the wet blackness of the street *and* the closed doors of the small shops, the herb sellers, the stationery *and* the newspaper shops, the midwife – second class – *and* the hotel *where* Verlaine had died *where* I had a room on the top floor *where* I worked . . . .

Asyndeton can sound abrupt, like Julius Caesar's stoical "I came, I saw, I conquered" (reinforced in Latin by alliteration and repeated grammatical form and rhythm: *Veni, vidi, vici*). Polysyndeton can sound primitive, either in a childish way or in the manner of ritual, especially at the end of a poem. The end of William Wordsworth's "A Slumber Did My Spirit Seal":

> No motion has she now, no force;
> She neither hears nor sees;
> Rolled round in earth's diurnal course,
> With rocks, and stones, and trees.

Likewise with the slowing pace at the end of Hardy's "Channel Firing":

Again the guns disturbed the hour,
Roaring their readiness to avenge,
As far inland as Stourton Tower,
And Camelot, and starlit Stonehenge.

(Here, as often, alliteration reinforces repetition.)

These variations of conjunction usually accompany parataxis, which is more flexible in its conjunctions. In **HYPOTAXIS**, however, which uses many more conjunctions with more definite meanings (such as *if* and *unless*), the conjunction is rarely omitted. In some cases of speech or rather informal uses, a subordinate conjunction can be omitted. "You pay me, I wash your car" (omitted *if* or *when*); "No shirt, no shoes, no service" (ellipsis compressing something like "If you are not wearing a shirt and shoes, you get no service" – abetted, once again, by alliteration).

Vocabulary and syntax can both be either simple or complex, which means that a given sentence may display one of four combinations of qualities. Samuel Johnson's humorous quatrain cited in Chapter 1 –

I put my hat upon my head
And went into the strand.
There I met another man
Whose hat was in his hand.

– combines relatively simple vocabulary and syntax. T. S. Eliot's "Mr. Eliot's Sunday Morning Service" maintains relatively simple syntax, but the vocabulary is outlandish:

Polyphiloprogenitive
The sapient sutlers of the Lord
Drift across the window-panes.

Dylan Thomas's "A Refusal to Mourn the Death, by Fire, of a Child in London," already quoted in this chapter, follows through on the promise of its elaborate title with complications of vocabulary and syntax:

> Never until the mankind making
> Bird beast and flower
> Fathering and all humbling darkness . . . .

and that is just the subject of the subordinate clause; the prodigious sentence goes on for sixty-nine more words. One compelling combination is simple vocabulary with slight complexity of syntax, as in two familiar opening lines by Robert Frost:

> Something there is that doesn't love a wall . . . .
> Whose woods these are I think I know . . . .

The words are ordinary, never more than two syllables. But, with subtle displacements, the syntax may require some work by the reader or hearer. Such first lines work as teasers or hooks for a reader, who may be curious about where such a beginning could lead.

These lessons about vocabulary and syntax will probably be more useful to a writer than to a reader, and more during revision than during original creation. Much imaginative writing is fluent, effortless, and almost automatic, but fairly often, on re-reading, a writer may feel that something is wrong. Coordinate syntax, involving much parataxis, may give the effect of just one thing happening after another, without shading or nuances. Coordination places material on equal footing, a playing field possibly *too* level. "The crowd watched in anticipation. The champion established a new world record." Except in extraordinary circumstances, establishing a new record matters much more than merely watching. That relationship can be registered by putting subordinate material in subordinate clauses: "As the crowd watched in anticipation, the champion established a new record." But it would seem disproportionate to say "The crowd watched in anticipation as the champion established a new record" – that puts the main idea in a subordinate clause. The difference can be shown by sizes of type:

The crowd watched in anticipation. The champion established a new world record.

As the crowd watched in anticipation, **the champion established a new record.**

The crowd watched in anticipation as the champion established a new record.

⚘ **Deft control of syntax can subtly put characters in their place.** The last sentence of Chapter 32 of William Makepeace Thackeray's *Vanity Fair*, concerning Amelia Sedley Osborne and her husband George, who is in the battle of Waterloo, is masterful: "Darkness came down on the field and city: and Amelia was praying for George, who was lying on his face, dead, with a bullet through his heart." It matters that George dies in a subordinate clause, which diminishes his importance even before his body is cold.

Grammarians classify sentences as **SIMPLE, COMPOUND,** or **COMPLEX.** A simple sentence consists of one independent clause. "I sat down." A compound sentence consists of two or more independent clauses joined by a coordinating conjunction or a semicolon. "I sat down, and I took off my shoes." "I sat down; I took off my shoes." ✗ **A complex sentence, including one or more dependent or subordinate clauses, may be either LOOSE or PERIODIC.** The loose sentence has the subordinate clause or clauses at the end, with an effect of fading away. Such is the case with the handling of George Osborne's death in *Vanity Fair*. A periodic sentence has its subordinate clause or clauses at the beginning, with an effect of suspense and climactic building. One could make the George Osborne sentence periodic by slight alterations of wording: "As darkness came down on the field and city: even while Amelia was praying for him, George was lying on his face, dead, with a bullet through his heart." But that might give too much importance to the character, who deserves some comeuppance for his silly misconduct.

The Index of Titles and First Lines in the most recent *Oxford Book of English Verse* (1999) lists seven poems beginning "If," thirteen beginning "As," and twenty-seven beginning "When." The class of poems beginning "When" includes a number of sonnets by Shakespeare. The grammatical anatomy of Hardy's "Hap" may demonstrate the operation of subordinate clauses and periodic sentences:

> If but some vengeful god would call to me   [*Antecedent*]
>   From up the sky, and laugh: "Thou suffering thing,
> Know that thy sorrow is my ecstasy,
>   That thy love's loss is my hate's profiting!"   [*33-word subordinate*
>   *clause, with an*
>   *included sentence*]

> Then would I bear, and clench myself, and die, [*Consequent*]
>   Steeled by the sense of ire unmerited;

Half-eased, too, that a Powerfuller than I
   Had willed and meted me the tears I shed.   *[33-word main clause with an included subordinate clause]*

But not so. How arrives it joy lies slain,   *[Sentence fragment; two questions]*

   And why unblooms the best hope ever sown?
   – Crass Casualty obstructs the sun and rain,   *[compound sentence]*
   And dicing Time for gladness casts a moan . . . .
   These purblind Doomsters had as readily strown
Blisses about my pilgrimage as pain.

As noted in Chapter 3, the components of the If-then construction are called antecedent and consequent. The antecedent is a subordinate clause at the beginning of a periodic sentence; the consequent is the succeeding main clause. As it happens, both clauses in "Hap" are thirty-three words long. The reversal of sentiment signaled by "But" at the beginning of the sestet also features a change of grammar, from complete clauses to an abrupt fragment of three monosyllables. Then come a pair of awkward questions, with the archaic "How arrives it" (meaning "How does it happen") and the unique coinage "unblooms" (classified as a "nonce word" in the *Oxford English Dictionary*). The final rather bitter sentence is accentuated by percussive repetition of bilabial consonants (*b, p, m*): "*B*lisses a*b*out *my* *p*ilgri*m*age as *p*ain." Six out of ten syllables – all of the stressed syllables – with bilabial sounds may have the effect of spitting dismissively.

With some of the resources available online today, you can with relative ease search for poems with almost any feature. With a site like the Columbia Granger's World of Poetry online, for example, you can look for sonnets beginning "When . . .". It is likely that most of them begin with a periodic sentence, which is more dramatic than any other kind. The results of such a search are interesting:

Edmund Spenser (1552?–1599)

When I behold that beauties wonderment
When my abodes prefixed time is spent

Fulke Greville, first Baron Brooke of Beauchamps (1554–1628)

When gentle Beauties over-wanton kindnesse

When all this All doth passe from age to age
When as Mans life, the light of humane lust

Sir Philip Sidney (1554–1586)

When my good angel guides me to the place
When far-spent night persuades each mortal eye
When sorrow (using mine own fire's might)
When Nature made her chief work, Stella's eyes
When I was forced from Stella ever dear

George Chapman (1559?–1634)

When all our other Starres set (in their skies)

Samuel Daniel (1562–1619)

When men shall finde thy flower, thy glory passe
When Winter snows upon thy golden hairs

William Shakespeare (1564–1616)

When most I wink then do mine eyes best see
When thou shalt be dispos'd to set me light
When my love swears that she is made of truth
When forty winters shall besiege thy brow
When I do count the clock that tells the time
When I have seen by Time's fell hand defaced
When I consider every thing that grows
When, in disgrace with fortune and men's eyes
When to the sessions of sweet silent thought
When in the chronicle of wasted time

William Drummond of Hawthornden (1585–1649)

When Nature now had wonderfully wrought

Mary Sidney Wroth, Countess of Montgomery (1587?–1651?)

When nights black mantle could most darknes prove
When last I saw thee, I did not[t] thee see

John Milton (1608–74)

When I consider how my light is spent
When Faith and Love which parted from thee never

Richard Lovelace (1618–1658)

When I by thy faire shape did sweare
When gentle Beauties over-wanton kindnesse

Samuel Taylor Coleridge (1772–1834)

When they did greet me Father, sudden Awe

Henry Kirke White (1785–1806)
When I sit musing on the chequer'd past

John Keble (1792–1866)

When I behold yon arch magnificent

The scrutiny of bilabial consonants in the last line of "Hap" added another element to those already explored, and we can see how acoustic effects can compound the effects of diction and how they, in turn, represent the thoughts and feelings that comprise the characters that make an action move. Accordingly, it is time to concentrate on sound in poetry.

5 The Arts of Sound

For many readers and possibly even for some writers, what we are here calling the fifth element of poetry is the only element: sound effects. That is, poetry is whatever rhymes and alliterates, or otherwise possesses an audible pattern of rhythm or meter or both. Their sentiment amounts to this: "If it rhymes, it's a poem." And that may be true, but only in a limited sense. Here sound effects will be considered as one functional part of a larger process, whereby abstract diction, which may remain silent as long as it is only written, becomes an audible physical reality. Acoustic and graphic effects furnish a poem with its distinctive physical qualities: it can be perceived by the ear and by the eye, and in some ways poetry combines the appeals of music and painting. Many poems have titles, at any rate, that suggest kinship with other arts: *song, prelude, rhapsody, hymn, anthem, quartet, canto, portrait, landscape, still life, nocturne, serenade*, and several others. (Some with such titles must be ironic: "The Love Song of J. Alfred Prufrock" is not a song and is not about love. It seems, in fact, to be more about the absence of music and love.)

🔲 **From another angle, we can say that action is realized in character, character in thought, thought in diction, and diction in sound: we hear sounds and interpret them as language; we hear language and interpret it as the expression of thought and feeling; we interpret thought and feeling as defining components of character; and we understand character as the agent of action.**

☠ **A further warning may be in order: the study of speech sounds has become forbiddingly scientific, with an elaborate system of exotic symbols that some may find obnoxious or irrelevant.** But others find them exciting. Some, resembling Molière's Monsieur Jourdain (in *Le*

The Poetry Toolkit: For Readers and Writers, First Edition. William Harmon.
© 2012 William Harmon. Published 2012 by Blackwell Publishing Ltd.

Bourgeois Gentilhomme), who is impressed to learn that all his life he has been speaking *prose* without knowing it, may be impressed that they have been practicing empirical phonologists. For convenience here, however one may feel about such things, a summary will suffice. (Some of the refinements available to poets in the English language are tabulated at the end of this chapter in Appendix B: Summary of Prosody.)

✗ METER, in a narrow sense, refers to the number of RHYTHMIC units ("FEET") in a given LINE. Any number of units is theoretically possible, but the majority of lines in English have three, four, or five feet. The names of the meters all end in *–meter*, preceded by a Greek number. ✗ The most familiar are MONOMETER (one), DIMETER (two), TRIMETER (three), TETRAMETER (four), PENTAMETER (five), HEXAMETER (six), and HEPTAMETER (seven). In many narrative and dramatic forms, the meter is consistent throughout; in others, especially lyric stanzas, the meter changes from line to line, usually according to an established pattern.

✗ A familiar example of mixed meter is alternation of tetrameter and trimeter (called the "BALLAD STANZA" or the "COMMON MEASURE" or "COMMON METER" of some hymnals). A very common effect is heard in "The boy stood on the burning deck/Whence all but he had fled" – a tetrameter line provides a main independent clause, then a trimeter line provides a subordinate dependent clause.

Similarly, what Samuel Taylor Coleridge called "the grand old ballad," "Sir Patrick Spens," exploits the same format:

> The King sits in Dunfermline town,
> Drinking the blood-red wine;
> "O where shall I get a skeely skipper
> To sail this ship of mine?"

We are given an immediate present-tense introduction to a situation of perplexity: the king has a problem, and, as he thinks, he drinks. The tetrameter lines – numbers one and three – are independent clauses that carry the most important information; the trimeter lines – two and four – add elaboration and refinement on a grammatically lower level: a participial phrase ("Drinking...") and an infinitive phrase ("To sail..."). In performance, the odd-numbered lines may be a little bit louder and at a slightly higher pitch:

The King sits in Dunfermline town,
Drinking the blood-red wine;
"O where shall I get a skeely skipper
To sail this ship of mine?"

The drama is heightened by the immediate direct quotation instead of a bland paraphrase, and what the king says attracts more attention by its status as a question. The drama is mainly in the action and character, to be sure – kings with problems are always interesting – but the presentation is much advanced by the expression by means of grammar and versification.

�֤ Rhythm is a much more complex concept than meter, in Modern English having mostly to do with patterns of ACCENTED and UNAC-CENTED SYLLABLES. Accented syllables are usually represented by an ictus mark (slash, or acute accent on text), and unaccented syllables by a breve mark (open semicircle). The commonest rhythm since the fourteenth century is the IAMB, diagrammed thus: ∪/).

⌘ Other rhythms may be used in poems on their own but also may appear as substitutions and variations within a basically iambic line: tro-chee (/∪), spondee (//), pyrrhic (∪∪), anapest (∪∪/), dactyl (/∪∪), amphibrach (∪/∪), and amphimacer (/∪/). A line in a mostly iambic poem could contain no iambs at all, as in the opening of Eliot's "Gerontion":

Hére Í | ám ăn | óld mán | ĭn ă | drý mónth –

Here the sequence is spondee, trochee, spondee, pyrrhic, spondee. ✗ SCANSION will always be inexact, especially with words of one syllable, but most speakers will agree on where accents belong. ☠ There is little excuse for distorting or wrenching accent for effect.

The earlier parts of a line are more subject to variation than the later, and many lines (called "headless") of iambic tetrameter omit the first unac-cented syllable entirely:

Tí | gĕr Tí | gĕr búr | nĭng bríght
Ín | thĕ fór | ĕst ŏf | thĕ níght . . .

The iambic rhythm is so percussive here that one is almost forced to accent prepositions (*in* and *of*) that are normally unaccented. In these lines, position suggests that *in* should be accented but that *of* can remain unaccented. Some of these choices are matters of individual interpretation. ♪ **We can relax in the recognition that not all feet in an iambic poem need to be iambic or even complete.**

♪ **Feminine endings are fairly common in pentameter lines, especially in BLANK VERSE (unrhymed iambic pentameter).** Here is a line chosen at random from John Milton's *Paradise Lost*:

That durst dislike his reign, and me preferring –

which illustrates such an ending.

Thăt dúrst | dĭslíke | hís réign, | ănd mé | prĕférrĭng . . .

The first two feet are strongly iambic, the third is either spondaic or iambic, the fourth is again strongly iambic, and the fifth is iambic plus an extra unaccented syllable, which could be said to convert the foot into an amphibrach, or just an iamb with a feminine ending.

♪ **As a rule, in an iambic line, any foot with an accented second syllable will suffice as a substitution: iamb, spondee, or, at the end, amphibrach.** Early, a trochee may replace an iamb, as in the opening line of Frost's "The Death of the Hired Man," which, although it is almost all in unrhymed iambic pentameter, begins with an irregular line of hexameter:

Mary sat musing on the lamp-flame at the table . . .

with one possible scansion thus:

Márў | sát mú | sĭng ŏn | thĕ lámp-| fláme ăt | thĕ táblĕ . . .

in which only one foot – the fourth – is certainly iambic; the likeliest pattern is trochee, spondee, pyrrhic, iamb, trochee, amphibrach. Such variations become part of a signature style. In Frost's case, the subtle deployment of spondees and accented syllables is most distinctive and distinguished:

Bĕgín | thĕ hóurs | ŏf thís | dáy slów,
Máke thĕ | dáy séem | tŏ ús | léss bríef . . .

Thĕ wáy | thĕ wír | y̆ gáng- | bóss líked | thĕ lógjàm. . . .
Báck óut | ŏf áll | thís nów | tóo múch | fór ús. . . .

(⚒ A grave accent ['] is used for syllables, such as the second of "logjam,"
that receive SECONDARY ACCENT.)

✗ A rare and peculiar rhythmic effect, known as SCAZON, is
heard when the last foot in an iambic line is in an alien rhythm, such
as trochee or dactyl. If Milton's line just cited –

Thăt dúrst | dĭslíke | hís réign, | ănd mé | prĕférrĭng. . .

be changed to

Thăt dúrst | dĭslíke | hís réign, | ănd mé | fávŏrĭng. . .

a dactyl replaces an amphibrach. When a **FALLING RHYTHM** thus
supersedes a **RISING RHYTHM** at the end of a line, the effect is so
unusual as to be arresting. *Scazon* means "limping" or "halting," and that
effect can be sensed in the abrupt shift with "fávŏrĭng." Something similar
happens in Tennyson's "Lucretius":

a noiseless riot underneath
Strikes through the wood, sets all the tops quivering. . . .

and Poe's "Annabel Lee":

A wind blew out of a cloud, chilling. . .

A *double* scazon ends the first line of John Crowe Ransom's "Bells for
John Whiteside's Daughter":

There was such speed in her little body. . . .

Divided into feet:

There was | such speed | in her | little | body. . . .

With accents marked:

Thĕre wăs | súch spéed | ĭn hér | líttlĕ | bódy̆. . . .

Another double scazon may be heard in a line from Frost's "West-Running Brook":

Below the point, and were at last driven wrinkled...
Below | the point, | and were | at last | driven | wrinkled...
Bĕlów | thĕ póint, | ănd wĕre | ăt lást | drívĕn | wrínklĕd...

Likewise in John Frederick Nims's "Love Poem":

My clumsiest dear, whose hands shipwreck vases...
My clum- | siest dear, | whose hands | shipwreck | vases...
Mý clúm- | sĭest déar, | whŏse hánds | shípwrĕck | vásĕs...

One line in Philip Larkin's "Mr Bleaney" may be a *triple* scazon –

That how we live measures our own nature...
That how | we live | measures | our own | nature...
Thăt hów | wĕ líve | méasŭres | óur ŏwn | nátŭre...

but at that point the line has probably just become ambiguous or trochaic. In any event, the change can be arresting, diverting, and ironic.

The end of Pound's "Exile's Letter" (based on a Chinese original) seems to have a pensive effect:

I call in the boy,
Have him sit on his knees here
To seal this,
And send it a thousand miles, thinking.

Anybody with ears is already familiar with the various sound effects of spoken language, and anybody with feelings knows that sounds can have an emotional effect, although it remains extremely difficult to connect certain sounds with certain feelings.

⚒ **Among the fundamental principles of sound in language are the ideas of consonant, vowel, and syllable.** Although all three defy precise definition, we can make a stab. (For now, this discussion has to do mostly with *sounds* and not letters, since the two do not necessarily coincide. For example, the *h* in *have* and *heart* is not the same as that in *hour* and *honor* or French *haricot*. The *th* in *hothouse* differs from those in both *thigh* and *thy*. (Appendix A at the end of this chapter presents a version of the special alphabet of symbols that approximate most of the common sounds of English.)

🔊 **Vowel sounds begin in the larynx ("voice box") and acquire their particular quality by the shape of the mouth through which they are sounded – especially the rounding of the lips and the placing of the tongue – and the specific part of the mouth in which they resonate.** There are relatively few vowels but, compared with consonants, they vary a great deal over time and from place to place. British and American pronunciation differs most in the sounding of vowels, since consonants are relatively fixed. Vowel sounds may also come in groups of two or three (diphthong, triphthong), which also differ from time to time and from place to place. The words "beat" and "beet" sound basically the same: /bit/, but in Britain the vowel is longer (/biːt/) than in America (/bit/). Vowels toward the front of the mouth are heard in *beet, bait, bet, bat* (slightly different in Britain and America); one toward the middle in the American sounding of *but*; those toward the back in *boot* and British *but*. According to the *Oxford Dictionary of Pronunciation for Current English*, the word spelled *bite* has the British sounding /bʌɪt/and American /bait/– with, as any speaker knows, considerable variation among speakers on both sides of the Atlantic. Visitors to New Zealand will recognize the sounding /sɪvn/ or /sɪvən/ for "seven," and so forth.

By a long-honored convention, promoted final syllables that end in -y or -ie are considered matching pairs with stressed syllables sounded like both "sea" and "sigh." There is little evidence, however, that the final vowel in "eternity," "symmetry," "company," and so forth was ever sounded like "tie," "try," or "nigh." Since such words are fairly common, this latitude increases the number of allowable rhymes, although the sounding like "sigh" has fallen somewhat out of favor since about 1950. A sampling of instances may be instructive:

Spenser (late 16th century): souerainty/ambitiously/principality/deny; be/Eternity/Mutabiltie/eternally.
Marvell (mid-17th century): try/virginity; lie/eternity.
Blake (late 18th century): eye/symmetry.
Hardy (late 19th century): me/equanimity.
Auden (mid-20th century): lie/poetry.

In Gilbert and Sullivan's *Iolanthe* the variation is mocked. Strephon sings:

> A shepherd I –
> Of Arca*dy*, [*die*]

A chorus of Peers responds:

> A shepherd he!
> Of Arca*dee!*

Writers may as well shape their acoustic designs to their native soundings. Readers and performers, on the other hand, may want to learn some historical and regional information, so that Pope, say, in the eighteenth century may have sounded "tea" to rhyme with "obey." Through the seventeenth century, writers often pronounced the verb "character" (meaning "inscribe") with the accent on the second syllable, as suggested by the scansion of a passage from *Hamlet*: "These few Precepts in thy memory/See thou Character" and another from *Two Gentlemen of Verona*: "The Table wherein all my thoughts/Are visibly Character'd, and en-grau'd." In Sonnet CVIII, however, which may be earlier than either of those plays, another sounding prevails:

> What's in the brain, that ink may character
> Which hath not figur'd to thee my true spirit?
> What's new to speak, what new to register,
> That may express my love, or thy dear merit?

Somewhat later, in 1634, John Day's *Parliament of Bees* suggests a scansion like that in Shakespeare's plays:

> The Author in his Russet Bee,
> Charrecters hospitallity.

⌂ **Some peculiarities of spelling and sounding can be blamed on what is called the GREAT VOWEL SHIFT, unique in English, which differenti-ates Modern from Middle English as well as Modern English from most other Indo-European languages.** The shift involves a more or less systematic change in long vowels, with inconsistent results for later speak-ers. It is especially important for rhyme, which we shall get to in time. The letter "a" in English often represents a sound /eɪ/, which in other languages is represented by the letter "e" (as in "Beethoven"). The letter "e" in English often represents a sound /iː/, which in other languages is represented by the letter "i" (as in "Lima" in Peru, not as "lima bean"). The letter "i" in English often represents a sound /aɪ/, which in other languages is represented by the letters "ei" or "ey" (as in "Einstein"). The *Oxford English Dictionary* indicates that *libido* is currently unsettled, with one choice representing values before the shift (/lɪˈbiːdəʊ/), another those after (/lɪˈbaɪdəʊ/). (There is humorous exploration of fluctuations in the libidinal drive and the word itself in Kingsley Amis's *Jake's Thing*.)

We may also notice that some languages distinguish front and back vowels: the former represented in general by *e* and *i*, the later by *a*, *o*, and *u*. The letters *c* and *g* represent different sounds before front vowels, but this effect is inconsistent. *Gerrymander* and *margarine* have two pronunciations: The letter "g" can represent either the /g/ sound in *get* or the /dʒ/ sound in *gem*. But usually these things behave themselves. In some word formations, change of vowel alone can affect meaning, as between singular and plural (*foot/feet, goose/geese, man/men*) or various forms of a verb (*sing, sang, sung*). In the case of the verb *read*, the present and past forms sound different but look the same. Later we shall look at how vowel quality can change with change in accentuation, but this is enough for now.

Consonants on the whole remain more constant than vowels, changing less from time to time and region to region; and there are more of them (as the alphabet testifies). What we spell as *undertake* was spelled much the same way by Chaucer, more than six hundred years ago, but every single vowel was different in sound and the final -*e* was sounded, while the consonants have stayed much the same. We classify some consonants according to which part of the total speech apparatus is involved in their sounding: **BILABIAL** (both lips), **ALVEOLAR** (gum ridge), **VELAR** (soft palate), and so forth.

We further distinguish degree of voicing, from **VOICELESS** to **VOICED** to **VOICED-NASAL**. Three sets of three furnish examples of all: bilabial /p b m/, alveolar /t d n/, and velar /k g ŋ/. Others have only the voiceless and voiced forms: **SIBILANT** /s z/, **SPIRANT** /f v/. Note once again that these are *sounds* and not necessarily letters. The *s* letter in "his" represents a *z* sound; that in "hiss" an *s* sound. Likewise the *f* in "of" represents a *v* sound; that in "off" an *f* sound. (Doubling some consonants can have the effect of changing voiced to unvoiced.)

Speakers assign physical and even emotional meanings to certain sounds, but it is very difficult to be exact about such things. The regular voiceless consonants (p, t, k) may be physically more abrupt and definite than their voiced counterparts (b, d, g), and such words as *pitchfork* may so strongly **DENOTE** sharpness and danger that the sounds seem to **CONNOTE** the same qualities, but the sounds themselves mean very little in isolation, and no one can conclusively separate objective meanings ("sharp-pointed") from subjective responses ("dangerous" for some, "effective" for others, even "pretty" for some). We habitually think of sounds as light or heavy, bright or dark, happy or sad, and *dormitory* and *mortuary* may suggest negative feelings such as loneliness or sorrow, but the sounds themselves are also found in *grocery store* and *motor boat*, which for most people probably suggest more pleasure than pain.

Edgar Allan Poe's essay "The Philosophy of Composition" offers itself as an explanation of how "The Raven" was written. A famous passage discusses sound effects:

> The question now arose as to the *character* of the word. Having made up my mind to a **REFRAIN**, the division of the poem into **STANZAS** was of course a corollary, the *refrain* forming the close to each stanza. That such a close, to have force, must be sonorous and susceptible of protracted emphasis, admitted no doubt, and these considerations inevitably led me to the long *o* as the most sonorous vowel in connection with *r* as the most producible consonant.
>
> The sound of the *refrain* being thus determined, it became necessary to select a word embodying this sound, and at the same time in the fullest possible keeping with that melancholy which I had pre-determined as the tone of the poem. In such a search it would have been absolutely impossible to overlook the word "Nevermore." In fact it was the very first which presented itself.

The vowel in "Poe" is a back vowel, and when followed by a glide such as /r/ can be extended and drawn out – which is what meant by "producible." Given that vowel, one can experiment with different situations, from the abrupt stoppage in *pope*, a longer finish in *probe*, even longer in *pome*, and longest of all in *pore* and *pole*. Even if poets do not customarily choose sounds before they find words to fit them, Poe's general principles seem sound enough, and "The Raven" has been around for more than 150 years.

One can hardly doubt the durability of a poem that has given its name to a professional football team.

There have been serious linguistic studies of connections between sounds and meanings, and one may identify common elements in words with similar meanings, such as *slide, slip, slick,* and so on. But much of this area includes irreducibly subjective responses that vary from speaker to speaker or even with the same speaker, so that we seem better off assuming that semantic associations have nothing particular to do with sounds. *Big* is not as big as *small; back* is in the front of the mouth, *front* farther back. The American poet John Crowe Ransom remarked that Tennyson's line "And murmuring of innumerable bees" does not sound much different from "And murdering of innumerable beeves." The French poet Stéphane Mallarmé famously lamented the *perversité* of French in which *jour* (/ʒuːr/), the word for "day," sounds dark while *nuit* (/nɥi/) "night," sounds bright. Even so, the sounds of syllables can create powerful emotional effects, although the causes remain complex and mysterious.

On the matter of subjective impressions of a language, Mark Twain made interesting remarks about "The Awful German Language":

> I think that a description of any loud, stirring, tumultuous episode must be tamer in German than in English. Our descriptive words of this character have such a deep, strong, resonant sound, while their German equivalents do seem so thin and mild and energyless. Boom, burst, crash, roar, storm, bellow, blow, thunder, explosion; howl, cry, shout, yell, groan; battle, hell. These are magnificent words; they have a force and magnitude of sound befitting the things which they describe. But their German equivalents would be ever so nice to sing the children to sleep with, or else my awe-inspiring ears were made for display and not for superior usefulness in analyzing sounds. Would any man want to die in a battle which was called by so tame a term as a *Schlacht*? Or would not a consumptive feel too much bundled up, who was about to go out, in a shirt-collar and a seal-ring, into a storm which the bird-song word *Gewitter* was employed to describe? And observe the strongest of the several German equivalents for explosion – *Ausbruch*. Our word Tooth-brush is more powerful than that. It seems to me that the Germans could do worse than import it into their language to describe particularly tremendous explosions with.

�֤ The basic syllable in many languages consists of three parts: ONSET, NUCLEUS, and CODA. The onset, which comes first, consists of one, two, or three consonant sounds; if there are three, the first is always *s*. (Here as elsewhere, we are talking about *sounds*, not letters. Sometimes two letters, such as *th*, may represent a single sound (θ or ð, as in *ether/either* and *thigh/thy*); sometimes one letter (such as *x*) will represent two sounds (*ks*). ֆ The nucleus, which comes second, is always a vowel sound: it is the one *necessary* part of the syllable. The coda, which comes third, is one, two, three, or four consonant sounds; if there are four, the fourth is always *s*.

The **x** symbol will be used for any consonant or consonant cluster; **o** will be used for any vowel or group of vowels within a single syllable. Parentheses will indicate optional elements. The diagram for any syllable is thus **(x) o (x)**. In many cases, such as with *tea* and *eat*, the onset or the coda may be missing, in which case we may speak of a "zero-consonant," of which we shall have more to say later on.

Given the basic **(x) o (x)** anatomy, we can use another couple of symbols to indicate relations between syllables: + for "same," – for "different." For example, we could display the relation between *catch* (/kætʃ/) and *king* (/kɪŋ/) as:

> **(x) o (x)**
> + – –

since the onsets are the same (+) and the nucleus and coda differ (– –). Thus, with three positions and two notations, there are eight (2^3) possible configurations. Of these, two are most common in poetry: alliteration –

> **(x) o (x)**
> + – –

and rhyme –

> **(x) o (x)**
> – + +

which are complementary: ֆ **Alliterating syllables begin (onset) the same but end differently; rhyming syllables begin differently but end (nucleus and coda) the same.** "Big" and "bear" alliterate; "big" and "pig" rhyme. Here is the general breakdown:

Pattern (x) o (x)	Description	Example
+ + +	Same throughout	
	1. Repetition (same word)	main/main
	2. Redundant (different words)	main/mane
+ + −	Alliteration plus assonance	main/mate
+ − −	Alliteration	main/mode
+ − +	Alliteration plus consonance	main/mean
− + +	Rhyme	main/rain
− − +	Consonance rhyme	main/roan
− + −	Assonance rhyme	main/tame
− − −	No relation	main/peel

The term "**IDENTICAL RHYME**" is sometimes applied to the effect that involves syllables that are no different in sound, which here are called "repetition" (same word repeated) and "redundant" (same sound, different words). Strictly, repetition occurs at the level of diction and does not qualify as rhyme, which ought to suggest difference somewhere instead of sameness at every level. But the case is difficult to maintain. We can say that "rain," "rein," and "reign" can constitute a proper redundant rhyme while "rain" (noun) merely repeated is only proper repetition. But what about "rain" (noun) and "rain" (verb)?

In no case here does the difference between British and American soundings matter in the description, although for some examples the difference could matter: in much of Britain, *clerk* and *lark* rhyme; in most of America they make only a consonance rhyme.

♭ Note that assonance in general refers to any repetition of vowel sounds, whether in a rhyming position or not; consonance in general refers to any repetition of consonant sounds, whether in a rhyming position or not.

♭ Many acoustic relations involve patterning of two elements (*a* and *b*); the three main possibilities are SUCCESSIVE (*a a b b*), ALTERNATING (*a b a b*), and CHIASTIC (*a b b a*). With assonance involving two vowel sounds, for example, there can be succession ("kn*ee* d*ee*p in the s*a*lt m*a*rsh" – Eliot, "Gerontion"), alternation ("l*e*ft m*y* neckt*ie*" – A. E. Housman, "Terence, This Is Stupid Stuff"), and chiasmus ("R*ai*n has f*a*llen *a*ll the d*ay*" – James Joyce, *Chamber Music* xxxii); "You w*a*lk b*y*, and *I* f*a*ll to pieces" – Harlan Howard and Hank Cochran). With alliteration involving two consonant sounds, likewise, there can be succession ("*b*lushed with *b*lood of *q*ueens and *k*ings" – John Keats, "The Eve of St.

Agnes"), alternation ("One of the brightest wealth has bred" – Thomas Hardy, "Ah, Are You Digging on My Grave?"), and chiasmus ("Reck'd not of boughten prayers, nor passing bell" – Robert Southey, Madoc; "guidon flags flutter gaily" – Walt Whitman, "Cavalry Crossing a Ford"). The patterns sometimes involve repetition of four or five sounds, as in Erasmus Darwin's The Botanic Garden ("Love out their hour and leave their lives in air"), William Barnes's "Linden Lea" ("Do lean down low in Linden Lea. . . ."), A. E. Housman's A Shropshire Lad, XLVI ("Break no rosemary, bright with rime"), and Robert Frost's "Never Again Would Bird's Song Be the Same" ("When call or laughter carried it aloft"). **⌂ Sometimes the Welsh CYNGHANEDD is used for alternating and chiastic patterns of alliteration.** Both sorts can be seen and heard in the last lines of Hopkins's "God's Grandeur": ". . . the Holy Ghost over the bent/World broods with warm breast and with ah! bright wings." It was Hopkins's practice to repeat all parts of initial consonant clusters – as in "dragonflies draw flame" – but a single consonant sound is sufficient to qualify as alliteration. In some stricter systems, the clusters sp-, st-, and sk- were regarded as fixed units. With some other clusters, however, it was possible to link any component with a component in another consonant or cluster, so that sleep might be grouped with sane and loose.

Acoustic relations such as alliteration and rhyme do not seem necessarily to have much to do with grammatical or semantic meanings, but there are some connections that have emerged over time. **⌂ Alliteration tends to associate words for ideas that are already associated, such as house, home, hut, hovel.** Alliteration tends to emphasize harmony, similarity, and family resemblances (as in the pairs of siblings in Wagner's Ring: Fafner and Fasolt, Fricka and Freya, Siegmund and Sieglinde [twins and lovers], Gunther and Gutrune, Woglinde and Wellgunde). Some alliterative combinations – time and tide, have and hold – seem to repeat the same idea (this is called "alliterative reduplication"). On the other hand, antithetical alliterative pairs such as thick/thin and nature/nurture seem to be fairly rare.

⌂ Rhyme, although it does sometimes connect related ideas (such as breast and chest, spine and chine), most strikingly puts together ideas that seem to belong asunder: hire and fire, womb and tomb, germinate and terminate, town and gown, night and light.

⌂ Alliteration is a much older effect than rhyme, at least in Germanic languages, and it is structurally simpler. Alliteration involves only repeated initial consonants (onsets), unlike rhyme, which can involve repeated vowels _and_ consonants (nuclei and codas). Furthermore,

alliteration is heard regardless of stress or accent, since those features concern only vowel sounds. The iambic phrase "*foundations fled*" (Housman, "Epitaph on an Army of Mercenaries") offers full alliteration, even though the *f* sounds do not occur in equally accented syllables. But alliteration seems to be more limited in its reach, seldom extending more than ten syllables. Besides, alliteration comes up frequently in ordinary uses of language, as in everyday expressions like *cup of coffee.* ⌂ **It is worth noting in passing that in Old Germanic languages that use alliteration as a structural device, all syllables that begin with vowel sounds, no matter what, alliterate with one another.** In *eat* and *are*, we hear only a nucleus and a coda; the onset is blank. But the Old Germanic practice seems to treat that blank as a sort of "zero-consonant," so that *eat* and *are* have a + − − design: that is, alliteration. Likewise, *eat* and *ate* have a + − + design: alliteration plus consonance. (An example is line 33 of *Beowulf*:

*i*sig ond *u*tfus, *æ*þelinges fær [ice-flecked, outbound, atheling's barge]

The initial vowels *i, u,* and *æ* all count as alliterating together.

Rhyme, rare in Sanskrit, Greek, and Latin verse of classical antiquity, was not much used in European poetry until about a thousand years ago, and even then it had to struggle for recognition. Since about 1300, however, it has become so much a staple of verse-writing that *rhyme* itself means "poem." Possibly rhyme developed later because it is more complicated than alliteration, and because it comes up much less often in ordinary speech. You will no doubt say things like "for food" during any day; you will not say "pound of ground round" so often. Rhyme is also sensitive to accent, whereas, as we saw above, alliteration is not. In most cases, syllables that rhyme have the same level of accent, usually primary.

⌂ **In this notation we shall recognize four levels of stress: primary (acute mark: á), secondary (grave mark: à), weak (breve mark: ă), and promoted (combining acute and breve: ắ).** The majority of rhymes in English connect two primary accents: *ăppéar/ĕndéar*. Now and then, rhyme will connect a primary and a secondary accent: *ăppéar/réindèer*. The rhyme between a primary and a weak accent may be hard to hear, as in *síng/mórnĭng* (Marlowe, "The Passionate Shepherd to His Love") and *kíng/wávĭng* (Auden, "Miranda's Song").

⌂ **Sometimes, as we have already seen in Chapter 2, for the sake of rhythm or rhyme, we bestow a sort of "courtesy accent" on a syllable normally unaccented. Such "promotion" normally occurs at the end of a**

word of three or more syllables configured as a dactyl: *cóurtĕsў̆*. In the usual practice, promotion (1) gives virtually primary accent to the last syllable and (2) changes the vowel quality. What now scans as *cóurtĕsý* may rhyme with *tea* or *tie*. The first rhyme in Thomas Hardy's "The Darkling Thrush" is between *gate* and the adjective *desolate*. The latter is normally sounded *désŏlăte* (a dactyl), but with promotion it becomes *désŏlăte* (an amphimacer); the sound may changes from /ˈdɛsələt/ to /ˈdɛsˌleɪt/ or /ˈdɛsə ˈleɪt/ (which is the usual accent on the verb *desolate*, but not the adjective).

☙ **An accented rhyming syllable with nothing following is called "MASCULINE" – as with** *make* **and** *take*. **If the accented rhyming syllable is followed by an unaccented undifferentiated syllable, the effect is called "DOUBLE" or "FEMININE" – as with** *making* **and** *taking*. With additional unaccented syllables, the effect is called "**TRIPLE**" (*medicate/dedicate*), "**QUADRUPLE**" (*medicated/dedicated*), and, most rarely, "**QUINTUPLE**" (*medicatedly/dedicatedly*).

"**MOSAIC**" or "**HETEROMEROUS**" rhyme occurs when a single word, such as *visit*, is put in a rhyming position with more than one word, such as *is it*:

> Oh, do not ask, "What is it?"
> Let us go and make our visit.
> > (T. S. Eliot, "The Love Song of J. Alfred Prufrock")

Rudyard Kipling's "If – " contains these pairs: *sinew/in you*; *virtue/hurt you*; *minute/in it*. William Butler Yeats's "The Tower" includes a rhyme between "barrel" and "star, all." Taken to exotic extremes, the effect of such sound effects can be ridiculous, especially in the hands of a comic genius like Byron:

> But – Oh! ye lords of ladies intellectual,
> Inform us truly, have they not hen-peck'd you all?
> > (*Don Juan*, Canto the First, xxii)

Many uses of feminine endings seem random. Hamlet's celebrated soliloquy goes for four pentameter lines before having a masculine ending:

> To be, or not to be – that is the *question*:
> Whether 'tis nobler in the mind to *suffer*
> The slings and arrows of outrageous *fortune*
> Or to take arms against a sea of *troubles*
> And by opposing end them. To die, to sleep. . . .

In many rhyming lyric poems, however, masculine and feminine endings show a pattern of alternation, as in this anonymous sixteenth-century song:

> While that the sun with his beams hot
> > Scorchéd the fruits in vale and mountain,
> Philon the shepherd, late forgot,
> > Sitting beside a crystal fountain,
> > > In shadow of a green oak-tree
> > Upon his pipe this song play'd he:
> Adieu Love, adieu Love, untrue Love,
> Untrue Love, untrue Love, adieu Love;
> Your mind is light, soon lost for new love.

♫ The rhyme between *suitcase* and *bootlace* in the Lennon-McCartney song "Lady Madonna" illustrates another rare variety: COMPOUND RHYME, in which primary accented syllables as well as secondary accented syllables rhyme: *bóotlàce* and *súitcàse*. That is, there are rhymes between *boot* and *suit* and between *lace* and *case*. A song in *King Lear* rhymes *wear rags* and *bear bags*. Philip Larkin once rhymed *careworn* and *airborne*.

Given four degrees of accent – primary, secondary, promotion, and weak – there are many possible combinations. Some are **ISOBARIC** ("equal weight"), as when primary matches primary, and so forth, the most common sort of rhyme in English by far. Others are **ANISOBARIC** ("unequal weight"), as when primary is linked to secondary; that was in evidence earlier with the *ăppéar/réindĕer* rhyme. When one element has only a weak accent, as Marlowe's *síng/mórnĭng* rhyme, the effect is called "**PUNY**," since one does not hear it as a full rhyme of the sort heard, say, in *mórnĭng/scórnĭng*. Marlowe's poem makes fun of a rustic youth possibly as inept with rhetoric and versification as he is with the rhetoric of courtship.

Very rarely rhyming positions will be occupied by words that do not really rhyme, because all of the syllables in question have only weak accent. They may look like a rhyme, but they fail to meet one of the qualifications which stipulates that at least one of the rhyming syllables have at least a minimal level of accent. Their presence suggests something ironic, cynical, or dissonant. The conscripting of weak syllables to do the job of rhyming involves aligning the same or similar *unaccented* syllables, as when *wíndŏw* and *shádŏw* fall at the ends of lines (as in John Crowe Ransom's "Bells for John Whiteside's Daughter"). ✖ **This general effect is called HOMEOTELEUTON.** The accented syllables *wín-* and *shá-* have nothing in common. The repeated unaccented syllable -*dŏw* is a mere repetition. *Nárrŏw* and *Féllŏw* are juxtaposed in a poem by Emily Dickinson – a poem in which, by the way, there is no perfect rhyme until the end:

A narrow Fellow in the Grass
Occasionally rides –
You may have met Him – Did you not
His notice sudden is –   *partial consonance rhyme*

The Grass divides as with a Comb –
A spotted Shaft is seen,
And then it closes at your Feet
And opens further on –   *consonance rhyme*

He likes a Boggy Acre
A Floor too cool for Corn –
But when a Boy, and Barefoot
I more than once at Noon   *partial consonance rhyme*

Have passed, I thought, a Whip lash
Unbraiding in the Sun
When stooping to secure it
It wrinkled, and was gone –   *consonance rhyme*

Several of Nature's People
I know and they know me –
I feel for them a transport
Of Cordiality –   *promotion rhyme*

But never met this Fellow
Attended or alone
Without a tighter Breathing
And Zero at the Bone.   *perfect rhyme*

A passage from Philip Larkin's "Poetry of Departures" presents an instructive rhyming situation:

... Such a deliberate step backwards
To create an object:
Books; china; a life
Reprehensibly perfect.

Both "object" and "perfect" can be pronounced in two ways, depending on the part of speech. If verbs, they would both be iambic: ŏbjéct, pĕrféct. (♫ **It is generally true of such options: the iambic form will be the verb, the trochaic form the noun or adjective. This applies to many words, including "accent," "addict," "contest," "defect," "reject," "permit," "insert," "progress," "subject," and scores of others. A few, such as "perfume," "romance," "address," and "research" may be exceptions.**)

Now, if the words as used by Larkin are iambic verbs, they rhyme perfectly, since -*jéct* and -*féct* are fully accented and conform to the pattern − + +, that is, their onsets are different but their nuclei and codas are the same. If one of the words is a verb and the other is not, either *ŏbjéct/pérfĕct* or *óbjĕct/pĕrféct*, then the rhyme is anisobaric, that is, the accents on the rhyming syllables do not match. The remaining possibly is the one that is actually present in Larkin's poem: *óbjĕct/pérfĕct* (the first is a noun, the second an adjective). Here, with no strong accent on either potentially rhyming syllable, we see homeoteleuton: same or similar unaccented syllables (the former in *window/shadow*, the latter in *object/perfect*). The effect, remote from the foursquare percussiveness of perfectly rhyming accented syllables, suggests s a degree of irony and understatement.

Such rhymes may seem to be a feature of twentieth-century verse, and they have continued into the twenty-first. Like Ransom and Larkin, Dylan Thomas experimented with anisobaric rhyme and homeoteleuton (rhyming *shelter* and *cancer*, for example); and it is difficult to find many examples from earlier centuries. But what happened in the twentieth century may represent little more than a recrudescence of a practice that had long been employed by poets in other languages (French especially) and may be observed in some sixteenth-century English poets heavily influenced by Italian and French practice. Sir Thomas Wyatt (1503–1542) was among the most original of poets and translators, and both his rhythms and rhymes could be inconsistent and oblique – with a very subtle sort of enchantment. A quick scan of Wyatt's poems will yield many rhymes of what could be called a "strange fashion": *chamber/remember/danger*; *gentleness/goodness*; *harbor/banner/suffer/displeasure*; *fashion/reason*.

A large number of great poets have written thousands of memorable poems that adhere reasonably well to the traditional conventional canons of meter, rhythm, and rhyme; and many poets continue to do so in the twenty-first century. But it ought to be recognized that, especially since about 1850, an impressive number of supremely accomplished poets all over the world have chosen to write prose poems, which look just like printed prose; and many have written verse that can be described as "free." It may be free of strictly measured qualities, but, as long as it uses a common language, it is not exactly free of the facts of language. There may be no audible alliteration or rhyme, and the meter may fluctuate, but there is bound to be rhythm, because the patterns are inherent to speech and carry over into habits of reading and writing. In English speech today, iambic rhythm is unavoidable – a statement that in itself is almost all iambic. (Ĭn Énglĭsh spéech tŏdáy, ĭámbĭc rhýthm ĭs únăvóidăblĕ.) Besides, many practitioners of free verse have themselves written measured verse of great distinction. John Milton famously pooh-poohed "the troublesome and modern bondage of riming" but did himself write hundreds of lines of notable rhymed verse.

No sound effect operates in isolation. The various acoustic devices work together, and they function in a cause-and-effect, form-and-matter, end-and-means relation with other parts of a literary work. The overall plots of action depend on subordinate plots of character, which in turn depend on intellectual, psychological, and moral states inside the character, and those in turn determine rhetoric and diction. A certain kind of character in a certain situation can be expected to think certain thoughts and feel certain feelings, which are expressed by rhetorical and grammatical means consistent with the whole discourse. (One always ought to allow for surprise and contradiction in all these matters.) The choice of words then determines the speech sounds.

A concrete example, preferably familiar, may help. Here are some words from the end of the second act of *Hamlet*:

> The spirit that I have seen
> May be the devil, and the devil hath power
> To assume a pleasing shape; yea, and perhaps
> Out of my weakness and my melancholy,
> As he is very potent with such spirits,
> Abuses me to damn me. I'll have grounds
> More relative than this: the play's the thing
> Wherein I'll catch the conscience of the king.

The speech is something spoken aloud by a character, in this case a character alone on stage outwardly expressing inward thoughts and feelings. It is a soliloquy, an utterance by convention assumed to be true, in which a character supposedly reveals real sentiments, motives, and schemes.

The character, Hamlet, is part of a plot that follows a contour of revenge or crime-and-punishment. To gain dramatic power, the punishment must be justified, and that means that the crime itself must be clearly established. The facts are that King Hamlet, Prince Hamlet's father, is dead, and his widow, Queen Gertrude, has married the King's brother, the Prince's Uncle Claudius. So far, at the end of the second act, Hamlet knows that his father is dead, his mother and uncle have married, and he dislikes his uncle. The Prince suspects murder only on the unreliable say-so of a ghost. Now, the conscientious hero – maybe *too* conscientious – needs to be certain of the facts before taking further action. A troupe of traveling players happens to arrive, and Hamlet contrives to add some lines to a speech in a play that includes a murder. He resolves to observe his uncle's reactions. In summarizing his plot, Hamlet explains why the play is needed to confirm suspicions aroused by a ghost. The act ends with a rhymed couplet:

> I'll have grounds
> More relative than this: the play's the thing
> Wherein I'll catch the conscience of the king.

Up until the last two lines, the words have been either prose or blank verse. The presence of rhyme is unusual, but it seems to add a degree of formality and finality to the verse. The last two lines are a rare display of acoustic devices that add levels of coherence and symmetry to the bare sentiment. The rhyme emphasizes the contrast between ordinary *thing* and extraordinary *king*; it may also hint that this king is just a "thing." The percussive iambic beat is abetted by an unusual degree of alliteration in "catch the conscience of the king." The verb *catch* means many things: "apprehend," "detect," "witness," "capture," "ensnare," "entrap," "deceive," and much else. Later, when Claudius asks, "What do you call the play?" Hamlet answers, "The Mouse-trap."

Most of the foregoing has to do with the rhymed or unrhymed qualitative verse written in Europe and America since about 1350. Such considerations, which apply to millions of poems in hundreds of languages, could suffice for a lifetime of satisfactory reading and writing. But they are not the whole story. They are not even most of the story. Most of the world's total of poems are not in **QUALITATIVE** verse and they know nothing of rhyme. **⚒ Sanskrit, Greek, and Latin poetry from classical antiquity mostly adhere to what is called QUANTITATIVE SCANSION: measuring verse by patterns of long and short syllables.** (There are many

differences among such languages. It is probable that Greek was quantitative while Latin may also have been accentual.) The long syllable,
represented by a macron, is regarded as twice the length of the short, and
a proper foot ought to be a whole number with no fractions. Hence, an
iambic foot consisting of one short and one long syllable, adding up to one
and a half units, would not qualify. In this system, it takes two iambs to
make a foot: $\cup - \cup -$, a total of two units and two halves, adding up to an
even three. ✻ **In epic verse, the usual measure is dactylic hexameter
with a CAESURA or pause after the seventh syllable:**

$$-\cup\cup \mid -\cup\cup \mid - \parallel \cup\cup \mid -\cup\cup \mid -\cup\cup \mid --$$

**(at any point in the first five feet a spondee can replace a dactyl; in the
sixth foot, a spondee is usual).** The pattern just given, including the mid-
line caesura, can be applied to the famous third strain of John Philip
Sousa's "The Stars and Stripes Forever."

Quantitative practice often combines a number of different feet and
meters in predetermined patterns. The versatile **SAPPHIC STANZA,** appearing first in Greek and later adapted in Latin, is a quatrain of three eleven-
syllabled lines and one five-syllabled line. Allowing for variations in certain
positions, the first three lines consist of two trochees, a dactyl, and two more
trochees. The fourth line, almost always, consists of a dactyl and a trochee.
The first poem in Thomas Hardy's first book of poetry, *Wessex Poems* (1898),
is the unrhymed Sapphic exercise entitled "The Temporary the All":

> Change and chancefulness in my flowering youthtime,
> Set me sun by sun near to one unchosen;
> Wrought us fellowlike, and despite divergence,
>   Fused us in friendship . . .

It is often impossible to distinguish the quantitative (long-short) from the
qualitative (strong-weak), and Sapphics of one sort or the other have been
attempted by many before and after Hardy, including Sir Philip Sidney,
Thomas Campion, Isaac Watts, Algernon Charles Swinburne, Ezra Pound,
E. E. Cummings, and even Allen Ginsberg.

A fully loaded English syllable can contain as many as eight sounds: three
consonant sounds in the onset, one vowel sound in the nucleus, and four
consonant sounds in the coda. That extreme is uncommon but not
unthinkable. The word *strengths* (/strɛŋθs/) with seven sounds approaches

the limit. In some languages, typical syllables consist of single consonants or clusters before and after the nucleus; in others, typical syllables consist of a single vowel combined with a single consonant preceding or following. In the former there are fewer syllables per word than in the latter. Compare English *cockroach* (two syllables) with its Spanish cognate *cucaracha* (four). One consists of two bulky bound syllables, the other of four airy open syllables. Or compare German *Friedrich* with Italian *Federico*, English *orchestra* with Japanese *ōkesutora*.

In languages, eastern and western, that favor words of many small syllables – a single vowel, a single vowel preceded by a single consonant, or a single vowel followed by a single consonant – the uniform syllables will not receive very audible quantitative or qualitative distinction. That is, the syllables will receive more or less uniform accents and occupy more or less equal durations. In that case, as happens in Italian and Japanese among quite a few other languages, scansion will normally be a matter of counting the syllables without discrimination. The number of sounds in a syllable is known as its **MASS**.

In Dante's *Comedy*, most of the lines contain eleven syllables, as here from Canto XXVI of the *Inferno*: "Fatti non foste a viver come bruti, /ma per seguir virtute e canoscenza" ("You were not born to live as beasts, /but to pursue virtue and learning"). Here, the single-letter words *a* and *e* are counted as part of the preceding syllables, so that "foste a" and "virtute e" count as two and three syllables respectively. In a moment of wit elsewhere, Dante mentioned a single farfetched Italian word that in itself contained eleven syllables:

Sovramagnificentissimamente –

meaning "super-most-magnificently."

✗ **In Japanese, the most celebrated verses are in lines of five, seven, five syllables, without much regard to alliteration, rhyme, or rhythm. The more serious poems in the form are the haiku, the more comical or satirical, as we have seen in Chapter 1, are the senryu.** The classic models date from the late seventeenth century, such as this famous example from Bashō:

kono michi ya
yuku hito nashi ni
aki no kure

with a prismatically clear syllabic breakdown (ko no mi chi ya/yu ku hi to na shi ni/a ki no ku re). The meaning is roughly "(On) this road/no one goes/autumn evening."

Obviously, the average Japanese syllable is much shorter than the average English syllable, so that the spoken duration of seventeen English syllables may exceed the same number in Japanese by two to one. Even so, many distinguished English poets have written poems in seventeen syllables. W. H. Auden's later poems are an example, although they are almost never factored into five-seven-five. The must usual pattern is five-six-six, as in some parts of "Elegy for JFK" (1964):

> When a just man dies
> Lamentation and praise,
> Sorrow and joy are one.

The added ornament of rhyme, almost never present in Auden, does turn up in Paul Muldoon's "News Headlines from the Homer Noble Farm":

> Behind the wood bin
> a garter snake snaps itself,
> showing us some skin.

As a curiosity, Ezra Pound's "Fan-Piece, For Her Imperial Lord," supposedly based on a Chinese original, keeps the five-seven-five Japanese design but fits it to the number of *words*, not syllables:

> O fan of white silk,
> clear as frost on the grass-blade,
> You also are laid aside.*

As it happens, the dying words of the charismatic Confederate General T. J. "Stonewall" Jackson compose a seventeen-syllable sentence: "Let us cross over the river and rest under the shade of the trees." (That, by the way, is the source of the title of Ernest Hemingway's novel about a dying soldier, *Across the River and into the Trees.*)

---

*Ezra Pound: "Fan-Piece, For Her Imperial Lord" from *Personae*, © 1926 Ezra Pound. Reprinted by permission of New Directions Publishing Corporation.

Appendix A: Simplified Phonetic Alphabet

Vowels (**American**, **British**) [variable from region to region]			Consonants (both areas)	
A	**B**	**Example**	**Symbol**	**Example**
i	i:	m*ea*t	p	*p*aper
i	i	meat*y*	b	*b*arber
ɪ	ɪ	d*i*m	t	*t*arget
ɛ	ɛ	d*e*bt	d	*d*ig
æ	a	h*a*t	k	con*c*ur
ɛ	a	m*a*rry	g	su*g*ar
ɑ	ɑ:	f*a*ther	f	*f*an*f*are
ɑ	ɒ	b*o*ther	v	*v*iva
ɔ,ɑ	ɔ:	h*a*wk	θ	*th*igh
ɔ	ɔ:	f*o*rge	ð	*th*y
ə	ʌ	f*u*n	s	*s*aucer
ʊ	ʊ	p*u*ll	z	*z*oo, ro*s*e
u	u:	s*ou*p	ʃ	*sh*oe
ə	ə	f*a*ther	ʒ	re*g*ime
ər	ə	g*er*m	h	a*h*ead
ɪ(ə)r	ɪə	h*e*re	tʃ	*ch*urch
ɛ(ə)r	ɛ:	h*ai*r	dʒ	*j*udge
eɪ	eɪ	r*ai*n	m	*m*ur*m*ur
aɪ	ʌɪ	r*i*nd	n	*n*oon
ɔɪ	ɔɪ	b*oy*	ŋ	wro*ng*
aʊ	aʊ	h*ou*se	l	*l*i*l*y
oʊ	əʊ	h*o*me	r	*r*oaring
			j	*y*o*y*o
			w	*w*ish

Appendix B: Summary of Prosody

The syllable governs much of measurement of language. The one necessary component is the **nucleus**, always a vowel sound. The nucleus may be preceded by an **onset**, consisting of one, two, or three consonants, and followed by a **coda**, consisting of one, two, three, or four consonants. These concepts have to do with *sounds*, not necessarily with letters. The letter "x" usually represents two consonant sounds (ks), while the letters "th" usually represent a single consonant sound (θ or ð as in "thigh" and "thy").

The **mass** of a syllable represents the total number of sounds: as few as one (as in the unaccented single vowel at the end of "idea"), and theoretically as many as eight (three consonants in the onset, one vowel, four consonants in the coda). "Strengths" approaches the practical limit in English, with seven sounds (strɛŋθs). **Accent** is the relative emphasis on a syllable: the noun "accent" is accented on the first syllable: /ˈæksənt/, the verb "accent" on the second: /ækˈsɛnt/. Accent, unlike **stress**, does not vary much. Stress is variable emphasis that one can place on any syllable for a number of rhetorical or semantic reasons. The two terms are often confused.

A binary system of **weak** (⌣) and **strong** (/) emphases may be used in scansion, but speakers clearly pronounce more than two levels of stress. The phrase "a reindeer" contains three syllables, each with a different level of accent: weak, primary, secondary: ă réindèer. In certain words of three or more syllables, we sometimes hear a **promotion** of an unaccented syllable so that it is given a stronger accent. The requirements of rhythm or rhyme may alter a word like "désŏlăte" so that it sounds more like "désŏláte," along with a change in vowel quality (as at the end of the third line of Hardy's "The Darkling Thrush," where the word rhymes with "gate"). The main vowel of promoted syllables will be marked with a special symbol combining acute and breve ("désŏlắte").

Meter is best kept to indicate the tally of feet per line: **monometer, dimeter, trimeter, tetrameter, pentameter, hexameter, heptameter,** and so on.

Rhythm in modern English poetry is almost always a pattern of syllables with varying levels of accent. The units are called **feet**. The commonest foot by far is the **iamb** (⌣/). Other feet possible in English are the **anapest** (⌣⌣/), the **trochee** (/⌣), the **dactyl** (/⌣⌣), the **spondee** (//), the **pyrrhic** (⌣⌣), the **amphibrach** (⌣/⌣), and the **amphimacer** (/⌣/). There are others, but they are insignificant. The conventional description of a verse form will include terms for the rhythm and meter, such as "iambic pentameter," meaning a five-foot line of iambs. Terms such as "iambic" concern the prevailing foot in a poem; it is not necessary that every foot be iambic. **Rhyme scheme** uses italicized lower-case letters to represent different patterns, such as *aabb* and *abab*. Repeated recurrent patterns of rhythm, meter, and rhyme are called **stanzas**, some having specific names (the **heroic quatrain**, for example, contains four lines of iambic pentameter rhyming *abab*). Other patterns are rhyme royal (*ababbcc*), ottava rima (*abababcc*), Spenserian stanza (*ababbcbcc*), Italian sonnet (*abba abba cde cde* or a variation), English sonnet (*abab cdcd efef gg*), and Anglo-Italian sonnet (*abab cdcd efg efg* or a variation). All those are usually in iambic pentameter.

Scanning best begins with a look at polysyllabic words about which there is no doubt. Blake's line "I wander thro' each charter'd street" can be approached in steps:

1. Mark accents on words of more than one syllable:
   I wánder thro' each chárter'd street
2. Mark strong accents on monosyllabic nouns and verbs:
   I wánder thro' each chárter'd stréet
3. Mark strong accents on sizable monosyllables used as adverbs and adjectives:
   I wánder thro' éach chárter'd stréet
4. Decide how you probably sound monosyllabic articles, prepositions, and conjunctions:
   I wánder thrŏ' éach chárter'd stréet
5. Decide how you sound monosyllabic pronouns (not usually stressed but maybe):
   Í wánder thrŏ' éach chárter'd stréet
6. Inspect the pattern:
   //∪∪//∪/
7. Insert likely foot boundaries:
   //| ∪∪ |//| ∪/

The line is tetrameter. The poem as a whole is iambic, but in this line the first foot is either spondaic or iambic (depending on the weight given to "I"), the second foot is either pyrrhic or iambic (depending on the weight given to "thro'"), the third foot is either spondaic or iambic (depending on the weight given to "each"), and the fourth foot is certainly iambic.

To tabulate the possible **acoustic relations** among syllables, let "x" represent any consonant or cluster of consonants, "o" any vowel, " + " sameness, "–" difference. The basic accented syllable would be (x) o (x), with nine permutations, as we have seen earlier in this chapter.

Alliteration tends not to be closely related to accent, although plenary alliteration would connect adjacent accented syllables (as in Hopkins's "**gr**éat **gr**áy"). Alliteration may be patterned or not; nearly all Old Germanic verse, including Old English, has a pattern of alliteration involving four accented syllables in a line: 1 2 3 4. Alliteration joins

syllables 1, 2, and 3; 1 and 3; 2 and 3; in all of these, the fourth accented
syllable is customarily outside the pattern of alliteration. Occasionally,
patterns will join 1 and 3 as well as 2 and 4, or 1 and 4 as well as 2 and 3. The
basic pattern persists in an early modern line such as "**Wé**stern **wí**nd, when
wíll thou **bl**ów," with alliteration joining accented syllables 1, 2, and 3 but
not 4. *Cynghanedd* is a Welsh word for various complex patterns; we shall
use it for arrangements called **alternating** (*xyxy*) and **chiastic** (*xyyx*). The
last line of Hopkins's "God's Grandeur" –"**W**orld **br**oods with **w**arm **br**east
and with ah! **br**ight **w**ings" shows both patterns: alternating in
/**w–br–w–br**–/ and chiastic in /**w–br–br–w**–/. Subtler patterns shape
sounds in Hardy's "The Darkling Thrush," as in "And **w**inter's **d**regs made
desolate/The **w**eakening eye of **d**ay" and "So **l**ittle **c**ause for **c**arolings."

Other patterns, which resemble alliteration, join initial consonants that,
without being identical, belong to the same family. The bilabial consonants
/p/, /b/, and /m/, for example, are all formed the same way, with the two lips
brought together. The last line of Hardy's "Hap" – "**Bl**isses a**b**out **m**y
pilgri**m**age as **p**ain" – presents four accented or stressed syllables that all
begin with bilabials, along with a probably unaccented "-mage" and "my."
Other such families are /t/,/d/,/n/ and /k/,/g/,/ŋ/. Those three threesomes
are the only groups in English with unvoiced, voiced and voiced-nasal
members. Unvoiced-voiced pairs include s/z, f/v, θ/ð (again, we are talking
about sounds, not necessarily about letters).

These zones show that rhyme fits between two classes of not-rhyme:

NO RHYME		RHYME		NO RHYME
Repetition				Homeoteleuton

Homeoteleuton is not rhyme proper but the rhyme-like relation between
unaccented syllables that (1) begin differently and end alike (e.g. "narrow/
fellow") or (2) sound the same throughout (e.g. "window/shadow"). For
musical or comic effects, word-accent can be **wrenched** to conform to
rhythmic patterns or create rhyme, as in Roger Miller's

Westminster Abbey, the tower of Bìg Bén,
The rosy-red cheeks of the little chìldrén.

"**Isobaric**," which means "having equal pressure," applies to syllables that
have the same accent; "isobaric rhyme" is between syllables that both bear
primary, secondary, or promotion stress. In the rare cases of **compound**

rhyme ("bootlace/suitcase"), the primary-accented syllables rhyme *and* the secondary-accented syllables rhyme. **An ambiguous rhyme** seems to be between two promotion-accented syllables ("family/history"). But, with no primary accent for guidance (as with "thée/líbĕrtў"), you will not know whether "family" is going to rhyme on the main syllable (with, say, "clammily") or on the third syllable. In songs, the rhythm of the tune guides the placement of accent and stress. Strictly speaking, even so, "family" and "history" may belong in the category of homeoteleuton, since the normally accented syllables have nothing in common and the rhyme-like relation ("-ly/-ry") is between unaccented syllables.

"**Anisobaric**" means "not having equal pressure," so that anisobaric rhyme would be between the following pairs: primary and secondary ("ăppéar/réindèer"); primary and promotion ("gáte/désolăte"); secondary and promotion ("ínmàte/désolăte"); secondary and unaccented ("Pópèye/fámĭlў"); promotion and unaccented ("révĕrĕnce/sílĕnce"). (The latter rhyme occurs in Philip Larkin's "Church Going.") If "reverence" be sounded with three syllables, the effect, as indicated, involves the aniso-baric rhyme "révĕrĕnce/sílĕnce." If "reverence" be compressed to two syllables, as happens in most people's casual speech, then the effect is homeoteleuton: "rév'rĕnce/sílĕnce." Anisobaric rhymes that include one unaccented syllable are also called **puny** (as well as "Simpsonian" in honor of a 1943 article by Percy Simpson called "The Rhyming of Stressed with Unstressed Syllables").

Multiple rhyme is that in which the rhyming accented syllable is followed by one or more undifferentiated unaccented syllables. The commonest such rhymes are **double** or **feminine** (e.g. "greatly/lately") and **triple** (e.g. "history/mystery"). A special instance of multiple rhyme is the **heteromerous** or **mosaic** rhyme, involving rhymes between one word and two, or two and three, and so forth (e.g. "minute/in it"). Hopkins's poetry presents a few exotic types: **broken** rhyme (e.g. "sing/ing-[ering]") and **fused** rhyme (e.g. "Irish/sire he Sh[ares]").

Scazon is a special rhythmic effect whereby a falling foot, such as a trochee, takes the place of a rising foot, such as an iamb, at the end of a line. Consider Larkin's line "Their parchment, plate and pyx in locked cases," plausibly scanned as:

Thĕir párch | mĕnt, pláte | ănd pýx | ĭn lócked | cásĕs.

That is, the sequence is iamb | iamb | iamb | iamb | trochee.

Note that the scazontic substitution of trochee for iamb in the last foot of the line differs from the ordinary **feminine ending**, in which the place of the iamb is taken by an amphibrach. There are no scazons here:

> To be or not to be – that is the question:
> Whether 'tis nobler in the mind to suffer
> The slings and arrows of outrageous fortune
> Or to take arms against a sea of troubles...

The idea of **thick scansion** exploits the border between prosody and diction, so that the normal order of "We trust in God" is probably iambic ("Wĕ trúst ĭn Gód") while the syntactic inversion of "In God we trust" may invite a slower pace and a more regular distribution, yielding two spondees ("Ín Gód wé trúst").

6 The Arts of Layout

We hear before we see, and we hear speech long before we learn to read writing. The ear is less directional and also less definite – we may say, "What's that sound?" but we seldom say, "What's that sight?" We usually know what we are looking at better than we know what we are listening to. The sound /juːz/ can be eleven different things: *yews, yew's, yews', ewes, ewe's, ewes', use, you's, yous, youse, U's*. But the written *use* can be only two: /juːz/ (verb: "Use your head") or /juːs/ (noun: "what's the use?"). Accordingly, the poem you see on the page may be only a two-dimensional shell or shadow of a much richer poem you might hear in the air. Monotonous speech is more animated than vivacious writing.

♫ **A speaker has an arsenal of devices – volume, pitch, pace, accent, tone, as well as gestures and expressions – that are beyond the reach of print.** A speaker also enjoys the advantage of possibly being near, since the unaided ear cannot hear things very far away, although the unaided eye may see them. The eye enjoys the advantage of sharpness of focus and concentration on this or that direction, and it is able right away to distinguish "the girl with colitis goes by" from "the girl with kaleidoscope eyes," which has confused more than one hearer; but the eye is relatively crude as an interpreter of sound. A musical score, however copiously annotated and fulsomely detailed, remains silent until the music is realized in performance. The writer has the alphabet, some pieces of punctuation, a few spaces, and some such devices as capitals and italics, but that is about all; a few hundred devices to try to represent millions of shades of meaning. Every time you say "five," for example, it sounds infinitesimally different from every other time; and your voice is distinctive enough for a telephone caller to recognize you immediately from nothing more than the way you whisper "Hi."

The Poetry Toolkit: For Readers and Writers, First Edition. William Harmon.
© 2012 William Harmon. Published 2012 by Blackwell Publishing Ltd.

With a written record, you do not need so much repetition. In deliberate, conscious writing, once is enough; in talking, once is seldom enough. Listen to any conversation, and then look at any verbatim transcript. Here is an archival transcription from one of Richard Nixon's typical taped conversations in the Oval Office: "Of course, this is a, this is a, Hunt, you will – that will uncover a lot of things . . ." (www.watergate.info/tapes/72-06-23_smoking-gun.shtml – accessed online July 2011). That is probably close to the way most people talk in unguarded moments.

Many ancient writing systems somehow recorded words and other units of speech but without indication of word divisions (*scripta continua*):

NEQVEPORROQVISQVAMESTQVIDOLOREMIPSVMQVIADO
LORSITAMETCONSECTETVRADIPISCIVELIT
[Neque porro quisquam est qui dolorem ipsum quia dolor sit amet, consectetur, adipisci velit (Cicero). "Neither is there anyone who loves grief itself since it is grief and thus wants to obtain it."]

Many of these writings were little more than prompt-sheets for reading aloud, which was the norm for centuries. Late in the fourth century, St Augustine was impressed by St Ambrose's unusual ability to read silently. The Old English poems preserved in what is known as the *Exeter Book* clearly adhere to alliterative patterning of four-stress lines – the norm for Old Germanic poetry – but they are written margin-to-margin, just as prose is written. That a poem need not be written or printed in any special way is attested by a modern text with these two prose paragraphs:

The last light fades and drifts across the land – the low, long land, the sunny land of spires; the ghosts of evening tune again their lyres and wander singing in a plaintive band down the long corridors of trees; pale fires echo the night from tower top to tower: Oh, sleep that dreams, and dream that never tires, press from the petals of the lotus flower something of this to keep, the essence of an hour.

No more to wait the twilight of the moon in this sequestered vale of star and spire, for one eternal morning of desire passes to time and earthy afternoon. Here, Heraclitus, did you find in fire and shifting things the prophecy you hurled down the dead years; this midnight my desire will see, shadowed among the embers, furled in flame, the splendor and the sadness of the world.

Those paragraphs, from F. Scott Fitzgerald's novel *This Side of Paradise*, had earlier been printed as two Spenserian stanzas (that term will be discussed below). Fitzgerald cleverly gave them a change of costume and reused them.

With prose, *line* means only an arbitrary line of characters with pre-formatted margins. Prose fiction and prose nonfiction *look* just alike, and the question of how **LINES** end is unimportant, except possibly to printers. With many poems, however, *line* is both an acoustic and a graphic concept, and what a line looks like can influence what the line will sound like when pronounced. 🖰 **The relation of graphic array to acoustic array is one of analogy: the look of a line, with its punctuation and spaces, suggests how the line will sound.** The poem looks a certain way because it sounds a certain way; it sounds a certain way because it contains certain words; it contains certain words because it expresses certain thoughts and feelings; those thoughts and feelings come from the nature of a certain character; and that character takes part in a certain action.

The look and sound of the graphic and acoustic arrays may suggest the syntactic array. Speech itself is unpunctuated: it is a messy stream that moves fast or slow, smoothly or turbulently. But punctuation is the property of writing – unless an unresourceful speaker resorts to drawing quotation marks in the air or adding a spoken "period," "full stop," or "stop" at the end of a sentence. Some poems are heavily punctuated in a way that insists on their status as a written text. Consider this typical passage from Alexander Pope's *Essay on Criticism*:

'Tis with our judgments as our watches, none
Go just alike, yet each believes his own.
In poets as true genius is but rare,
True taste as seldom, is the critic's share;
Both must alike from Heaven derive their light,
These born to judge, as well as those to write.
Let such teach others who themselves excel,
And censure freely who have written well.
Authors are partial to their wit, 'tis true,
But are not critics to their judgment too?

These ten lines contain five rhymed couplets of iambic pentameter with all rhymes masculine. The rhyme between *none* and *own* belongs in the category of consonance rhyme – that is, the vowels are not quite the same but the final consonants are the same – but all other rhymes are **PERFECT**. The placement of rhyme words every ten syllables itself works as a kind of zoning that may suggest a slight addition of emphasis followed by a long or short pause. The first line ends with no punctuation, but all the others have *something*: period, comma, semicolon, comma, period, comma, period, comma, question mark.

As with Frost's "Provide, Provide," this poem avoids monotony by varying the part of speech of most of the rhyme words: *rare* [adjective]/ *share* [noun]; *light* [noun]/*write* [verb]; *excel* [verb]/*well* [adverb]; *true* [adjective]/*too* [adverb].) Except for the question, the other marks of punctuation prompt a falling voice in most speakers. The spelling *'tis* suggests that we may have a transcript of somebody talking, but little else suggests anything but deliberate writing with abundant printed punctuation and a good deal of lexical and syntactic complication and compression. Translation into regular prose might change the wording to something like this:

> Judgments are like watches: no two quite agree, but people believe their own. Just as true genius is rare in poets, true taste is rare in critics. Both poets and critics derive their light from heaven, the former ["those"] to write, the latter ["these"] to judge. Let those who excel teach others, and let those who have written well censure freely. Authors are partial to their wit, but are critics not also partial to their judgment?

This mildly dogmatic writing, of a sort common in the eighteenth century, may require a blocky dogmatic presentation with parallel ideas registered in parallel phrases and clauses. The end-stopped lines may themselves slow the pace, since the marks of punctuation ("stops") seem to invite some change of tone and tempo.

If a poem minimizes or eliminates most punctuation, the effect comes closer to the norms of speech, since readers have fewer reminders that they are reading writing: they may have the sensation of hearing speaking. Here are specimens of prose and poetry in which punctuation has been diminished or eliminated:

> The figure seated on a large boulder at the foot of a round tower was that of a broadshouldered deepchested stronglimbed frankeyed redhaired freelyfreckled shaggybearded widemouthed largenosed longheaded

deepvoiced barekneed brawnyhanded hairylegged ruddyfaced sine-
wyarmed hero.
                                                    – James Joyce, *Ulysses*

... and the gagging chloride and the puky dirtstench of the yearold
dead...
                                                    – John Dos Passos, *USA*

According to Brueghel
when Icarus fell
it was spring
a farmer was ploughing
his field...
        – William Carlos Williams, "Landscape with the Fall of Icarus"

Typography is mostly an invisible instrument of little inherent interest,
although we sometimes may notice that "Mountains" begins with a picture
of mountains – M – and "Valleys" with a picture of a valley – V. The word
PIVOT seems to have a pivot in the middle. In some striking instances,
extraordinary capitals map uncommon volume or emphasis:

"MISS JEMIMA!" exclaimed Miss Pinkerton, in the largest capitals. "Are
you in your senses? Replace the Dixonary in the closet, and never
venture to take such a liberty in future."
                                    – W. M. Thackeray, *Vanity Fair*, Chapter I

In his version of parts of the *Iliad*, Christopher Logue brilliantly let capitals
register the voice of loud god, Apollo:

...Across the rucked, sunstruck Aegean, the Mousegod's voice,
Loud as ten thousand crying together,
Cried:
"Greek,
Get back where you belong!"

In Canto LXXXVI, Ezra Pound records what a correspondent said about
Franklin Roosevelt:

"Don't write me any more things to tell him
(scripsit Woodward, W. E.)

"on these occasions

 talks."

The best known modern experimenter with the look of writing remains E. E. Cummings, who seems to have amused himself and his readers with meditations on the keyboard that can be made to register many actions and moods (he was also, like Thackeray, an accomplished graphic artist):

l(a
le
af
fa
ll
s)
one
l
iness*

There remain many other ways to exploit the look of writing, and there are anthologies of what is called **CONCRETE POETRY** and **SHAPED POETRY** to demonstrate them. For now, we can note that the words *canoe* and *ocean* are **ANAGRAMS**: they share the same five letters, which represent, however, radically different sounds (only the *n*-sound is common to both words). Moreover, those lower-case letters are about the same height, without the ascenders (as with "b") or descenders (as with "y"). And oceans and canoes are related in substance as well, since an ocean is a body of water and a canoe is a water craft (though, admittedly, canoes stay mostly on rivers and lakes). Accordingly, one could create a picture of a canoe floating on an ocean by printing the words in a display:

oceanoceanoceanoceanocean
oceanoceancanoeoceanocean
oceanoceanoceanoceanocean

Voilà: "Seascape." Something similar has been done with "boredom" and "bedroom."

---

*"l(a" is reprinted from *E. E. Cummings: Complete Poems 1904–1962*, edited by George J. Firmage, by permission of W. W. Norton & Company. Copyright © 1991 by the Trustees for the E. E. Cummings Trust and George Firmage. Reprinted with permission of W. W. Norton & Company Ltd UK.

✄ A stanza is something you can both see and hear: it is best defined as "a regular, rhymed, recurrent unit" distinguished by rhythm, meter, and rhyme. Other less regular graphic-acoustic units are best called **STROPHES.** In long poems, some of the subdivisions of lines qualify as **VERSE-PARAGRAPHS.**

Since in English almost all stanzas – like much of European poetry in general – rely on the iambic rhythm, that particular property will usually be omitted from descriptions. As with other arrays, stanzas can be treated as having patterns of succession (*aabb*), alternation (*abab*), or chiasmus (*abba*) – a series of increasing complexity requiring a greater reach of memory.

The stanzas evolved over time, especially during the three centuries between 1300 and 1600, and by 1600 most of the important stanzas were in place. What has followed during the four centuries after 1600 has mostly been refinement and variation.

A primitive grouping is a rhymed **COUPLET** of dimeter, along the lines of:

When the cat's away
The mice will play.

Beyond that, growth comes in (1) number of couplets, which can be piled up indefinitely: *aabbccddee...*; (2) number of feet per line, settling mostly on units of three, four, or five feet; (3) rhyme scheme, usually diagrammed in lower-case italics (*abab* and so forth).

✄ **Two-lined forms are the couplet or DISTICH.** They are very common in tetrameter and pentameter couplets. **The latter, also called "HEROIC COUPLET," became the staple verse form between 1660 and 1800. These couplets tend to be end-stopped.**

✄ **Three-lined forms are the TRIPLET or TERCET.** *Triplet* also applies to a set of three rhymed lines inserted in a poem mostly using rhymed couplets, as in this example from Alexander Pope's "Epistle to Dr. Arbuthnot":

His Wit all see-saw between *that* and *this*,
Now high, now low, now Master up, now Miss,
And he himself one vile Antithesis.

For his *Comedy*, Dante designed a long poem in three parts – hell, purgatory, paradise – occupying three days of the year 1300 – Good Friday, Holy Saturday, Easter Sunday – dealing with a divine trinity; and for that design he adopted the verse form called **TERZA RIMA**, usually printed in three-lined graphic units and rhyming *aba bcb cdc ded* and so on. The form has been used in English from time to time, beginning with Sir Thomas Wyatt in the early sixteenth century and continuing through "Cuchulain Comforted," one of William Butler Yeats's very last poems. The rhyme pattern was adapted more recently in Paul Muldoon's "News Headlines from the Homer Noble Farm," in which the three-lined units have the 5-7-5 syllabic pattern of haiku but the rhyme scheme of terza rima.

� **Four-lined forms are the QUATRAIN.** It is probable that the standard unrhymed four-stress alliterated line common in medieval Germanic poetry evolved smoothly enough into a rhyming four-stress line in modern languages, and it persists today in many **RAP** lyrics. Grouping into quatrains fits the usual foursquare design of songs, so that many musical verses are in quatrains of one sort or another.

Some hymnals contain a **METRICAL INDEX**, which typically gives the line-by-line breakdown of syllables, on the principle that any 8.8.8.8 verse, say, can be sung to any 8.8.8.8. melody. For example, "How Firm a Foundation," designated "11.11.11.11" (four lines of eleven syllables each) can be sung either to the tune called "Foundation" or to "Adeste Fideles."

Three hymn forms quatrains have special names:

✖ **LONG MEASURE (or Long Meter): all lines tetrameter (8.8.8.8), rhyming *aabb*, *abcb*, or *abab*.** ("All creatures that on earth do dwell"). Also in T. S. Eliot's seven "Quatrain poems."

✖ **COMMON MEASURE (or Common Meter) (also called Ballad Measure) (8.6.8.6), alternating tetrameter and trimeter, rhyming *abcb* or *abab*.** ("Amazing Grace"). Used in hundreds of hymns and other **VERSES**.

✖ **SHORT MEASURE (or Short Meter) (6.6.8.6), usually rhyming *abab*.** ("Blest Be the Tie That Binds"). Also used in many poems by Emily Dickinson ("There's a certain slant of light") and a few by Thomas Hardy ("I look into my glass," "The Man He Killed"). ᗑ **This verse form is also related to POULTER'S MEASURE (couplets of alternating hexameter and heptameter), very popular around 1575. A variant, sometimes divided into five lines (trimeter, trimeter, dimeter, dimeter, trimeter), became the modern LIMERICK, very popular for two hundred years.**

Although the tetrameter quatrain rhyming *abba* had been employed earlier, it gained special distinction from its use in Alfred, Lord Tennyson's

In Memoriam (1850), which consists of 131 sections that all use such a stanza, now sometimes even called the "*IN MEMORIAM* STANZA." Each section contains at least three quatrains, and all rhymes are masculine.

⚒ **Both the HEROIC QUATRAIN (*abab*) and the RUBÁIYÁT STANZA (*aaba*) are pentameter quatrains differing only in rhyme scheme.** (*HEROIC* is a vague term: in Greek and Latin poetry, it means hexameter; in French, twelve-syllabled **ALEXANDRINES**; in English, German, and Italian, pentameter or just ten syllables).

The Heroic or Elegiac Quatrain seems suitable for memorial poetry, since the reader has to keep the *a*-rhyme in mind while registering the first *b*-rhyme. The rhyming sounds are twenty syllables apart, so that the memory has to do some work. The Heroic Quatrain was used in the Earl of Surrey's elegy for Sir Thomas Wyatt (around 1542), in seventeenth-century heroic poems by Sir William Davenant and John Dryden, and later in memorial or funereal poems by Henry Wadsworth Longfellow ("The Jewish Cemetery at Newport") and Allen Tate ("Mr. Pope"). With some irony, the heroic measure was also used in an elegy for people who were not at all heroic: Thomas Gray's celebrated "Elegy Written in a Country Churchyard." With even more irony, the measure is heard in a quatrain by A. E. Housman, as though spoken by the dead:

Here dead lie we because we did not choose
To live and shame the land from which we sprung.
Life, to be sure, is nothing much to lose,
But young men think it is, and we were young.

Rubáiyát is the plural of Farsi *ruba'i*, "quatrain." In the famous version by Edward FitzGerald (1859), the rhyme scheme is *aaba*, which adheres to the pattern in some if not all of the stanzas in the original language.

⚒ **Most five-lined stanzas work as an extension and elaboration of a quatrain**, as in the *abcbb* stanza in A. E. Housman's "When smoke stood up from Ludlow." **CINQUAIN**, a generic name for a group of five, has been applied to a particular format devised by the American poet Adelaide Crapsey: monometer, dimeter, trimeter, tetrameter, monometer, as in this recent **BAGATELLE** called "Irresolution and Dependence":

I *do*!
I *know* I do.

I *think* I know I do.
I *guess* I think I know I do . . .
I don't.

⚒ **Many six-lined stanzas, likewise, work as elaborations of a basic quatrain**, as in the *ababab* pattern of Thomas Hardy's "Drummer Hodge," which has the alternating tetrameter and trimeter of Common or Ballad Measure. In the course of *The Rime of the Ancient Mariner*, which is mostly in Ballad Measure quatrains, Samuel Taylor Coleridge introduces stanzas of five or six lines that either repeat a rhyme word or extend the basic *abcb* scheme to *abcbdb*. That scheme also turns up in some poems by William Butler Yeats, including "Crazy Jane Talks with the Bishop." William Shakespeare's *Venus and Adonis* reads like a quatrain followed by a couplet – *ababcc* – which has a rather agitated effect consistent with the turbulence of the subject matter. The last six lines of a classical Italian sonnet, ideally rhyming *cdecde*, are called the **SESTET** (a version of **SEXTET**), and some six-lined stanzas with an *abcabc* pattern seem to carry on the tradition, although usually in shorter lines than the pentameter of a sonnet. Dylan Thomas used that scheme in "A Refusal to Mourn the Death, by Fire, of a Child in London," with an approximate metrical scheme of tetrameter, trimeter, tetrameter, tetrameter, dimeter, tetrameter. Here the rhymes are reasonably close: "*making/flower/darkness/breaking/hour/harness*." In a similar stanza used by others, however, the rhyme is more relaxed. In the typical first poem in John Berryman's *The Dream Songs* the rhyme words are "*day/sulked/over/thought/away/talked*." Likewise in Randall Jarrell's "Next Day": "*All/box/hens/identical/flocks/James*." (Thomas, Berryman, and Jarrell were all born in 1914.)

⚒ **There is only one noteworthy seven-lined stanza, but it is noteworthy indeed: the RHYME ROYAL is the only stanza used in common by Geoffrey Chaucer, Sir Thomas Wyatt, William Shakespeare, John Milton, William Wordsworth, William Morris, John Masefield, and W. H. Auden.** The usual meter is pentameter throughout, but with some poets – Milton and Wordsworth – the seventh line is expanded to hexameter. (This effect is also called *Alexandrine*.) The rhyme scheme is *ababbcc*.

⚒ **Some eight-lined stanzas act like doubled quatrains,** as in the *ababcdcd* heard in Thomas Hardy's "The Darkling Thrush" and many other poems as well. Hymnals may abbreviate such a design to "C.M.D," for "Common Meter Doubled." ⚒ **Many BALLAD STANZAS are in** eight lines rhyming *ababbcbc*. Ottava Rima, usually rhymed *abababcc*, has been used with distinction by Sir Thomas Wyatt, Lord Byron, and William Butler Yeats. Yeats also adapted an earlier eight-lined stanza rhymed *aabbcddc* for a few of his poems, including "A Prayer for My Daughter." The meter is pentameter except in lines four, six, and seven, which are either trimeter or tetrameter. A variation of that stanza was adapted by John Berryman for *Homage to Mistress Bradstreet*, in which the syllable count ranges from three to twelve and the rhyme scheme is usually *abcbddba*.

�засX Only one nine-lined stanza is well-known. Devised by Edmund Spenser for *The Faerie Queene*, the SPENSERIAN STANZA rhymes *ababbcbcc* with an extra foot in the last line. It was used by some of Spenser's successors, then revived in the early nineteenth century by Byron, Shelley, and Keats. Since then it has fallen into disuse.

✗ The KEATS ODE STANZA is usually ten lines long, with the first four lines always a heroic quatrain (*abab*) and the remainder in some variation of the sestet of an Italian sonnet (*cdecde*). Most of Keats's odes are pentameter throughout, but in "Ode to a Nightingale" the eighth line is trimeter. Keats's "To Autumn" resembles his other odes but has eleven lines instead of ten, here rhyming either *ababcdedcce* or *ababcdecdde*. Philip Larkin's "The Whitsun Weddings" employs a ten-lined pentameter stanza rhyming *ababcdecde* with dimeter in the second line, a pattern scrupulously aped in Gavin Ewart's parody, "The Larkin Automatic Car Wash." Two of Matthew Arnold's best-known poems, "The Scholar Gypsy" and "Thyrsis," use a ten-lined stanza rhymed *abcbcadeed* with trimeter in the sixth line.

✗ "CURTAL SONNET" is the name given to a poem of ten lines plus a half-line – which amounts to a curtailed sonnet – the first six lines rhyming *abcabc* and the remainder either *dbcd* or *dcbd*. It came about when Gerard Manley Hopkins experimented with a variation of the Italian sonnet that preserved the 8:6 ratio of the original but began with a sestet. The formula is 8:6::6:4.5. R. S. Gwynn has written a rare modern version of the form.

The sonnet, as we have seen in earlier chapters, is a regular rhymed verse form but seldom recurrent within a longer poem, so that it may technically fall short of being a stanza, but it satisfies enough of the requirements to fit in here. ✗ Most sonnets consist of fourteen pentameter lines, although both features can be changed. Among the variations, however, only one dimension changes: that is, sixteen-lined sonnets (such as those in George Meredith's *Modern Love*) are pentameter and those in tetrameter or hexameter (such as Shakespeare's Sonnet 145 or Sonnets 76 and 77 in Sir Philip Sidney's *Astrophil and Stella*) have fourteen lines. ✗ **The senior sonnet form is the ITALIAN or PETRARCHAN, usually with an 8 + 6 design; the former section (OCTAVE) rhyming *abba abba*, the latter (sestet) *cde cde*; the sestet varies more often than the octave, but the form seldom uses more than five rhyme sounds. The ENGLISH or SHAKESPEAREAN follows a 12 + 2 design, consisting of three heroic quatrains and a couplet: *abab cdcd efef gg*.** As has been seen in Chapter III, in both basic formats a change in thought is often marked by a "but" or "yet," called a volta (Italian for "turn"), which typically falls at the beginning of the ninth line of the Italian and the thirteenth of the English. The Italian form is the older by two or three centuries, and, while more demanding in its rhyme scheme, it is shapelier than the English, which can sound blocky and perfunctory. If one omits Shakespeare's sonnets from the tally, it is possible that, paradoxically, most worthy English sonnets are Italian. The **SPENSERIAN SONNET** varies the English model in its rhyme scheme: *abab bcbc cdcd ee*. (It resembles the interlaced rhyme of the Spenserian Stanza.) Thomas Hardy's "Her Reproach" and Richard Wilbur's "Praise in Summer" are later examples of the Spenserian sonnet, which remains, even so, a rare and exotic form. The so-called **MILTONIC SONNET** displaces or omits the volta but is always basically Italian. An interesting combination form is the **TERZA RIMA SONNET,** which uses the interlocking rhyme of terza rima with the fourteen lines of the sonnet, resulting in a poem rhyming along the lines of *aba bcb cdc ded ee*. Percy Bysshe Shelley's "Ode to the West Wind" is the earliest important example, consisting of five stanzas. A "Chorus of Ironic Spirits" in Hardy's *The Dynasts*, beginning "The Will Itself is slave to him," is a tetrameter version of the terza rima sonnet, and Robert Frost's "Acquainted with the Night" rhymes on only four sounds: *aba bcb cdc dad aa*, with the first line repeated as the last. Philip Larkin's "Whatever Happened?" is a later example.

For about the last ten years of his life, Robert Lowell (1917–1977) experimented with **BLANK VERSE SONNETS** that combine the breadth of ordinary blank verse, long associated with drama and epic, and the concentration of the sonnet, with its history in the somewhat more personal lyric. Lowell added to a note on the form: "Even with this license [not rhyming], I fear I have failed to avoid the themes and gigantism of the sonnet." Like many earlier sonnets, some of Lowell's have to do with history, contemporary politics, and personal perplexities – all typically involving conflict (one common theme of sonnets) and achieving grandeur of rhetoric and magniloquence of diction (possibly what he meant by "gigantism").

✂ **Beyond the sonnet, the only rhymed stanza needing to be mentioned here is the VILLANELLE, a form with nineteen lines and only two rhyme sounds. The format is usually printed as five tercets plus a quatrain:** *aba aba aba aba aba abaa.* Line 1 is repeated as lines 6, 12, and 18; line 3 as lines 9, 15, 19, so that the final couplet joins lines 1 and 3. The strict form calls for exact repetition of the recurring lines, but many poets adapt something less strict. William Empson's "Missing Dates" repeats everything exactly. Dylan Thomas's "Do Not Go Gentle into That Good Night" repeats the words as such, but the grammatical function shifts. In line 1 – "Do not gentle into that good night" – *Do* is imperative. Line 6 looks identical, but grammatically the *Do* is declarative, continuing line 5: "...they/Do not go gentle into that good night." Elizabeth Bishop's "One Art" is more relaxed, content to repeat rhyme words but with changes in the overall wording. The first American villanelle is "The Best Is Good Enough" (1883) by James Whitcomb Riley, a poet seldom associated with elaborate verse forms. It is in tetrameter:

> I quarrel not with destiny,
> But make the best of everything –
> The best is good enough for me.
>
> Leave discontent alone, and she
> Will shut her mouth and let you sing.
> I quarrel not with destiny.
>
> I take some things, or let 'em be –
> Good gold has always got the ring;
> The best is good enough for me.
>
> Since fate insists on secrecy,
> I have no arguments to bring –
> I quarrel not with destiny.
>
> The fellow that goes "haw" for "gee"
> Will find he hasn't got full swing.
> The best is good enough for me.
>
> One only knows our needs, and he
> Does all of the distributing.

I quarrel not with destiny:
The best is good enough for me.

A few years later, Edwin Arlington Robinson wrote the bleak trimeter villanelle "The House on the Hill" (1897):

They are all gone away,
The House is shut and still,
There is nothing more to say.

Through broken walls and gray
The winds blow bleak and shrill:
They are all gone away.

Nor is there one to-day
To speak them good or ill:
There is nothing more to say.

Why is it then we stray
Around the sunken sill?
They are all gone away,

And our poor fancy-play
For them is wasted skill:
There is nothing more to say.

There is ruin and decay
In the House on the Hill:
They are all gone away,
There is nothing more to say.

At about the same time, Ernest Dowson wrote his six villanelles, which range from trimeter to pentameter.

✂ An unrhymed form, the SESTINA consists of thirty-nine lines arranged as six six-lined units followed by a tercet in which all six terminal words are repeated either in mid-line or at the end of the line. The end-words recur according to a complicated pattern (using cardinal numbers for the end-words of the lines): 1–2–3–4–5–6; 6–1–5–2–4–3; 3–6–4–1–2–5; 5–3–2–6–1–4; 4–5–1–3–6–2; 2–4–6–5–3–1. Then words 1, 3, and 5 come in the middle of lines in the tercet, 2, 4, and 6 at the ends of lines. The form goes back to the sixteenth century, when Sir Philip Sidney and Barnabe Barnes produced estimable examples. After going into eclipse for about three hundred years, the form reemerged late in the nineteenth century. Thereafter, Algernon Charles Swinburne, Rudyard Kipling, Ezra Pound, W. H. Auden, John Ashbery, and James Merrill produced distinguished sestinas. In "The Dry Salvages," T. S. Eliot varied the sestina by using repeated rhyme-sounds instead of repeated words.

So far we have looked at relations among plots or arrays: a semantic plot of meanings, a verbal plot of words to express meanings, an acoustic plot of sounds to realize the words, and a graphic plot of visual signs to represent the sounds. In most poems, furthermore, there are resemblances among the plots. In

When the cat's away
The mice will play –

for example, the graphic array is a record of the acoustic array, marked by a rising rhythm of iambs and anapests and given further coherence by rhyme. The graphic and acoustic arrays both embody the grammatical array of a periodic sentence divided into a four-word dependent clause ("When the cat's away") followed by a four-word independent clause ("The mice will play"). The audible rhyme as well as the visible line break and capital letter map both the graphic and acoustic arrays. All these arrays may constitute what has been called a "surplus of signifiers" supporting one another as cause-and-effect, form-and-matter, and end-and-means. We know how a poem sounds because we know how it looks, we know what the words mean because we know how they sound – the process goes from eye to ear to mind or, for some, from eye to mind. Or, if we hear the poem without seeing it, we just move from ear to mind.

With those very common arrangements of signifiers, we are seeing what rhymes – what resembles what, what looks like and sounds like what. These relations are **ANALOGIES**: the graphic array is analogous to the spoken array, and the spoken array in turn is analogous to the grammatical array of this or that kind of sentence. The whole parcel of analogies works mostly in poetry, since in prose we do not much care where the written or printed line begins or ends. Prose is printed margin-to-margin, justified right and left, and our ears are more or less turned off to the signals of rhythm, alliteration, and rhyme. If the acoustic effects do obtrude in prose, most readers probably feel "crowded" by an overdetermined text that works too hard and does too much. In some cases, we cannot attend to the meaning while we are attending to the way something sounds or looks.

The most famous example is the first edition of William Whewell's *Elementary Treatise on Mechanics* (1819), which includes this: "There is no force, however great, can stretch a cord, however fine, into a horizontal line which is accurately straight." Those words of scientific prose can reasonably be scanned and printed as an *abba* tetrameter quatrain. (Once his attention had been called to the situation, Whewell changed the passage in subsequent editions. Whewell published poetry at about the same time, and it is possible that some habits lingered; but he was a prolific polymath, and it seems likelier that this case of surplus signifiers is a bizarre happenstance.)

Other instances, however, suggest other possibilities. The middle of the nineteenth century enjoyed prose texts of unusual power, and two of them fall into some of the repetitions of poetry. In Chapter XXXVI of Herman Melville's *Moby-Dick* (1851), Captain Ahab explains to his first mate, Starbuck, how strongly he feels the need to kill the whale that injured him: "I'd strike the sun if it insulted me." That scans as regular line of blank verse, and there is chiastic alliteration of consonants and vowels in the sequence "*sun if it insu*lted." Two years later, in Chapter XLVII of Charles Dickens's *Bleak House*, a poor homeless boy named Jo dies of pneumonia. He dies in the middle of reciting The Lord's Prayer, and the narrator turns the volume up all the way:

> The light is come upon the dark benighted way. Dead!
>   Dead, your Majesty. Dead, my lords and gentlemen. Dead, right reverends and wrong reverends of every order. Dead, men and women, born with heavenly compassion in your hearts. And dying thus around us every day.

The two outer sentences scan as iambic hexameter and pentameter, and they rhyme:

> The light is come upon the dark benighted way...
> And dying thus around us every day.

(One may hear an echo of the opening of Chapter LX of Isaiah: "Arise, shine; for thy light is come...") The effect is reinforced by internal rhymes: *light* and *-night-*, *thus* and *us*. In both cases, the extreme effects accompany extreme situations; otherwise, the heightening would be impossible to justify.

Abraham Lincoln's Second Inaugural Address (March 1865) has been called "poetic," probably because some passages – such as "Fondly do we hope, fervently do we pray, that this mighty scourge of war may speedily pass away" – can be printed as a fairly regular rhymed quatrain:

> Fondly do we hope,
> fervently do we pray,
> that this mighty scourge of war
> may speedily pass away.

Alliteration and syntactic parallelism link the first two lines, further alliteration connects "mighty" and "may," and "may" creates an internal rhyme with the line-ending "pray" and "away." A little of such prose goes a long way, and nobody – not even a Melville, a Dickens, or a Lincoln – can sustain it for long. (Lincoln's address is only about 700 words long.) A few years after the death of the novelist Thomas Wolfe in 1938, John S. Barnes published a volume of free verse poems that represent a re-casting of Wolfe's prose:

> . . . O waste of loss in the hot mazes, lost,
> Among the bright stars
> On this most weary unbright cinder, lost!
> Remembering speechlessly
> We seek the great forgotten language,
> The lost lane-end into heaven,
> A stone, a leaf, an unfound door.

What rhymes is what is analogous, one might say. Ezra Pound applied the term "subject rhyme" to subjects that may resemble each other, such as the mighty figures Samson and Hercules ("Herculean Samson," John Milton, *Paradise Lost*, Book IX). The extraordinary orders of any poetry furnish powerful alignments of what is seen and heard, on the one hand, and what is thought and felt, on the other.

In this respect, a poem resembles the readout on an analog device of some sort. The traditional timepieces common everywhere from about 1750 to 1975 involved an analog readout: the configuration of the face and hands – terms already suggesting analogy – was analogous to the place of the sun in the sky, and the circular motion of the moving hands was analogous to the movement of the sun. The interpretation of the readout was complicated, and it took years to master. Late in the twentieth century many analog readouts were replaced by digital readouts that displayed data directly. An analog clock face indicating 4 o'clock is understandable, even without numerals, because it is the configuration of long and short hands and not the numerals that "tells" the time:

The analog clock has a relatively simple mechanism but a relatively complicated readout; the *digital* clock is the opposite: relatively complicated mechanism but radically simple readout: 04:00.

At about the time such digital readouts were appearing on timepieces and telephone dials, poets began examining an analogous possibility in the appearance of poetry. Some of the poems by A. R. Ammons have an interesting graphic appearance, usually sets of three or four lines arranged in strophes with a justified left margin and an unjustified but orderly right margin. The graphic array is not related to the acoustic array, and a line can end on any word. There is little zoning by alliteration or rhyme, although there may be interesting acoustic activity of a subtle sort. And there may be grammatical arrays, but they are independent of the graphic and acoustic arrays.

The beginning of "The City Limits" will illustrate:

When you consider the radiance, that it does not withhold
itself but pours its abundance without selection into every
nook and cranny not overhung or hidden; when you consider...

The whole poem consists of almost two hundred words but is only one periodic sentence, a series of "when" clauses leading up to a "then" (five lines from the end). The lines end without regard to grammar or sound, just when the right margin comes near – the zone at which a little bell would sound on some manual typewriters of the sort that Ammons used for most of his career. The rhythm is subdued but, as in most English utterances, fundamentally rising, more organized toward the iambic end: "calmly turns to praise." There are some harmonies in the middle of lines, such as the subtle repetitions in "radiance" and "abundance," and a scrupulous ear may detect some resonance between the *r-d-n-s* skeleton of *radiance* and the *n-s-d-r* inside *consider*. But the signifiers are so controlled that the readout may qualify as anomalous or digital.

It is encouraging that the world of poetry is sufficiently abundant and the resources of imagination sufficiently varied that poets can still find original ways to design their works. With something so vivid and striking, much in poetry can devolve and deteriorate into formula and cliché, to which a reader may wearily respond with yet another cliché: "Been there, done that." Theodore Sturgeon's judgment that "... ninety percent of science fiction is crap; ninety percent of everything is crap" probably applies to poetry. Even if the figure is raised to ninety-five or ninety-nine percent, however, more than enough genuine poems remain to keep readers busy and entertained.

7 The Arts of Reaction

Do not let anyone tell you that poems are simple, direct, natural, smooth-flowing, or any such thing. All real poems are and always have been and always will be irreducibly complex, always indirect and convoluted, always radically unnatural, always rough-gaited, always extraordinarily perpendicular to the plane of ordinary life. Face it: Nothing sounds or looks like a poem, and nowhere else will you find such language as that in even the most primitive piece of lowest-level verse. Difficulties, obscurities, and obliquities abound, from the time when the thoughtful infant wonders, "How can these clowns even begin to think that they can put me to sleep by singing to me about a breaking bough and a falling cradle?" And it is all uphill from there.

A poem has designs on you. That may account for all its designs in the first place. A poem wants to sell you something, and it will remorselessly use high-pressure tactics. A poem will come at you. When that happens, the usual choice is between flight and fight, and many flee from the discomforts and perturbations that accompany any poem. We do not like losing our balance, our bearings, our footing, or our cool.

And some choose to fight. Whatever the first poem was, it is a sure thing that the second reacted to it, possibly mocking it, possibly attacking, possibly denying, possibly reversing or refuting, maybe just continuing, expanding, varying it. Any poem whatsoever behaves so assertively and immodestly that, unless you just run the other way to avoid confrontation, you have to do something about it.

Sometimes a text says all there is to say about something, but the writer realizes that only half of the story has really been told. Accordingly, along comes a second text that moves in the opposite direction. Consecutive

The Poetry Toolkit: For Readers and Writers, First Edition. William Harmon.
© 2012 William Harmon. Published 2012 by Blackwell Publishing Ltd.

verses in the Book of Proverbs say, "Answer not a fool according to his folly, lest thou also be like unto him" and then, "Answer a fool according to his folly, lest he be wise in his own conceit" (26:4–5). Such statements seem to amount to a pattern of "On the one hand" and "On the other hand" – and everybody says something like that often, because it sums up a very familiar state of affairs.

John Milton's "Il Penseroso" and "L'Allegro" deal with representative figures who are pensively melancholy or merrily unmelancholy; a similar contrast may even apply to *Paradise Lost* and *Paradise Regained*. Robert Browning seemed to delight in writing poems in sets of two or more: "Fra Lippo Lippi" is a spring morning poem set at the beginning of the Renaissance, while "Andrea del Sarto" is an autumn evening poem set at the end of the Renaissance. Both are dramatic monologues spoken by real painters in imagined circumstances. Browning also wrote "The Englishman in Italy" alongside "The Italian in England," "Before" alongside "After," "Meeting at Night" alongside "Parting at Morning," and a matched set of madhouse soliloquies called "Porphyria's Lover" and "Johannes Agricola in Meditation."

Sometimes an egregiously unilateral text seems to call out for direct refutation. An ecstatic romantic couplet –

It's spring! It's spring! It's spring!
The bird is on the wing!

invites a literalist response:

Absurd, absurd, absurd:
The wing is on the bird.

(It is possible that the provocative idiom comes from Edward FitzGerald's version of the *Rubáiyát of Omar Khayyám*: "The Bird of Time has but a little way/To fly and Lo! the Bird is on the Wing.")

The title of A. E. Housman's "Epitaph on an Army of Mercenaries" does not necessarily refer to the "soldiers of fortune" who cynically peddle their services in any cause regardless of moral worth. England's enemies in the First World War had dismissed its soldiers as a "contemptible little army" of conscripts, colonials, and mercenaries. Thereafter, in jolly exploitation of the rhetoric, the army of regulars and special reserves called themselves "the Old Contemptibles," and it is they to whom Housman's epitaph probably applies:

These, in the day when heaven was falling,
  The hour when earth's foundations fled,
Followed their mercenary calling,
  And took their wages, and are dead.

Their shoulders held the sky suspended;
  They stood, and earth's foundations stay;
What God abandoned, these defended,
  And saved the sum of things for pay.

The point is that, whether they were mercenaries or volunteers or con-scripts, they and they alone saved the day, and accordingly they deserve whatever rhetorical exaggeration is being thrown around so glibly. Nobody needs to be told that wartime breeds the most ridiculous patriotic rhetoric. (The resonant "sum of things," reaching back to Latin *summa rerum*, "the highest public interest," was earlier used in Milton's *Paradise Lost* and Tennyson's *In Memoriam*.) Willfully or not, Hugh MacDiarmid inter-preted Housman's poem without benefit of nuance or irony; he responded with blunt-force trauma:

It is a God-damned lie to say that these
Saved, or knew, anything worth a man's pride.
They were professional murderers and they took
Their blood money and impious risks and died.
In spite of all their kind some elements of worth
With difficulty persist here and there on earth.

The poise of Housman's stoic quatrains is trashed, and in its place there is a rather ragged set of lines irregularly rhymed and energetically enjambed. Note: it is more difficult to say "With difficulty persist here and there on earth" than "Persist with difficulty here and there on earth." The latter is perfectly iambic. The former answerably complicates the rhythm with a pyrrhic and a spondee: "Wĭth dĭf | fĭcúl | tў pĕr | síst hére..."

In most situations, subtlety works better than shouting. George Meredith's sonnet "Lucifer in Starlight" ends with a glorious vision of evil thwarted by righteousness:

... Soaring through wider zones that prick'd his scars
  With memory of the old revolt from Awe,

He reach'd a middle height, and at the stars,
Which are the brain of heaven, he look'd, and sank.
Around the ancient track march'd, rank on rank,
   The army of unalterable law.

(The last line is reinforced by powerful assonance in "army of unalterable law.") In 1909, the year after Meredith died, T. S. Eliot produced a sketch called "Cousin Nancy," about a young woman who dances and smokes while her baffled aunts look on, remnants of a generation that depended for guidance on Matthew Arnold and Ralph Waldo Emerson:

Upon the glazen shelves kept watch
Matthew and Waldo, guardians of the faith,
The army of unalterable law.

On the subject of attacking another text, it may help to remember something E. M. Forster said about book reviewing: "To break a butterfly, or even a beetle, upon a wheel is a delicate task. Lovers of nature disapprove, moreover the victim is apt to reappear each time the wheel revolves, still alive, and with a reproachful expression upon its squashed face . . ."

    One poem may QUOTE another outright, or refer to it directly (which is called "REFERENCE") or indirectly ("ALLUSION"), or ECHO it in some respect. William Wordsworth more than once said, "The child is father to the man," a paradox suggesting that what a child is determines what the adult will be. Gerard Manley Hopkins reacted in a repetitive verse form called **TRIOLET**:

"The child is father to the man."
How can he be? The words are wild.
Suck any sense from that who can:
"The child is father to the man."
No; what the poet did write ran,
"The man is father to the child."
"The child is father to the man!"
How *can* he be? The words are wild.

One of Shakespeare's sonnets, about the pressures of youth, begins, "Look in thy glass . . ." One of Thomas Hardy's poems, less flippant than

Hopkins's triolet, about the disappointments of age begins, "I look into my glass/And view my wasting skin . . ."

A poet can react by translating and adapting. One of Guido Cavalcanti's poems begins, "Perch' io no spero di tornar giammai" – "Because I never hope to return . . . ." T. S. Eliot's "Ash-Wednesday" begins, "Because I do not hope to turn again," replacing the idea of returning with that of turning again, which is not quite the same thing. More faintly, a line in *The Waste Land* – "And still she cried, and still the world pursues" – may echo a couplet about a schoolmaster in Oliver Goldsmith's "The Deserted Village": "And still they gazed, and still the wonder grew, /That one small head could carry all he knew."

There may be a middle ground of accommodation between flight and fight. **Some poems work as HOMMAGES, amiable imitations of earlier poems that do not mock the precursor.** Thomas Hardy's "Friends Beyond," for example, has attracted at least two acts of respectful homage. Hardy's poem concerns people who have died in his corner of the world (some are real, some from his own fiction):

> William Dewy, Tranter Reuben, Farmer Ledlow late at plough,
>   Robert's kin, and John's, and Ned's,
> And the Squire, and Lady Susan, lie in Mellstock churchyard now!

(The stanza, Hardy's adaptation of the terza rima rhyme scheme in tercets of octameter-trimeter-octameter, is original.) In 1937, nine years after Hardy's death, John Betjeman published "Dorset":

> . . . .
> Light's abode, celestial Salem! Lamps of evening, smelling strong,
> Gleaming on the pitch-pine, waiting, almost empty even-song:
> From the aisles each window smiles on grave and grass and yew-tree
>   bough –
> While Tranter Reuben, Gordon Selfridge, Edna Best and Thomas Hardy
>   lie in Mellstock Churchyard now.

(The first four words come from a **HYMN** by John Mason Neale. Gordon Selfridge, founder of the famous department store but in much reduced circumstances by the time of Betjeman's poem, was alive in 1937, as was Edna Best, a movie actress who was married to the actor Herbert Marshall.) About forty years later, in conscious imitation of both Hardy and

Betjeman, Kingsley Amis wrote "Farewell Blues," in honor of a kind of music that was waning by the 1970s:

> For Louis Armstrong, Mildred Bailey, Walter Page, and Sidney Catlett
>> lie in Brunswick churchyard now...
> While Muggsy Spanier, Floyd O'Brien, Sterling Bose, and Henry Allen
>> lie in Decca churchyard now...
> What replaced them no one asked for, but it turned up anyhow,
> And Coleman Hawkins, Johnny Hodges, Bessie Smith, and PeeWee
>> Russell lie in Okeh churchyard now.

(These churchyard names are revered record labels.)

Henry Wadsworth Longfellow's "Prelude" begins:

> Pleasant it was, when woods were green,
> And winds were soft and low,
> To lie amid some sylvan scene....

– clearly an echo of a passage in John Milton's *Paradise Lost* describing Paradise before the Fall:

> Insuperable highth of loftiest shade,
> Cedar, and pine, and fir, and branching palm,
> A sylvan scene...

– so that the appearance of the phrase "sylvan scene" in the second part of *The Waste Land* in connection with the rape of Philomel may seem doubly ironic. Longfellow's poetry also furnished the title of Robert Frost's first book, *A Boy's Will*, and an image from Longfellow's sonnet "Mezzo Cammin" – "The cataract of death far thundering from the heights" – reappears in Frost's "West-Running Brook" as "The universal cataract of death."

Technical features themselves, if sufficiently distinguished, can suggest kinship among works. A line in Christopher Marlowe's "Hero and Leander" has a peculiarly syncopated rhythm: "Búrns whĕre ĭt chérĭshed, múrdĕrs whĕre ĭt lóved." The placement of the break in mid-foot after the fifth syllable, the trochee in the first foot, and the pyrrhic in the fourth all combine to give the line a strange nervousness, which accentuates the typically extreme paradoxes of Marlowe. Much the same rhythm turns up in Robert Browning's "An Epistle Containing the Strange Medical Experience of Karshish, the Arab Physician," where the human body is presented as "Blówn lĭke ă búbblĕ, knéadĕd lĭke ă páste"; and again in T. S. Eliot's "Portrait of a Lady": "Crý lĭke ă párrŏt, chátter lĭke ăn ápe." Such patterns, seeming to preserve a sort of "tissue memory" from use to use, may go back to a line in the oldest English poem, known as "Caedmon's Hymn" – "méŏtódĕs méahtĕ ánd hĭs módgĕþánc" ("the might of the Measurer and His mind's purpose") – and forward to a line at the end of E. E. Cummings's "Poem, Or Beauty Hurts Mr. Vinal": "cŏmes óut lĭke ă ríbbŏn lĭes flát ŏn thĕ brúsh."

What now follows may be understood as a capricious **SATYR PLAY**, like the fourth part of a tetralogy entered in the competition of the Athenian Dionysia. After three solemn tragedies, there followed a shorter and possibly sillier drama as a relief from the terror. Almost all have perished, but we know that all the great tragic playwrights composed more than one, and the tradition is honorable. On to some fun, then.

CARICATURE involves exaggeration of some salient feature. Big ears get bigger and small eyes get smaller. If a poet seems to overuse a device, then a caricature can expand the overuse to ridiculous extremes. Algernon Charles Swinburne seems to have been addicted to anapestic alliteration in the service of grotesquely superheated emotions. Arthur Clement Hilton's "Octopus" caricatures all these Swinburnian vices:

> . . . O breast, that 'twere rapture to writhe on!
>   O arms 'twere delicious to feel
> Clinging close with the crush of the Python,
>   When she maketh her murderous meal!

But Swinburne himself could out-Swinburne any caricaturist:

> From the depth of the dreamy decline of the dawn through a notable
>   nimbus of nebulous noonshine,
> Pallid and pink as the palm of the flag-flower that flickers with fear of the
>   flies as they float,
> Are they looks of our lovers that lustrously lean from a marvel of mystic
>   miraculous moonshine,
> These that we feel in the blood of our blushes that thicken and threaten
>   throbs through the throat?
>
> ("Nephelidia")

TRAVESTY and BURLESQUE cover much, but here they will be restricted to texts that preserve a serious level of subject matter but lower the style to comedy or DOGGEREL. Samuel Butler's *Hudibras* makes fun of a Presbyterian knight by recounting his exploits in jauntily unkempt couplets:

> When Gospel-Trumpeter, surrounded
> With long-ear'd rout, to battle sounded,
> And pulpit, drum ecclesiastick,
> Was beat with fist, instead of a stick;
> Then did Sir Knight abandon dwelling,
> And out he rode a colonelling.
> A wight he was, whose very sight wou'd
> Entitle him Mirror of Knighthood....

The noble seriousness of John Keats's "Ode on a Grecian Urn" is subverted in Desmond Skirrow's "Ode on a Grecian Urn Summarized":

> Gods chase
> Round vase.
> What say?
> What play?
> Don't know.
> Nice, though.*

Keats's life and death themselves became the subject for literary treatment. During 1818 his *Endymion* received rough treatment in the *Edinburgh Magazine*, the *Quarterly Review*, and elsewhere, leading to suspicions that the unkind criticism led to his death at age twenty-five. Shelley's *Adonais* elevates Keats to the status of Adonis, mourned as a shepherd, in the traditional **PASTORAL ELEGY**, and as a darling of the gods. Lord Byron appears among the mourners as an exaggerated effigy called "the Pythian of the age" and "the Pilgrim of Eternity," and the unkindest critic is in for big trouble:

> the curse of Cain
> Light on his head who pierced thy innocent breast,
> And scared the angel soul that was its earthly guest!

*Desmond Skirrow: "Ode on a Grecian Urn Summarized" is reprinted from Amis, K. (1978) (ed.) *The New Oxford Book of English Verse*, p. 316. First printed in the *New Statesman* (30 July 1960). Reprinted by permission of the *New Statesman*.

Byron himself, however, was more down to earth. In a letter he wrote a travesty of the affair in the garment of a **NURSERY RHYME**:

> Who killed John Keats?
> I, says the Quarterly
> So savage & Tartarly
> 'Twas one of my feats....

And Byron's *Don Juan* is somewhat more benevolent but still skeptical about the diagnosis:

> John Keats, who was killed off by one critique,
> .... Just as he really promised something great,
> If not intelligible,—without Greek
> .... Contrived to talk about the Gods of late,
> Much as they might have been supposed to speak.
> .... Poor fellow! His was an untoward fate: –
> 'Tis strange the mind, that very fiery particle,
> Should let itself be snuffed out by an Article. (XI, 60)

Wendy Cope has nimbly reduced the five sections of Eliot's *The Waste Land* to five burlesque limericks, beginning:

> In April one seldom feels cheerful;
> Dry stones, sun and dust make me fearful;
> Clairvoyantes distress me,
> Commuters depress me –
> Met Stetson and gave him an earful.

Whereas travesty and burlesque make fun of a subject by lowering the style, PARODY makes fun of a style by lowering the subject. Many satirical works do both, and it is difficult to find a work that does only one or the other. **The MOCK EPIC, say, makes fun of a trivial event by treating it in a grand epic manner, but it also makes fun of the grand epic manner by applying it to a small matter.** Alexander Pope's *The Rape of the Lock*, for example, takes a petty episode involving the snipping of a lock of hair and blows it up into a big deal involving all the trappings of epic. At the same time, it displays some of the ridiculous features of John Milton's

Paradise Lost, in which angels fight but are not permanently wounded, as with Michael's sword striking Satan:

> ... But with swift wheele reverse, deep entring shar'd
> All his right side; then Satan first knew pain,
> And writh'd him to and fro convolv'd; so sore
> The griding sword with discontinuous wound
> Passd through him, but th' Ethereal substance clos'd
> Not long divisible ....

Pope mocks this with a miniature supernatural beautician caught in some scissors:

> Fate urg'd the Sheers, and cut the Sylph in twain,
> (But Airy Substance soon unites again).

In standard parody, all the sniper has to do is change the subject. William Butler Yeats produced an astrological couplet that some may judge ridiculous:

> If Jupiter and Saturn meet,
> What a crop of mummy wheat!

By relatively easy steps, a quick-witted parodist notes that Saturn is the name of a car, and so is Mercury, another Roman god who gave his name to a planet. "Mercury" has the same rhythm as "Jupiter." And cars can meet in a more interesting conjunction than that of planets. Accordingly:

> If Mercury and Saturn meet,
> What a mess is in the street!

This couplet is further fortified by the repeated initial consonants in Mercury/Saturn/meet/mess/street.

Emily Dickinson is as great a poet as Yeats and just as capable of saying things that make fat targets for parody:

> The Soul selects her own Society –
> Then – shuts the Door –
> To her divine Majority –
> Present no more –

Shifted only slightly to an American collegiate context, this becomes

> The Soul selects her own Sorority –
> Then – shuts the Dorm –
> From her divine Majority –
> Black balls – eclectic – swarm –

It is noteworthy that effective parody works best with small changes, not with hammer blows. Frost's "But I have promises to keep/And miles to go before I sleep" can be deflated by one change in the articulation of one phoneme: "But I have promises to keep/And piles." Another minute change converts Wallace Stevens's unseemly assertion, "The greatest poverty is not to live/in a physical world" ("Esthétique du Mal") into something more appropriate for a wealthy insurance lawyer: "The greatest poverty is not to live/in a fiscal world." Tennyson's "'Tis better to have loved and lost/Than never to have lov'd at all" can be improved by truncation: "'Tis better to have loved and lost." Robert Burns's "Should auld acquaintance be forgot, /And never brought to mind?" can be improved by augmentation: "Should auld acquaintance be forgot, /and never brought to mind or not?" or even ". . . and never brought to mind or what?" No text is safe, immune, sacred, or off-limits.

Two texts coincidentally from 1847 combine in Bayard Taylor's "Nauvoo" (1872), which is (1) a burlesque of the arrival of the Mormons at the Great Salt Lake, where Brigham Young supposedly said, "This is the place" as well as (2) a parody of Longfellow's *Evangeline*, which begins famously "This is the forest primeval." Two texts beginning "This is," accordingly, are all Taylor needed:

> This is the place: be still for a while, my high-pressure steamboat!
> Let me survey the spot where the Mormons builded their temple.
> Much have I mused on the wreck and ruin of ancient religions,
> Scandinavian, Greek, Assyrian, Zend, and the Sanskrit,
> Yea, and explored the mysteries hidden in Talmudic targums,
> Caught the gleam of Chrysaor's sword and occulted Orion,
> Backward spelled the lines of the Hebrew graveyard at Newport,
> Studied Ojibwa symbols and those of the Quarry of Pipestone . . .

The verse form is dactylic hexameter, also in Longfellow's "The Courtship of Miles Standish." (A half-dozen other poems by Longfellow are alluded to here as well.)

It is possible for one work to parody a style or manner and at the same time burlesque a poet. Wordsworth's famous lines:

She dwelt among the untrodden ways
Beside the springs of Dove,
A maid whom there were none to praise
And very few to love:

A violet by a mossy stone
Half hidden from the eye!
—Fair as a star, when only one
Is shining in the sky...

provoked a response from Hartley Coleridge, the eldest son of Wordsworth's friend Samuel Taylor Coleridge:

He lived amidst th' untrodden ways
To Rydal Lake that lead;
A bard whom there were none to praise,
And very few to read.

Behind a cloud his mystic sense,
Deep hidden, who can spy?
Bright as the night when not a star
Is shining in the sky.

Wordsworth is among the most parodied of poets, along with Longfellow, Tennyson, and Robert Browning. Against Browning's *The Ring and the Book*, which begins:

Do you see this Ring?
'T is Rome-work, made to match
(By Castellani's imitative craft)
Etrurian circlets found, some happy morn,
After a dropping April....)

C. S. Calverley wrote "The Cock and the Bull":

You see this pebble-stone? It's a thing I bought
Of a bit of a chit of a boy i' the mid o' the day –

I like to dock the smaller parts-o'-speech,
As we curtail the already cur-tail'd cur
(You catch the paronomasia, play 'po' words?)

Fairly often, a poet or group will produce parodies and burlesques in an organized set. Rejected Addresses (1812) by Horace and James Smith mocks the competition for a dedicatory ode for the reopening of the Drury Lane Theatre, which had burned and been rebuilt. The Smiths provided bogus entries signed with initials hinting at Scott, Byron, Southey, Wordsworth, and Coleridge, and even included, as a bonus, a piece of prose supposedly by the ghost of Samuel Johnson, who had died in 1784, easily within living memory. Here the Johnsonian manner is applied to a theater's snack bar:

> Our refectory will be found to contain every species of fruit, from the cooling nectarine and luscious peach to the puny pippin and the noxious nut. There Indolence may repose, and Inebriety revel; and the spruce apprentice, rushing in at second account, may there chatter with impunity; debarred, by a barrier of brick and mortar, from marring that scenic interest in others, which nature and education have disqualified him from comprehending himself.

The volume was such a success that Thomas Campbell was disappointed to have been left out, and Sir Walter Scott evidently believed that he had really written the entry attributed to him but forgotten it.

> A poetic entry is a speech assigned to someone playing Macbeth:
> When spoonys on two knees implore the aid of sorcery,
> To suit their wicked purposes they quickly put the laws awry;
> With Adam I in wife may vie, for none could tell the use of her,
> Except to cheapen golden pippins hawk'd about by Lucifer.

Later in the nineteenth century, Bayard Taylor, whom we saw earlier in this chapter in a treatment of Longfellow and Brigham Young, wrote an elaborate set of parodies called Diversions of the Echo Club, with names and personalities for the fictional members. Eventually, Carolyn Wells wrote The Re-Echo Club, in the course of which a number of well-known poets submit their versions of a familiar text. In one instance, the base verse is Gelett Burgess's "The Purple Cow's Projected Feast":

I never saw a Purple Cow,
I never hope to see one;
But I can tell you, anyhow,
I'd rather see than be one.

These are the versions attributed to the poets:

Wordsworth:

She dwelt among the untrodden ways
Beside the springs of Dee;
A Cow whom there were few to praise
And very few to see....

Shelley:

Hail to thee, blithe spirit!
Cow thou never wert...

Gray:

The curfew tolls the knell of parting day,
　　The lowing herd winds slowly o'er the lea;
I watched them slowly wend their weary way,
　　But, ah, a Purple Cow I did not see.

Keats:

A cow of purple is a joy forever.

Swinburne:

Oh, Cow of rare rapturous vision,
　　Oh, purple, impalpable Cow,
Do you browse in the Dream Field Elysian,
　　Are you purpling pleasantly now?

And another from Swinburne:

Only in dim, drowsy depths of a dream do I dare to delight in deliciously
　　dreaming
Cows there may be of a passionate purple,—cows of a violent violet hue;

Ne'er have I seen such a sight, I am certain it is but a demi-delirious
    dreaming—
Ne'er may I happily harbour a hesitant hope in my heart that my dream
    may come true.
Sad is my soul, and my senses are sobbing so strong is my strenuous
    spirit to see one.
Dolefully, drearily doomed to despair as warily wearily watching I wait;
Thoughts thickly thronging are thrilling and throbbing; to see is a
    glorious gain—but to be one!
That were a darker and direfuller destiny, that were a fearfuller,
    frightfuller fate!

G. K. Chesterton's "Variations of an Air" presents versions of "Old King
Cole," again attributed to well-known poets:

Tennyson:

Cole, that unwearied prince of Colchester,
Growing more gay with age and with long days
Deeper in laughter and desire of life
As that Virginian climber on our walls
Flames scarlet with the fading of the year;
Called for his wassail and that other weed
Virginian also, from the western woods
Where English Raleigh checked the boast of Spain,
And lighting joy with joy, and piling up
Pleasure as crown for pleasure, bade me bring
Those three, the minstrels whose emblazoned coats
Shone with the oyster-shells of Colchester;
And these three played, and playing grew more fain
Of mirth and music; till the heathen came
And the King slept beside the northern sea.

Whitman:

Me clairvoyant,
Me conscious of you, old camarado,
Needing no telescope, lorgnette, field-glass, opera-glass, myopic
    pince-nez,
Me piercing two thousand years with eye naked and not ashamed;

The crown cannot hide you from me,
Musty old feudal-heraldic trappings cannot hide you from me,
I perceive that you drink.
(I am drinking with you. I am as drunk as you are.)
I see you are inhaling tobacco, puffing, smoking, spitting
(I do not object to your spitting),
You prophetic of American largeness,
You anticipating the broad masculine manners of these States;
I see in you also there are movements, tremors, tears, desire for the
    melodious,
I salute your three violinists, endlessly making vibrations,
Rigid, relentless, capable of going on for ever;
They play my accompaniment; but I shall take no notice of any
    accompaniment;
I myself am a complete orchestra.
So long.

    **Now and again, in reaction to a school, movement, or journal, someone
will concoct a HOAX that combines features of parody and burlesque.**
Such hoaxes may involve the creation of a fictitious poet who is presented
as a practitioner of a certain type of poetry. Sometimes, serious editors,
publishers, and readers are taken in, with a degree of humiliation and
embarrassment. Early in the twentieth century, amid many new schools
and -isms, such as Imagism and Symbolism, the American poets Witter
Bynner and Arthur Davison Ficke, calling themselves "Emanuel Morgan"
and "Anne Knish" respectively, produced *Spectra: a Book of Poetic Experi-
ments* (1916), illustrating the Spectric or Spectrist movement. Their poems
were untitled except for "Opus" numbers. "Morgan" was a rhymer:

If I were only dafter
    I might be making hymns
To the liquor of your laughter
    And the lacquer of your limbs. ("Opus 6")

"Knish" more experimental:

If bathing were a virtue, not a lust
I would be dirtiest.
To some, housecleaning is a holy rite.

For myself, houses would be empty
But for the golden motes dancing in sunbeams.

Tax-assessors frequently overlook valuables.
Today they noted my jade.
But my memory of you escaped them. ("Opus 118")

Later, Bynner and Ficke were joined by Marjorie Allen Seiffert ("Elijah Hay"), and the movement received praise and encouragement from Edgar Lee Masters, Harriet Monroe, Alfred Kreymborg, William Carlos Williams, John Gould Fletcher, Amy Lowell, and others. (Ezra Pound was not taken in.)

That was in America at the time of the First World War. In Australia at the time of the second, an even more elaborate hoax was perpetrated: "Ern Malley" was a fictitious poet created by James McAuley and Harold Stewart as a way to show up the folly of *Angry Penguins*, a modernist magazine. The magazine was completely taken in and devoted a special issue to Malley's poems. It may be that what McAuley and Stewart fabricated was better poetry than what Bynner and Ficke produced, since the Malley controversy went on longer, and some insisted on taking the poems seriously. (**Note that such hoaxes involve the creation of a fictional poet and his or her poetry. Clifford Irving's *Hoax*, about his fabrication of texts supposedly written by Howard Hughes, is technically about a *forgery*, not a hoax. In a forgery, you fake a real person's signature to a document or instrument, such as a check.**)

Conservatives and traditionalists may point to hoaxes as scandalous confirmation of the silliness of the new and modern, and even genuinely new movements and artists are called hoaxers by someone. The very first issue of *Time* magazine, March 3, 1923, included this:

SHANTIH, SHANTIH, SHANTIH

Has the Reader Any Rights Before the Bar of Literature?

There is a new kind of literature abroad in the land, whose only obvious fault is that no one can understand if. Last year there appeared a gigantic volume entitled *Ulysses*, by James Joyce. To the uninitiated it appeared that Mr. Joyce had taken some half million assorted words – many such as are not ordinarily heard in reputable circles – shaken them up in a colossal hat, laid them end to end. To those in on the secret the result represented the greatest achievement of modern letters – a new idea in novels.

The Dial has awarded its $2,000 prize for the best poem of 1922 to an opus entitled *The Waste Land*, by T. S. Eliot. Burton Rascoe, of *The New York Tribune*, hails it as incomparably great. Edmund Wilson, Jr., of *Vanity Fair*, is no less enthusiastic in praise of it. So is J. Middleton Murry, British critic.

Here are the last eight lines of *The Waste Land*:

London Bridge is falling down falling down falling down
Poi s'accose nel foco che gli affina
Quando fiam uti chelidon – O swallow swallow
Le Prince d'Aquitaine a la tour abolie
These fragments I have shored against my ruins
Why then He fit you. Hieronymo's mad againe.
Datta. Dayadhvam. Damyata
Shantih Shantih Shantih

The case for the defense, as presented by the admirers of Messrs. Eliot, Joyce, *et al.*, runs something like this:

Literature is self-expression.It is up to the reader to extract the meaning, not up to the writer to offer it. If the author writes everything that pops into his head – or that is supposed to pop into the head of a given character – that is all that should be asked. Lucidity is no part of the auctorial task.

It is rumored that *The Waste Land* was written as a hoax. Several of its supporters explain that that is immaterial, literature being concerned not with intentions but results.

Soon enough, to be sure, *Time* joined the fan clubs of Joyce and Eliot, both of whom were eventually honored with cover stories. **This is one of those "cautionary tales" warning all not to be taken in too readily or to condemn too easily.** If you are a genuinely sincere and original artist conscientiously doing your work as well as you can, then somebody is sure to condemn you as a faker and hoaxer. And the more brilliant you are, the more assured you can be of such treatment.

That's life in the world of poetry – enjoy it.

Glossary

ACCENT
The relative emphasis or prominence of a syllable. The noun accent is accented on the first syllable, the verb accent on the second. See **SECONDARY ACCENT, PROMOTION.**

ACTION
That aspect of a work that has to do with doing, making, or thinking. Actions include loving, fighting, recovering, and so forth.

ALEXANDRINE
In English, a line of six feet or twelve syllables, commonly found as the ninth line in the **SPENSERIAN STANZA** and sometimes as the seventh in the **RHYME ROYAL** stanza. Also, a line of six feet added as a variation to a **COUPLET** of **PENTAMETER**.

A needless Alexandrine ends the Song,
That like a wounded Snake, drags its slow Length along. (Pope)

ALLITERATION
The repetition of the sound or sounds in the **ONSET** or beginning of a syllable. In most cases this involves **CONSONANTS** and **CONSONANT CLUSTERS**, but in some it involves any **VOWEL** sound at the beginning of a syllable that lacks the onset. Both sorts can be heard in Housman's line "The *hou*r when *earth*'s *f*oundations *fl*ed" (vowel alliteration in *hour* and *earth's*, consonant and consonant cluster in *foundations fled*).

The Poetry Toolkit: For Writers and Readers, First Edition. William Harmon.
© 2012 William Harmon. Published 2012 by Blackwell Publishing Ltd.

ALLUSION

An indirect reference in one work to another. Eula Varner's exclamation to her schoolteacher Labove in William Faulkner's *The Hamlet* – "You old headless horseman Ichabod Crane" – is an allusion to Washington Irving's "The Legend of Sleepy Hollow." In T. S. Eliot's "The Love Song of J. Alfred Prufrock," the line "I have heard the mermaids singing" may be an allusion to John Donne's "Go and Catch a Falling Star": "Teach me to hear mermaids singing" or to a passage in Robert Louis Stevenson's "Crabbed Age and Youth": "We sail in leaky bottoms and on great and perilous waters; and to take a cue from the dolorous old naval ballad, we have heard the mermaidens singing, and know that we shall never see dry land any more."

ALTERNATING

A configuration in the pattern *abab*. Usually applied to rhyme schemes but also applicable to alliteration ("*now burn new born*"), assonance ("*left my necktie*"), and other acoustic or graphic phenomena.

ALVEOLAR

Sounds produced by some part of the tongue in contact with the ridge just behind the upper front teeth: the three main alveolar consonant sounds are the voiceless (*t*), the voiced (*d*), and the voiced nasal (*n*). All three are heard in *tendon*.

AMPHIBRACH

A rhythmic foot consisting of a long or strong syllable flanked on both sides by a short or weak syllable, represented by ∪ – ∪ or ∪ / ∪. "Ohio" is an example.

AMPHIMACER

A rhythmic foot consisting of a short or weak syllable flanked on both sides by long or strong syllables, represented as – ∪ – or / ∪ /.

ANAGRAM

A word resulting from rearranging the letters of another word, as with *berate*, *rebate*, and *beater*.

ANALOGY

A resemblance or similarity, especially when used to explain or illustrate a principle. Thus, modern *software* has been formed by analogy with earlier *hardware*. In some cases, we suggest an analogy between something abstract and something concrete, such as the relation of life in general to a road, wherein the *milestones* are analogous to years.

ANAPEST
A rhythmic foot consisting of two unaccented syllables followed by one accented syllable: ∪ ∪ /, audible in such lines as "'Twas the night before Christmas, when all through the house..."

ANAPHORA
Repeating the beginning word or words of a line. Whitman is the most conspicuous employer:

> Out of the cradle endlessly rocking,
> Out of the mocking-bird's throat, the musical shuttle,
> Out of the Ninth-month midnight...

ANGLO-ITALIAN
A type of sonnet that somehow combines the Italian design (octave-sestet, rhyming *abbaabbacdecde*) with the English (three heroic quatrains plus a couplet, rhyming *ababcdcdefefgg*). Examples are Thomas Hardy's "Hap" (*ababcdefeffe*), W. B. Yeats's "Leda and the Swan" (*ababcdcdefgefg*), and W. H. Auden's "Who's Who" (*ababcdcdefggfe*).

ANISOBARIC
Showing unequal weight or pressure. Opposite of **ISOBARIC**. Applied to rhyming syllables that do not receive the same level of accent, as with "áll" and "fóotfàll" in Yeats's "The Cap and Bells," "áre" and "gás-tàr" in Lawrence's "When I Read Shakespeare," and "séem" and "íce-crèam" in Stevens's "The Emperor of Ice-Cream." All these examples, which come toward the end of poems, pair a primary accent (´) with a secondary (`).

ANTECEDENT
In grammar, normally the noun to which a pronoun refers. In "Sarah gave me her book," Sarah is the antecedent of "her." In logic, the conditional statement (beginning with a word like "if") that precedes the **CONSEQUENT** (beginning with a word like "then").

ASSONANCE
Repetition of vowel sounds, as in "*a*rmy of un*a*lterable l*a*w" or "you can't h*i*de your l*y*ing *ey*es."

ASSONANCE RHYME

A rhyme in which the vowel **NUCLEUS** of two words match but the succeeding consonant sounds in the **CODA** do not, as in "Leave them al*one*, /And they will come h*ome*."

ASYNDETON

The omission of a conjunction. Often with **COORDINATING CONJUNCTIONS** (as in "I came, I saw, I conquered," in which "and" is omitted), less often with subordinating conjunctions (as in "You don't pay, you suffer," in which an initial "if" is omitted).

BAGATELLE

A trifle.

BALLAD STANZA

A quatrain of alternating tetrameter and trimeter rhymed either *abab* or *abcb*; also called common measure or common meter in hymnals. Here is a famous example:

> The King sits in Dunfermline town,
> Drinking the blood-red wine;
> "O where shall I get a skeely skipper
> To sail this ship or mine?"

BALLADE

The ballade (not be confused with the **BALLAD**) has been one of the most popular of the French verse forms. Early usage most frequently demanded three **STANZAS** and an **ENVOY**, though the number of lines per stanza and of syllables per line varied. Typical earmarks of the ballade have been: (1) the **REFRAIN** (uniform as to wording) recurring regularly at the end of each stanza and of the envoy; (2) the envoy, a peroration of climactic importance and likely to be addressed to a patron; and (3) the use of only three (or at the most four) rhymes in the entire poem, occurring at the same position in each stanza and with no rhyme-word repeated except in the refrain. Stanzas of varied length have been used in the ballade, but the commonest is eight lines rhyming *ababbcbc*, with *bcbc* for the envoy. A good early example of English ballade form is Chaucer's "A Ballade against Woman Inconstant." One of the best known later ballades is Dante Gabriel Rossetti's rendering into English of François Villon's "Ballade of Dead Ladies," with its refrain, "But where are the snows of yester-year?" The

SPENSERIAN STANZA was developed in the late sixteenth century as a variation of the ballade, adding a hexameter ninth line (rhyming *c*): *ababbcbcc*.

BILABIAL
A consonant sound produced with the lips, best known in three articulations: voiceless (*p*), voiced (*b*), and voice nasal (*m*). The end of Hardy's "Hap" contains six instances: "*B*lisses a*b*out *m*y *p*ilgri*m*age as *p*ain."

BLANK VERSE
Unrhymed **IAMBIC PENTAMETER**. The basis of much **DRAMATIC, EPIC, NARRATIVE**, and meditative poetry since 1550.

BLANK VERSE SONNET
An unrhymed fourteen-lined poem, usually in **IAMBIC PENTAMETER**; seldom used except for hundreds of late poems by Robert Lowell (1917–1977) for about the last ten years of his life.

BURLESQUE
An ancient form of comedy characterized by ridiculous exaggeration and distortion: the sublime may be made absurd; honest emotions may be turned to sentimentality; a serious subject may be treated frivolously or a frivolous subject seriously. The essential quality is the discrepancy between subject matter and style. That is, a style ordinarily dignified may be used for nonsensical matter, or a style very nonsensical may be used to ridicule a weighty subject.

CAESURA
A distinct pause in the middle of a line, often marked by a comma or other punctuation. From Pope's *Essay on Criticism*:

To err is human, ‖ to forgive, divine.

CARICATURE
In poetry as in drawing, the exaggeration of features of someone or something for generally comic effect. The main characters in Edward Arlington Robinson's "Miniver Cheevy" and "Mr. Flood's Party" are caricatures of a crazed antiquarian and a codger, both of whom drink too much.

CATALOG
A list, usually of proper names, such as the genealogies ("begats") in the Old Testament and the tally of ships and kings in the *Iliad*, II.

Ovid's *Metamorphoses*, III, tells the story of how Actaeon was attacked by his own hounds, and lists the names of almost forty. In Brookes More's translation, these include Blackfoot, Tracer, Glutton, Quicksight, Surefoot, Killbuck, Tempest, Hunter, Wingfoot, Chaser, Woodranger, Wildwood, Harpy, Racer, Barker, Spot, Tiger, Stout, Blanche, Smut, Storm, Quickfoot, Wolfet, Snap, Blackcoat, Bristle, Towser, Wildtooth, Babbler: "these and others, more than patience leads us to recount or name."

CHARACTER

That element of an artistic creation having to do with a person or personality, usually human but sometimes animal, machine, or supernatural entity. Character contributes the subject of the sentence that is a plot, while the action contributes the predicate. "An ordinary woman overcomes obstacles and defeats enemies while searching for her lost child," for example.

CHIASMUS, CHIASTIC

A mirror image arrangement of components with the general configuration *abba*. It can apply to vowel sounds ("You w*a*lk b*y*, and *I* f*a*ll to pieces" – Howard and Cochran), consonant sounds ("...he felt somehow the *sh*adow of a *ch*ange and the *ch*ill of a *sh*ock" – Henry James), parts of a syntactic pattern ("*Out* went the taper as she hurried *in*" – Keats; "*Part* steals, lets *part* abide" – Hardy), or a rhyme scheme (*abba*).

CINQUAIN

Although sometimes applied to any group of five lines, usually reserved for a particular pattern invented by Adelaide Crapsey: the metrical design is monometer, dimeter, trimeter, tetrameter, and monometer. An example is "Irresolution and Dependence":

> I *do*!
> I *know* I do.
> I *think* I know I do.
> I *guess* I think I know I do...
> I don't.

CODA

Any end or tail. With syllables, coda is the final consonant sound or sounds. In *gap*, for example, the coda is /p/.

COMMON MEASURE or METER
A hymnal designation corresponding to the **BALLAD MEASURE**: a quatrain of alternating tetrameter and trimeter rhyming *abab* or *abcb*. Isaac Watts wrote one well-known example:

> Our God, our help in ages past,
> Our hope for years to come,
> Our shelter from the stormy blast,
> And our eternal home.

COMPOUND RHYME
A rhyme of polysyllables with primary-accented and secondary-accented syllables rhyming, as in *wíldwood/chíldhood* and *másticàte/cástigàte.*

CONCRETE POETRY
The exploitation of the visual and tactile qualities of writing, as in this exercise in significant **ANAGRAMS**:

BEDROOMBEDROOMBEDROOM
BEDROOMBOREDOMBEDROOM
BEDROOMBEDROOMBEDROOM

CONJUNCTION
A word that conjoins and indicates a relation, such as addition (*and*) or contrast (*but*) or alternation (*or*). Coordinating conjunctions join more or less equal units, phrases, and independent clauses; subordinating conjunctions introduce subordinate or dependent clauses or other units. The latter is a larger group, and some members can be arranged in antithetical pairs (*if/unless, when/until, because/although*).

CONNOTE, CONNOTATION
The opposite of "denote," which means to indicate directly. To connote is to imply or suggest indirectly. "Grecian," say, may have a more formal connotation than "Greek," but the words denote the same thing.

CONSEQUENT
As a complement to **ANTECEDENT**, consequent means the second part of an *if/then* proposition.

CONSONANCE

The repetition of consonant sounds. Julius Caesar's line "Le*t* me have men abou*t* me tha*t* are fa*t*" contains four *t* sounds in a largely monosyllabic line – with a most emphatic effect. The line "Be*t*ween *t*wo Og*d*en, I*n*diana, *d*u*n*es" contains five *n* sounds, along with some *t* and *d* sounds, and all of them are alveolar articulations, though not quite the same consonant.

CONSONANCE RHYME

RHYME in which the final elements (**CODA** – usually consonant sounds) do match but the vowel sounds (**NUCLEUS**) are different. In many cases, the words look like rhymes, but, because of the notorious ambiguity of the *o* letter, do not sound the same: *food/good/blood, tomb/comb/bomb, come/home, word/lord, ward/lard,* and so forth.

CONSONANT

A speech sound, made in the mouth and nose, which is produced by contact of some sort between various parts of the oral cavity, unlike a **VOWEL**, which is produced in the larynx and consists of pure sound.

CONSONANT CLUSTER

A set of two or more consonant sounds occupying either the onset or the coda of a syllable. "Starts," for example, has clusters at the beginning and the end. In English, an onset can contain as many as three consonant sounds, a coda as many as four.

COUPLET

A unit consisting of two lines, often rhymed between themselves.

CURSE

An invocation that calls on a supernatural power to visit evil on someone or some enterprise. It is one ancient function of poetry.

CURTAL SONNET

Gerard Manley Hopkins's name for a sonnet that has been curtailed. The challenge, according to Hopkins, was to shorten the **OCTAVE** to a **SESTET** while preserving the numerical ratio of the first subdivision to the second. Since 8:6::6:4.5, a curtal sonnet is divided into parts consisting of six lines and four and a half lines. The octave is shortened to a sestet and rhymes *abcabc*. The sestet is shortened to an augmented quatrain and rhymes either *dbcd* or *dcbd*. A half-line rhyming *c* ends the poem. Hopkins's "Pied Beauty" is the most famous example.

CYNGHANEDD

A medieval Welsh term covering a wide and sophisticated range of verse devices, revived in the late nineteenth century by Gerard Manley Hopkins to refer to various harmonious patterns of interlaced multiple **ALLITERATION**. Interlacing alliteration, in such patterns as *xyyx* and *xyxy* (much the commonest), sometimes occurs in vernacular phrases ("*tempest* in a *teapot*," "*partridge* in a *pear tree*") and the biblical collocation of *s*words-*p*loughshares and *s*pears-*p*runing-hooks. There is conspicuous and complex *cynghanedd* in Macbeth's description of life as a "*tale*/*Told* by an idiot, *full* of *sound* and *fury*, /*Signifying* nothing" and in Wordsworth's noble tribute to Milton: ". . . and yet thy *heart*/The *lowliest duties* on *herself did lay*." The device can be heard in "*studied fate stand forth*" (Richard Crashaw), "*sad heart*" and "*sick* for *home*" in one line of Keats's "Ode to a Nightingale." Other examples are in William Barnes's "*Ellen Brine* ov *Allenburn*," in "*guidon flags flutter gayly*" in Whitman's "Cavalry Crossing a Ford," and in "*Headed* with *flint*, or *hardened with flame*'s breath" in C. M. Doughty's *The Titans*. The most salient use is in the sonnet beginning "As *kingfishers catch fire*, *dragonflies draw flame*" and the end of "God's Grandeur":

> because the Holy Ghost over the *bent*
> World *broods* with *warm breast* and with ah! *bright wings*.

DACTYL

A foot consisting of one accented syllable followed by two unaccented, as in "mánĭkĭn."

DECASYLLABIC

A line composed of ten syllables. Iambic and trochaic pentameter lines are decasyllabic.

DECLARATIVE

One of the three main types of sentence, the others being interrogative and imperative. The declarative declares or states: "I eat." (Interrogative: "Do you eat?" Imperative: "Eat!")

DEMOTION

The reduction of stress on a syllable caused by the rhythmic environment. An established pattern of anapests can effect the demotion of a stressed syllable, as when one recites a phrase like "'Twăs thĕ nĭght bĕfŏre Chrĭstmăs," so that the normally iambic "before" is sounded as two weak syllables.

DICTION
Use of language in general, construed as being divided into **VOCABU-LARY** (words one at a time) and **SYNTAX** (words arranged in a certain order).

DIMETER
A line with two long or accented syllables.

DISTICH
Two verse lines.

DOGGEREL
Incompetent poetry, sometimes caused by ineptitude but sometimes produced with deliberately comic intention, marked by ragged rhythm, inexact rhyme, and fantastic exaggeration. Samuel Butler's seventeenth-century *Hudibras* is a burlesque of Presbyterians and Cromwellians in general. A number of amusingly clumsy versifiers have achieved a degree of fame. Mark Twain called readers' attention to the obituary effusions of Julia A. Moore (1847–1920), "The Sweet Singer of Michigan" and to the unstoppably prolific Bloodgood Haviland Cutter (1817–1906), "The Long Island Farmer Poet," whom Mark Twain nicknamed "The Poet Lariat." Cornelius Whur (1782–1853) and William Topaz McGonagall (1825–1902) likewise enjoyed celebrity among university wits. It may seem cruel to make fun of them, but it is impossible to take them seriously.

DOUBLE
Sometimes applied to rhymes in which the stressed rhyming syllable is followed by an undifferentiated, unstressed syllable, as in *double/trouble*. Usually called **FEMININE**.

DRAMATIC MONOLOGUE
A poem, often in blank verse, offered as a single sustained speech by a character, usually in a situation requiring self-revelation. Since the mono-logue is all the reader has to go on, many such poems represent speeches by pre-existing characters, including real people (Lucretius, Andrea del Sarto, Fra Lippo Lippi), literary characters (Caliban), and figures from myth and legend (Tithonus, Ulysses). The heyday of such poems was the last two-

thirds of the nineteenth century, especially as done by Alfred, Lord
Tennyson and Robert Browning.

ECHO

A general effect whereby one thing sounds like another. Sometimes used
specifically in an "echo poem," such as George Herbert's "Heaven":

> O Who will show me those delights on high?
>   *Echo.*   *I.*
> Thou Echo, thou art mortall, all men know.
>   *Echo.*   *No.*
> Wert thou not born among the trees and leaves?
>   *Echo.*   *Leaves.*
> And are there any leaves, that still abide?
>   *Echo.*   *Bide.*
> What leaves are they? impart the matter wholly.
>   *Echo.*   *Holy.*
> Are holy leaves the Echo then of blisse?
>   *Echo.*   *Yes.*
> Then tell me, what is that supreme delight?
>   *Echo.*   *Light.*
> Light to the minde: what shall the will enjoy?
>   *Echo.*   *Joy.*
> But are there cares and businesse with the pleasure?
>   *Echo.*   *Leisure.*
> Light, joy, and leisure; but shall they persever?
>   *Echo.*   *Ever.*

Some of these echoes are perfect rhymes, others are identicals, with units
consisting of the same sounds but remaining different words (*know/no*). In
some pairs, such as *persever/ever*, the second component is included in the
first, rather like an echo.

ELLIPSIS

The omission of material, sometimes when a pattern is repeated. A stanza
of Hardy's "The Darkling Thrush" furnishes a good example:

> The land's sharp features seemed to be
>   The Century's corpse outleant,
> His crypt the cloudy canopy,
>   The wind his death-lament.

This compresses three assertions, the full form of which would be something like "The land's sharp features seemed to be the Century's corpse
outleant, the cloudy canopy seemed to be his crypt, the wind seemed to be
his death-lament." By ellipsis, the repeated "seemed to be" is omitted, with
a variation in the reversal in the third line.

END-STOPPED COUPLETS

Rhymed couplets with pauses at the end of many lines, often indicated by
punctuation. The beginning of Dryden's *Absalom and Achitophel* is an apt
illustration:

> In pious times, e'r Priest-craft did begin,
> Before Polygamy was made a sin;
> When man, on many, multiply'd his kind,
> E'r one to one was, cursedly, confind:
> When Nature prompted, and no law deny'd
> Promiscuous use of Concubine and Bride;
> Then, Israel's monarch, after Heaven's own heart,
> His vigorous warmth did, variously, impart
> To Wives and Slaves; And, wide as his Command,
> Scatter'd his Maker's Image through the Land.

Eight of the ten lines end with punctuation (comma, semicolon,
colon).

END-STOPPED LINES

Lines in which both the grammatical structure and the sense reach completion
at the end. The absence of enjambment or run-on lines, in Pope's

> All are but parts of one stupendous whole,
> Whose body Nature is, and God the soul.

Here is an example of *end-stopped* blank verse, from Antony's funeral
oration (*Julius Caesar* 3,2):

> He was my friend, faithful and just to me;
> But Brutus says he was ambitious,
> And Brutus is an honorable man.
> He hath brought many captives home to Rome,
> Whose ransoms did the general coffers fill.

Did this in Caesar seem ambitious?
When that the poor have cried, Caesar hath wept;
Ambition should be made of sterner stuff.
Yet Brutus says he was ambitious;
And Brutus is an honorable man.

ENGLISH SONNET (also SHAKESPEAREAN)

A sonnet consisting of three quatrains followed by a couplet, rhyming *abab cdcd efef gg*. Often called the Shakespearean sonnet because Shakespeare was its most distinguished practitioner.

ENJAMBMENT

Opposite of **END-STOPPED**: the carrying over of the sense from line to line, often with no punctuation, as in this passage from Robert Browning's "My Last Duchess":

    . . . so not the first
Are you to turn and ask thus. Sir, 'twas not
Her husband's presence only, called that spot
Of joy into the Duchess's cheek: perhaps
Fra Pandolf chanced to say "Her mantle laps
Over my lady's wrist too much," or "Paint
Must never hope to reproduce the faint
Half flush that dies along her throat": such stuff
Was courtesy, she thought, and cause enough
For calling up that spot of joy . . .

ENVOY (also *ENVOI*)

A conventionalized stanza appearing at the close of certain kinds of poems; particularly associated with the French **BALLADE**. An envoy comes as a shorter stanza at the end of the chant royal and the **SESTINA**. An envoy is someone or something *sent*, and many poems sound like instructions to an envoy that conveys a message, as in Edmund Waller's "Go, lovely rose" and Ezra Pound's poems that include phrases like "Go, my songs, seek your praise from the young and from the intolerant" (from "Ité" – which means "Go") and "Go, my songs, to the lonely and the unsatisfied" (from "Commission").

EPIC

A long narrative poem in elevated style presenting characters of high and even divine position in debate, conflict, and adventures, forming an organic whole through their relation to a central heroic figure or contest.

EPIGRAM
A pithy saying, often expressed as a rhymed couplet, as in this by William Blake:

> Her whole life is an epigram: smack smooth, and neatly penned,
> Platted quite neat to catch applause, with a sliding noose at the end.

EPIGRAPH
A quotation on the title page of a book or a motto heading a section of a work. Not to be confused with **EPIGRAM** or **EPITAPH**.

EPISODE, EPISODIC
An incident presented as one continuous action. Although having its own unity, an episode is usually accompanied by other episodes woven together to create a whole. Loosely, any item in a series.

EPISTLE
Any letter in general, but the term is usually limited to formal compositions written to a distant individual or group. The most familiar use of the term is to characterize certain books of the New Testament. The epistle may differs from the letter in that it is a conscious literary form rather than a spontaneous, chatty, private composition. Much poetry and quite a bit of fiction in the eighteenth century was epistolary.

EPITAPH
An inscription marking a burial place. Commemorative verses or lines appearing on tombs or written as if intended for such use.

EUPHEMISM, EUPHEMISTIC
A device in which indirectness replaces directness of statement, usually in an effort to avoid offensiveness. To say "at liberty" instead of "out of work," "senior citizens" instead of "old people," "in the family way" instead of "pregnant," "anti-Semite" instead of "Jew-hater," and "pass away" instead of "die" is to practice *euphemism* of one sort or another.

FABLE
Broadly, any story, but usually a brief tale told to point out a moral. The characters are frequently animals, but people and inanimate objects are sometimes central.

FALLING RHYTHM

A **FOOT** in which the first syllable is accented, as in a **TROCHEE** or **DACTYL**. Coleridge's lines on the poetic feet illustrate it:

Trochee is in falling double,
Dactyl is falling, like – Tripoli.

Thomas Hardy's "The Voice" is one of the few rhymed English poems that uses both of the chief falling rhythms – dactyls and trochees.

FEMININE ENDING

An extrametrical unstressed syllable added to the end of a line in iambic or anapestic rhythm. This variation, which may give a sense of movement and irregularity, is commonly used in blank verse. The most famous **SOLIL-OQUY** in English begins with four lines that all have feminine endings:

To be, or not to be – that is the question:
Whether 'tis nobler in the mind to suffer
The slings and arrows of outrageous fortune
Or to take arms against a sea of troubles
And by opposing end them . . .

FEMININE RHYME (also **DOUBLE RHYME**)

A rhyme in which the rhyming stressed syllables are followed by an undifferentiated identical unstressed syllable, as *waken/forsaken*. The phenomenon may be random, in which case feminine rhymes will almost always be in the minority, or there may be some patterned arrangement. In the latter case – as in Shakespeare's "Oh Mistress Mine," Longfellow's "Snowflakes," Browning's "Soliloquy of the Spanish Cloister," and Housman's "Epitaph on an Army of Mercenaries," the normal tendency is for **FEMININE** rhymes to precede **MASCULINE**.

FOOT, FEET

The basic unit of rhythm, whether quantitative or qualitative. The usual notation is binary, with some arrangement of long/short or strong/weak syllables. A foot is defined by the order of elements, such as the iamb, a weak syllable followed by a strong, diagrammed ∪ /.

FRAME, FRAMING

A story with another story inside. Common in fiction, also found in poems. Coleridge's "The Rime of the Ancient Mariner" has a present-tense outer story ("It *is* an ancient mariner . . .") in which a wedding-guest is halted by an old man, who insists on telling him a story, which is in the past tense ("There *was* a ship . . ."). Shelley's "Ozymandias" has a past-tense outer story that presents the teller of the present-tense inner story: "I *met* a traveller from an antique land/Who said: 'Two vast and trunkless legs of stone/*Stand* in the desert . . .'"

GRAPHIC EFFECTS

The whole range of effects that appeal to the eye, including punctuation, capitalization, line breaks, stanza design, indentations, margins, and other features peculiar to print or the written word.

GREAT VOWEL SHIFT

A large and important shift in the values of long vowels in English that took place in the decades after about 1350. The main result is that English differs from other ancient and modern European languages in the way it may pronounce certain words. The Peruvian city is called/ˈliːmə/, but in America the bean associated with it is called/laɪmə/. "Libido" has two soundings, one with the more traditional pre-Shift vowel/lɪˈbidəʊ/(most common in America), the other with the post-Shift/-lɪˈbaɪdəʊ/.

HAIKU

A form of Japanese poetry that states – in three lines of five, seven, and five syllables – a clear picture designed to arouse a distinct emotion and suggest a specific spiritual insight. Haiku poetry is deeply serious and also profoundly conventional. Every season, element, bird, flower, insect, and so forth comes equipped with a large set of associations that the haiku exploits.

HEPTAMETER

A verse line with seven feet, as in Thayer's "Casey at the Bat":

The outlook wasn't brilliant for the Mudville nine that day;
The score stood four to two, with but one inning more to play.

HEROIC

Applied to various devices and forms, most of which involve pentameter or hexameter lines.

HEROIC COUPLET

IAMBIC PENTAMETER lines rhymed in pairs. A favorite measure of Chaucer – *The Legend of Good Women* is an instance – this verse form did not come into its greatest popularity, however, until the middle of the seventeenth century, and from then through the early years of the nineteenth century it was a staple of serious verse.

HEROIC QUATRAIN
Four lines of iambic pentameter (or, much more rarely, tetrameter) rhyming *abab*, a component of the Shakespearean sonnet, used as a stanza by Dryden and others, but brought to perfection in Gray's "Elegy Written in a Country Churchyard," which is, ironically, about people who were not at all heroic. Another unheroic context is found in a poem by Housman:

> Here dead lie we because we did not choose
> To live and shame the land from which we sprung.
> Life, to be sure, is nothing much to lose;
> But young men think it is, and we were young.

In recent years the most notable use of the heroic quatrain has been in "Bridge for the Living" by Philip Larkin.

HETEROMEROUS
A term borrowed from biology to apply to something with mismatched parts; here, the same as **MOSAIC** (a rhyme like "visit / is it").

HEXAMETER
A line of six feet. In Latin and Greek, hexameter was the conventional medium for epic and didactic poetry. Some of the sonnets in Sir Philip Sidney's *Astrophil and Stella* are in hexameter lines:

> Loving in truth, and fain in verse my love to show,
> That she (dear she) might take some pleasure of my pain;
> Pleasure might cause her read, reading might make her know;
> Knowledge might pity win, and pity grace obtain; . . .
> Biting my truant pen, beating myself for spite,
> "Fool," said my muse to me; "look in thy heart, and write."

HOAX
An act of mischievous trickery designed to expose folly or exploit innocence. A literary hoax may involve a fabrication (of a work, a person, or a whole school) that is presented, often to a periodical or publisher, as genuine.

HOMEOTELEUTON
Sameness or similarity of endings of consecutive words or words near each other, often considered unsettling or graceless but sometimes unavoidable,

as in adjacent adverbs ("relatively easily"), verbal forms ("emerging meaning becoming fashionable"), accidental sameness of affixes ("truly holy family"), or echoic names (Lyndon Johnson, Dudley Bradley, Charlton Heston, Edward Woodward). Most instances of homeoteleuton have to do with unstressed syllables, so it can usually be distinguished from proper rhyme. In John Crowe Ransom's "Bells for John Whiteside's Daughter," "window" and "shadow" are placed in a rhyming position, but the only significant relation between them is homeoteleuton, because they share the same unstressed syllable (*-dow*) and their stressed syllables have nothing in common (*win-* and *sha-*).

HOMMAGE

A tribute or act of homage by one artist to another. Robert Lowell's "Ezra Pound" quotes Pound dismissing "an abomination, Possum's *hommage* to Milton" – referring to T. S. Eliot's tribute in an essay called "Milton II."

HYMN

A poem expressing religious or patriotic emotion and generally intended to be sung by a chorus. Originally the term referred to almost any song of praise, whether of gods or famous people. It has been suggested that typical "national anthems" are technically hymns.

HYPOTAXIS

Arrangement of clauses, phrases, or words in dependent or subordinate relationships. The phrase "hypotactic style" refers to writing that uses subordination to reflect logical, causal, temporal, or spatial relations. Occasionally, hypotaxis refers to the use of a subordinate clause in a place where one might normally expect a coordinate. Instead of the coordination of "'Twas the night before Christmas, *and* all through the house," for example, Clement Moore actually wrote ". . . *when* all through the house." In any event, parataxis is a feature of ordinary speaking – especially the naive, simple, rustic, or juvenile – and hypotaxis of writing. One might say aloud, "I tried, but I failed" (parataxis); one could write, "Although I tried, I failed" (hypotaxis).

IAMB (or IAMBUS)

A foot consisting of an unaccented syllable and then an accented (∪ /). The most common rhythm in English verse for more than 600 years.

IDENTICAL RHYME

A term sometimes applied to rhyming syllables that are no different in sound. See **REPETITION** and **REDUNDANT**.

IN MEMORIAM STANZA

A quatrain of iambic tetrameter rhyming *abba*. A few earlier poets, such as Ben Jonson, used such a stanza occasionally, but it remained for Tennyson to invest the form with singular dignity and variety. As an added constraint in Tennyson's *In Memoriam*, all the rhymes are **MASCULINE**, and all the constituent lyrics have at least three stanzas.

IRONY

A broad term referring to the recognition of a reality different from appearance. Verbal irony is a figure of speech in which the actual intent is expressed in words that carry the opposite meaning. We may say, "I could care less" while meaning "I couldn't care less."

ISOBARIC

Having equal weight or pressure. Most rhymes are between equally accented syllables.

ITALIAN SONNET (also PETRARCHAN SONNET)

A **SONNET** divided into an **OCTAVE** rhyming *abbaabba* and a **SESTET** rhyming *cdecde*. That is the classic form, which asserts the avoidance of rhyme in couplets in the sestet and a limiting of the overall number of rhymes to five. Ideally, the sense of the lines falls into groups different from the rhyme groups, thus: *ab-ba-ab-ba-cde-cde*, so that nowhere do we encounter a pat couplet. The least objectionable departures are the *abbaacca* octave and the *cdcdcd* sestet, but there are many exceptions and innovations.

KEATS ODE STANZA

A stanza of ten or eleven lines developed by John Keats for some of the odes he wrote towards the end of his life. Almost all of the lines are pentameter, and the first seven lines always rhyme *ababcde*. The rhyme scheme in the concluding lines may be *cde, dce, ced, dcce,* or *cdde*. Similar patterns have been adopted by Matthew Arnold ("The Scholar Gypsy" and "Thyrsis"), Philip Larkin ("The Whitsun Weddings"), and Gavin Ewart ("The Larkin Automatic Carwash").

LEXICAL

Involving words or other such units considered one at a time.

LIMERICK

A form of light verse that usually follows a definite pattern: five **ANAPESTIC** lines of which the first, second, and fifth, most often consisting of three feet, rhyme; and the third and fourth lines, consisting of two feet, rhyme.

There seem to be associations among the limerick, **POULTER'S MEASURE,** and the **SHORT MEASURE** of the hymnals. (Limericks can be sung to the tune of "Blest Be the Tie That Binds.")

LINE
A fundamental conceptual unit, normally realized as a single spoken or written sequence of elements and possibly zoned by various sorts of punctuation, meter, rhyme, and other devices. Necessarily, prose is printed in conventional lines, but the lines are seldom distinguished by demarcation except that dictated by justified right and left margins. A line of poetry conventionally equates a spatial measure with a temporal, but the two arrays need not be closely linked. Some poems, including the Old English poems in the *Exeter Book* and other manuscript sources, can be written out as prose; two paragraphs printed as ordinary prose in Scott Fitzgerald's *This Side of Paradise* turn out, on inspection, to be **SPENSERIAN STANZAS.** As a rule, however, poems look like poems. (Jeremy Bentham once playfully suggested that "when the lines run all the way to the right margin it is prose"; when not, the result is poetry.)

LITOTES
A form of **UNDERSTATEMENT** in which a thing is affirmed by stating the negative of its opposite. To say "She was not unmindful" when one means that "She gave careful attention" is to employ litotes. Although a common device in ironic expression, litotes was also one of the characteristic figures of speech in Old English poetry. In Tennyson's "Ulysses," the heroic speaker resorts to litotes several times, with an effect of stoic restraint and (this is still the trickster) subtlety: "little profits" for "profits not at all," "not least" for "great," "not to fail" for "succeed splendidly," and "not unbecoming" for "thoroughly appropriate." Auden's "The Wanderer" calls a noisy bird "unquiet" and the sea "undried." Many today express the idea "good" by saying "not bad."

LONG MEASURE or METER
A stanza of four lines of **IAMBIC TETRAMETER** rhyming either *abab* or *abcb.*

LOOSE
A sentence grammatically complete before the end; the opposite of **PERIODIC.** A complex loose sentence consists of an independent clause followed by a dependent clause. Most of the complex sentences we use are loose (the term implies no fault in structure), the periodic sentence being

usually reserved for emphasis, drama, and variety. Loose sentences with too many dependent clauses become limp. "Although I just ate, I'm still hungry" is periodic; "I'm still hungry, although I just ate" is loose, ending with more whimper than bang.

LYRIC POEM
A brief subjective poem strongly marked by imagination, melody, and emotion, and creating a single, unified impression. It is the result of trimming away plots of action and character, to concentrate chiefly on thoughts and feelings in an individual sensibility.

MASCULINE (ENDING, RHYME)
With an accent on the final syllable: applied to the ending of lines (such as the **IAMBIC** and **ANAPESTIC**) and to rhymes in which nothing follows the rhyming syllable. The predominant ending of lines and rhymes in English for many centuries. Contrasted with **FEMININE**. "Mount / fount" is a masculine rhyme, "Mountain / fountain" feminine.

MASS
A measure of the total number of consonant and vowel *sounds* in a syllable. Sometimes considered in determining the length of a syllable in quantitative scansion.

MENTAL STATE
Sensibility: the combination of inner elements that make up one's consciousness, including more or less intellectual things – "sunrise is at 6:04 a.m. today" – along with possible emotional coloring – "I am happy that my parents arrive at sunrise," "Unfortunately, my parents arrive at sunrise," etc.

METAPHOR
An **ANALOGY** identifying one object with another and ascribing to the first object one or more of the qualities of the second. When Shakespeare writes:

> That time of year thou mayst in me behold
> When yellow leaves, or none, or few, do hang
> Upon those boughs which shake against the cold,
> Bare ruined choirs where late the sweet birds sang –

old age is likened to late fall or early winter, conveyed through a group of images unusually rich in implications. According to a fairly ingenuous notion of language, abstractions can be treated only in terms that are not abstract, presumably because the primitive mind cannot handle abstractions. But no evidence establishes the existence of any such limitations. To presume that any human being has to have a grasp of physical "pulling away" (*abs* + *trahere*) before being able to grasp an abstract "abstraction" is little more than bigotry. Even so, mentally negotiable systems of signs do resemble metaphoric displacements and substitutions enough for Emerson to assert, "Every word was once a poem... Language is fossil poetry."

METER

The recurrence in poetry of a rhythmic pattern, or the **RHYTHM** established by the regular occurrence of similar units of sound. Meter nowadays refers mostly to accentual-syllabic rhythm, and the number of feet in a line furnishes a means of describing the meter as a count of the number of feet per line. The standard English meters are: **MONOMETER**, one foot; **DIMETER**, two; **TRIMETER**, three; **TETRAMETER**, four; **PENTAMETER**, five; **HEXAMETER**, six (also called the **ALEXANDRINE**); **HEPTAMETER**, seven (also called "fourteener" when the feet are iambic); **OCTAMETER**, eight.

METRICAL INDEX

A feature of some hymnals that identifies the syllabic profile of a given hymn by name, syllable count, or designation. The stanza of the familiar hymn "Eternal Father, strong to save" ("The Navy Hymn"), for example, consists of four lines of iambic tetrameter plus a two-lined iambic tetrameter refrain. Since a line of iambic tetrameter contains eight syllables, the index may annotate this hymn as 8.8.8.8.8 or in some cases 8.8.8.8 with 8.8 refrain. The 8.8.8.8 quatrain is also called Long Measure or Meter, abbreviated "L M.," so that the index may say "L.M. with 8.8 refrain." "L.M. D." means "Long Measure Doubled" (8.8.8.8.8.8.8.8). "S.M." is "Short Measure" (6.6.8.6), "C.M." "Common Measure" (8.6.8.6), and both may be doubled or augmented with a refrain. "Eternal Father" also has the tune name "Melita," the ancient name of Malta, which is the island where St Paul found refuge from a storm at sea.

MILTONIC SONNET

A variation of the **ITALIAN SONNET** devised by Milton, in which the rhyme scheme is kept but the **VOLTA** or "turn" between the **OCTAVE** and the **SESTET** is eliminated.

MOCK EPIC (or **MOCK HEROIC**)
Terms for a literary form that burlesques the epic by treating a trivial subject in a grand style or uses the epic formulas to make a trivial subject ridiculous by ludicrously overstating it. A brilliantly executed mock epic has a manifold effect: to ridicule trivial or silly conduct; to mock the pretensions and absurdities of epic proper; to bestow an affectionate measure of elevation on low or foolish characters; and to bestow a humanizing, deflating, or debunking measure of lowering on elevated characters.

MONOMETER
A line of verse consisting of one **FOOT**.

MOSAIC
A term sometimes used for a rhyme between a single word and two or more words, such as those between "minute" and "in it" (Kipling) and "is it" and "visit" (Eliot). Also called "heteromerous rhyme."

MULTIPLE RHYME
Any rhyme in which the rhyming stressed syllable is followed by one or more undifferentiated, unstressed syllables.

NARRATIVE POEM
A poetic account of events; a poem that tells a story. **EPICS, BALLADS,** and metrical romances are among the many kinds of *narrative poems*. Such poems are driven by a plot of action, to which all else is subordinate.

NUCLEUS
The heart of a syllable; almost always a vowel sound. A paradigmatic syllable consists of a *nucleus* necessarily, and possibly an **ONSET** (consonant matter) before and a **CODA** (consonant matter) after.

NURSERY RHYME
A brief verse, often anonymous and traditional, with percussive rhythm and frequent, heavy rhyme, written for young children. The first important collection in English was made in the eighteenth century by "Mother Goose," whose actual identity remains unknown.

OCCASIONAL (POEM, POETRY, VERSE)
Poetry written for some particular occasion, such as a wedding, birthday, or funeral. Poems with titles like "September 1913," "Easter 1916," "Ash Wednesday," and "September 1, 1939" suggest at least a genesis on an occasion.

OCTAMETER

A line of eight feet. It is fairly rare in English verse. Of the rhythm and meter of "The Raven," Edgar Allan Poe said, "The former is trochaic – the latter is octameter acatalectic, alternating with heptameter catalectic repeated in the refrain of the fifth verse, and terminating with tetrameter catalectic." ("The Philosophy of Composition," 1846). These lines from Tennyson's "Locksley Hall" illustrate **IAMBIC OCTAMETER**:

In the spring a fuller crimson comes upon the robin's breast;
In the spring the wanton lapwing gets himself another crest.

OCTAVE

An eight-lined stanza. The chief use of the term, however, is to denote the first eight-lined division of the Italian sonnet as separate from the last six-lined division, the **SESTET**. In this sense it is a synonym for octet. In strict usage the octave rhymes *abbaabba,* serves to state a position resolved in the sestet, and comes to such a complete close at the end of the eighth line as to be marked by a period.

ONSET

One of the three components of a syllable. The *onset,* which is optional, consists of one or more consonants and comes before the **NUCLEUS** (vowel), which in turn comes before the optional **CODA** (consonant matter again).

OTTAVA RIMA

A stanza consisting of eight iambic pentameter (or hendecasyllabic) lines rhyming *abababcc.* Some English poets using *ottava rima* are Wyatt (the earliest in English), Spenser, Milton, Keats, Byron, Longfellow, Browning, and Yeats.

OVERSTATEMENT

Exaggeration; hyperbole. The figure may be used to heighten effect, or it may be used for humor. Macbeth is using *hyperbole* here in describing how bloody his hand is:

No; this my hand will rather
The multitudinous seas incarnadine,
Making the green one red.

PARATAXIS

An arrangement of sentences, clauses, phrases, or words in coordinate rather than subordinate constructions, often without connectives, as in Julius Caesar's "Veni, vidi, vici" ("I came, I saw, I conquered"), or with coordinate conjunctions, as in Hemingway's or Whitman's extensive use of "and" as a connective. Thus, **POLYSYNDETON** (especially in the form "and ... and ... and ...") often accompanies parataxis.

PARODY

A composition imitating another, usually serious, piece. It is designed to ridicule a work or its style or author. Parody makes fun of some familiar style, typically by keeping the style more or less constant while markedly lowering or debasing the subject.

PASTORAL ELEGY

A poem employing conventional pastoral imagery, written in dignified, serious language, and taking as its theme the expression of grief at the loss of a friend or important person. In some of the best – Milton's "Lycidas," Shelley's "Adonais," Arnold's "Thyrsis" – one poet laments the death of another.

PENTAMETER

A line of verse of five feet. Serious verse in English since the time of Chaucer (epic, drama, meditative, narrative) and many conventional forms (terza rima, heroic quatrain, rhyme royal, ottava rima, the Spenserian stanza, and the sonnet) have made pentameter the staple measure.

PERFECT

Said of a rhyme that fully satisfies the requirements: the syllables involved have different onsets but identical nuclei and codas, as with *last* and *mast*. Distinguished from deficient rhymes, such as assonance rhymes (*last* and *bath*) and consonance rhymes (*last* and *mist*).

PERIODIC SENTENCE

A sentence not grammatically complete before its end; the opposite of a loose sentence. The first stanza of Longfellow's "Snowflakes" is *periodic*, beginning with a succession of adverbial phrases and not grammatically complete until the very last word, which is the subject:

> Out of the bosom of the Air,
> > Out of the cloud-folds of her garments shaken,

> Over the woodlands brown and bare,
>   Over the harvest-fields forsaken,
>   Silent, and soft, and slow,
>   Descends the snow.

PETRARCHAN SONNET
Another name for the **ITALIAN SONNET**.

PLAIN
The simplest level of style, in which statement and meaning coincide.

PLOT
The overall design of the action of a work. The plot may rearrange elements, so that the work begins in the middle of things, then goes back into the past for background, then returns to the present for completion.

POLYSYNDETON
The use of many conjunctions, possibly in excess of the usual expectations. A normal sentence may say, "I got up, I got dressed, and I had breakfast." With **ASYNDETON**, that becomes "I got up, I got dressed, I had breakfast." With **POLYSYNDETON**: "I got up, and I got dressed, and I had breakfast." Alan Dugan's "On A Seven-Day Diary" sounds like an exercise in polysyndeton to convey monotony:

> Oh I got up and went to work
> and worked and came back home
> and ate and talked and went to sleep.
> Then I got up and went to work
> and worked and came back home
> from work and ate and slept. . . .

POULTER'S MEASURE
A couplet, now rarely used, with a first line in iambic hexameter and a second line in iambic heptameter. Queen Elizabeth I used the form:

> The doubt of future foes exiles my present joy,
> And wit me warns to shun such snares as threaten mine annoy;
> For falsehood now doth flow, and subjects' faith doth ebb,
> Which should not be if reason ruled or wisdom weaved the web.

PREDICATE

That part of a sentence that makes a statement about the subject; it usually contains the verb along with objects and other materials attached to the verb.

In "He walked to work this morning," the subject is "He," everything else belongs in the predicate.

PREQUEL (and SEQUEL)

After an initial work establishes a story, there may be sequels to tell about what has followed and prequels to account for how things came to be. Following *The Godfather* (1972), set during the period between 1945 and 1955, *The Godfather Part II* (1974) is both a prequel, narrating the story of the immigration of those who would become important later, as well as a sequel, narrating the story of what happened in the aftermath of the first part. *The Godfather Part III* (1990) is a sequel. J. R. R. Tolkien's *The Silmarillion* is a prequel to *The Hobbit* and *The Lord of the Rings*, and Tolkien is sometimes given credit for coining the word.

PROMOTION

The assignment of stress to an unstressed syllable, usually as the result of patterns of rhythm and rhyme. In many cases, a change of vowel quality also occurs. Promotion is most often encountered when a word of three or more syllables, ending as a dactyl, occurs at the end of a rhymed iambic line, as in the familiar

My country, 'tis of thee,
Sweet land of liberty....

The last word is normally stressed as a dactyl ("líbĕrtў") but, by promotion, picks up courtesy stress on the final syllable ("líbĕrtý"), along with a change of the final vowel to suggest a rhyme with "thee."

PUNY

Said of a rhyme in which one of the components is an unaccented syllable that cannot be promoted without wrenching. "Sweet land of liberty" permits PROMOTION, because "liberty" has three syllables. "Sweet land of beauty," however, does not, because adding accent to the second syllable would wrench it away from the first. In Marlowe's "The Passionate Shepherd to His Love," there is a puny rhyme in the lines

The shepherds' swains shall dance and sing
For thy delight each May morning:

PYRRHIC
A rhythmic foot consisting of two short or weak syllables, represented by
∪ ∪. Occurs almost exclusively as a common variation in an iambic or
trochaic environment, as in the second foot of "dáughtĕr | ŏf thĕ | árrŏw-
mákĕr."

QUADRUPLE
Applied to the rare rhyme in which the rhyming stressed syllable is followed
by three unstressed, undifferentiated syllables, as with *medicated/dedicated/
predicated.*

QUALITATIVE (SCANSION, VERSE, VERSIFICATION)
Versification based on patterns of accented and unaccented syllables. Most
European languages since about 1350, including English, have followed
some model of qualitative versification.

QUANTITATIVE (SCANSION, VERSE, VERSIFICATION)
A system based on rhythm determined by quantity, that is, relative length
or duration of sound. Classical poetry was quantitative, whereas almost all
English poetry has been qualitative or accentual-syllabic.

QUATRAIN
A **STANZA** of four lines, usually rhymed.

QUINTUPLE
A rare sort of rhyme in which the rhyming syllables are followed by four
unaccented and undifferentiated syllables, as with "dedicatedly" and
"medicatedly."

QUOTE
Exact words from another text that are included in something later, with or
without quotation marks. A passage in Eliot's *The Waste Land* – "And a
clatter and a chatter from within" – repeats several words from Emily
Brontë's *Wuthering Heights* ("a chatter of tongues, and a clatter of culinary
utensils, deep within") without quite reaching the point of quotation.
Matthew Arnold's "The Scholar Gypsy" describes one who seems to be
Alfred Tennyson:

> Yes, we await it!—but it still delays,
> And then we suffer! and amongst us one,
> Who most has suffer'd, takes dejectedly
> His seat upon the intellectual throne.... (1853)

Seven decades later, Robert Frost's "New Hampshire" ridicules "Matthew Arnoldism" as

> The cult of one who owned himself "a foiled
> Circuitous wanderer," and "took dejectedly
> His seat upon the intellectual throne" —

And that *is* a quotation.

RAP
Beginning in New York City in the 1980s, rap was the name for a style of performance that usually involved improvised rhymed verse sung or chanted to recorded instrumental music. The verse tends to be in rhymed lines of dimeter or tetrameter, often with adventurous rhymes (such as Ice T's "Jersey" and "heard me").

REDUNDANT
Another term for **IDENTICAL RHYME**, as in that between "cell" and "sell."

REFERENCE
The inclusion of part of one work in another, not necessarily a direct quotation. Samuel Taylor Coleridge's "Dejection: An Ode" quotes a quatrain from "The Ballad of Sir Patrick Spence [Spens]" and then begins with a further reference:

> Well! If the Bard was weather-wise, who made
> The grand old ballad of Sir Patrick Spence . . .

REFRAIN
One or more words repeated at intervals in a poem, usually at the end of a stanza. The most regular is the use of the same line at the close of each stanza (as is common in the ballad).

RHETORIC
In general, the ratio between statement and meaning. In plain style, statement and meaning coincide. In **OVERSTATEMENT**, the statement exceeds the meaning. In **UNDERSTATEMENT**, the statement falls short of the meaning. In **METAPHOR**, the statement converts the meaning into different terms. In **IRONY**, statement may invert the meaning.

RHETORICAL QUESTION

A question propounded for its rhetorical effect and not requiring a reply or intended to induce a reply. Most *rhetorical questions* generate strongly negative answers. Usually, when we ask "Who knows?" and "Who cares?" with a special intonation, we mean "Nobody knows" and "Nobody cares." Often, the negative element is built into the question: "Aren't we all patriots?"

RHYME ROYAL (or RIME ROYAL)

A seven-lined iambic pentameter stanza rhyming *ababbcc*, sometimes with an Alexandrine (hexameter) seventh line. Rhyme royal enjoys the unique distinction of being the only stanza used by all three poets customarily called the greatest in English – Chaucer, Shakespeare, and Milton – as well as by Wordsworth, Masefield, Auden, and others.

RHYTHM, RHYTHMIC

The pattern of some more or less recurrent features of sound, such as stress, duration, or some other quantitative or qualitative principle. Rhythm may be strict or loose, rapid or slow, in patterns perceived as rising (**IAMB, ANAPEST**) or falling (**TROCHEE, DACTYL**).

RISING RHYTHM

A foot in which the last syllable is accented; thus, in English the **IAMB** and the **ANAPEST**. Coleridge illustrates *rising rhythm* in these lines:

Iámbĭcs márch frŏm shórt tŏ lóng.
Wĭth ă léap ănd ă bóund thĕ swĭft Ánăpĕsts thróng.

RUBÁIYÁT STANZA

The iambic pentameter quatrain rhyming *aaba* employed in Edward Fitzgerald's translation of *The Rubáiyát of Omar Khayyám* (1859). Here is a familiar quatrain from the fifth edition (1889):

A Book of Verses underneath the Bough,
A Jug of Wine, a Loaf of Bread – and Thou
Beside me singing in the Wilderness –
Oh, Wilderness were Paradise enow!

RUN-ON LINES

Another name for **ENJAMBMENT**. Unlike the practice with **END-STOPPED LINES**, here the sense runs on from line to line without such pauses as may normally be indicated with commas, dashes, and so forth.

SAPPHIC STANZA

A stanzaic pattern named after the Greek poet Sappho. It has three lines of eleven or twelve syllables each $(-\cup\cup\,|--\,|-\cup\cup\,|-\cup\,|-\cup)$ and a fourth of five syllables $(-\cup\cup\,|-\cup)$. The pattern has been occasionally tried in English. Here is the opening stanza of the first poem in Thomas Hardy's first book of poetry, "The Temporary the All":

> Change and chancefulness in my flowering youthtime,
> Set me sun by sun near to one unchosen;
> Wrought us fellowlike, and despite divergence,
> Fused us in friendship.

SATYR PLAY

The fourth and final play in the bill of tragedies in Greek drama: so called because the chorus was made up of horse-tailed goat-men called satyrs. After the three solemn tragedies that preceded it, the satyr play was intended to bring comic relief, which evidently took the form of drunken ribaldry, grotesque distortions of sacred myths, and outlandish obscenity.

SCANSION

Scanning verse in general: giving a descriptive account of such matters as rhythm, meter, and rhyme scheme. A specific example would be: The scansion of the heroic quatrain is four lines of iambic pentameter rhyming *abab*.

SCAZON

A rare effect that occurs at the end of a line when a trochee or dactyl takes the place of the iamb or anapest that the ear has been conditioned to expect. It can be refreshing, surprising, and even shocking. Consider the line "that the wind came out of the cloud, chilling" in Poe's "Annabel Lee," wherein the trochaic "chilling" supplants the rising rhythm established by the rest of the poem. Line 186 of Tennyson's "Lucretius" shows the same effect, with a dactyl supplanting an iamb at the end: "Strikes through the wood, sets all the tops quivering." There is a dramatic reversal at the end of one line in Wallace Stevens's "Sunday Morning": "Elations when the forest blooms; gusty." There is a double scazon at the end of the first line of John Crowe Ransom's "Bells for John Whiteside's Daughter": "There was such speed in her little body."

SECONDARY ACCENT or SECONDARY STRESS

A stress that is medial in weight (or force) between a full (primary) stress and an unstressed syllable. It usually occurs in polysyllabic words but is sometimes the result of the cadence and sense of a line. In the word élĕmèntryč, the third syllable carries a stress, indicated by the mark ', lighter than that on the first syllable. However, in the scansion of English verse, the rhythmic pattern is formed of stressed and unstressed syllables, and those with secondary stress are conventionally resolved into one or the other. In actual practice, secondary stress creates effective variations within basically regular lines.

SENRYU

The senryu, named after the poet Karai Senryu (1718–1790), has the same form as the **HAIKU** – seventeen syllables arranged in lines of five, seven, and five syllables – but a different spirit, relying on humor or satire rather than conventions related to certain seasons.

SEQUEL
(see PREQUEL)

SESTET

The second, six-lined division of an Italian sonnet. Following the eight-lined division (octave), the *sestet* usually makes specific a general statement that has been presented in the octave or indicates the personal emotion of the author in a situation that the octave has developed. The preferred rhyme scheme is the *cdecde* (following the *abbaabba* of the octave).

SESTINA

One of the most elaborate, difficult, and complex of verse forms. The *sestina* consists of six six-lined stanzas and a three-lined envoy. This form is usually unrhymed, the effect of rhyme being taken over by a fixed pattern of end-words. These end-words in each stanza must be the same, though arranged in a different sequence each time. If we take 1–2–3–4–5–6 to represent the end-words of the first stanza, then the first line of the second stanza must end with 6 (the last end-word used in the preceding stanza), the second with 1, the third with 5, the fourth with 2, the fifth with 4, the sixth with 3 – and so to the next stanza. The order of the first three stanzas, for instance, would be: 1–2–3–4–5–6; 6–1–5–2–4–3; 3–6–4–1–2–5. The three-lined conclusion must use as end-words 5–3–1, these being the final end-words, in the same sequence, of the sixth stanza. But the poet must exercise even greater ingenuity than all this, because buried in each line of the envoy must appear the other three end-words, 2–4–6. So highly artificial a pattern affords a form that, for most poets, can never prove anything more than a prosodic exercise.

SEXTET or SEXTAIN
A stanza or strophe of six lines.

SHAKESPEAREAN SONNET
Another name for **ENGLISH SONNET**.

SHAPED POETRY
Poetry so printed or otherwise presented that the shape of the poem suggests an object. George Herbert's "The Altar" approximates the shape of an altar:

A broken A L T A R, Lord, thy servant reares,
Made of a heart, and cemented with teares:
Whose parts are as thy hand did frame;
No workmans tool hath touch'd the same.
A H E A R T alone
Is such a stone,
As nothing but
Thy pow'r doth cut.
Wherefore each part
Of my hard heart
Meets in this frame,
To praise thy Name;
That, if I chance to hold my peace,
These stones to praise thee may not cease.
O let thy blessed S A C R I F I C E be mine,
And sanctifie this A L T A R to be thine.

SHORT MEASURE
A **QUATRAIN** with its syllables arranged as 6-6-8-6, its feet as **TRIMETER**-trimeter-**TETRAMETER**-trimeter.

SIBILANT
A "hissing" consonant sound represented by /s/, /ss/(unvoiced) and /s/, /z/ (voiced), as in loose/lose and dose/doze.

SIMILE
A figure in which a similarity between two objects is directly expressed, as in Milton's "A dungeon horrible, on all sides round. /As one great furnace flamed . . ." Here the comparison between the dungeon (Hell) and the great furnace is directly expressed in the *as*. Most *similes* are introduced by *as* or *like* or even by such a word as "compare," "liken," or "resemble." In the

preceding illustration the similarity between Hell and a furnace is based on the great heat of the two.

SIMPLE, COMPOUND, or COMPLEX

The main categories of sentence: the simple contains one independent clause, the compound contains two or more independent clauses, and the complex includes one independent clause and any number of dependent clauses.

SOLILOQUY

A speech delivered while the speaker is alone (*solus*), calculated to inform the audience of what is passing in the character's mind. By convention, it can be assumed that what the character says in a soliloquy is what he really is thinking. The term was coined in its Latin form *sōliloquium* by St Augustine.

SONNET

A poem almost invariably of fourteen lines and following one of several set rhyme schemes. The two basic types are the Italian or Petrarchan and the English or Shakespearean. The Italian form is distinguished by its division into the octave and the sestet: the octave rhyming *abbaabba* and the sestet *cdecde, cdcdcd,* or *cdedce.* The octave presents a narrative, states a proposition, or raises a question; the sestet drives home the narrative by making an abstract comment, applies the proposition, or solves the problem. The octave–sestet division is not always kept; the rhyme scheme is often varied, but within the limitation that no Italian sonnet properly allows more than five rhymes or rhymed couplets in the sestet. Iambic pentameter is usual. Certain poets have, however, experimented with other meters.

SOUND EFFECTS

The whole collection of audible features of a work, including scansion as well as pitch, pace, and accent.

SPENSERIAN SONNET

A sonnet of the English type in that it has three quatrains and a couplet but features quatrains joined by the use of linking rhymes: *abab bcbc cdcd ee.* So-called because it was used by Edmund Spenser in his sonnet sequence, *Amoretti.* Modern instances are Thomas Hardy's "Her Reproach," Richard Wilbur's "Praise in Summer," and Paul Muldoon's "A Hummingbird."

SPENSERIAN STANZA

A stanza of nine iambic lines, the first eight in pentameter and the ninth in hexameter. The rhyme scheme is *ababbcbcc*. The name honors Edmund Spenser, who created the pattern for *The Faerie Queene*. Burns used the Spenserian stanza in *The Cotter's Saturday Night*, Shelley in *The Revolt of Islam* and *Adonais*, Keats in *The Eve of St. Agnes*, and Byron in *Childe Harold*. A part of Tennyson's "The Lotos-Eaters" is written in the stanza. Since Tennyson, however, it has fallen into disuse; except for two stanzas printed as paragraphs of prose in Scott Fitzgerald's *This Side of Paradise*, it is hard to find modern examples of any distinction.

SPIRANT

A "breathing" consonant sound produced usually by lower lip and upper teeth, commonly represented by /f/, /ff/ (unvoiced) and by /f/, /v/ (voiced).

SPONDEE

A rhythmic foot consisting of two long or strong syllables. A three-foot passage in T. S. Eliot's "Gerontion" exhibits two spondees: "Knée déep ĭn thĕ sált mársh."

STANZA

A recurrent grouping of two or more verse lines in terms of length, metrical form, and, often, rhyme scheme. For convenience, the term *stanza* is limited to units that are regular, rhymed, and recurrent; other subdivisions are called **STROPHES**.

STOCK CHARACTERS

Conventional character types. A feature of modern art is its tendency to take stock characters from the past, move them from the periphery to the center of attention, and reveal new complexities. Shaw's St Joan begins as a standard ingénue, for example. Eliot's "Gerontion" is a gerontion – the word itself is the name of a favorite stock character of Greek (and later) comedy: the geezer, codger, "little old man."

STORY

Any account of actions in a sequence; any narrative of events in a sequential arrangement.

STROPHE

Some writers limit *stanza* to regular, recurrent, and usually rhymed subdivisions of a poem, leaving *strophe* to cover irregular and possibly unrhymed subdivisions.

SUBJECT

That part of a sentence that represents the subject or agent of the overall statement, normally a noun or pronoun with associated matter. In "The Speaker of the House called for order," the subject is "The Speaker of the House."

SUCCESSIVE

Any pattern in which one pair of effects is followed or succeeded by another, as in the rhyme scheme *aabb* or the assonance in stressed syllables in Eliot's "Gerontion" ("Knée déep in thĕ sált mársh"). "A *c*up of *c*offee and a *p*iece of *p*ie" exhibits successive alliteration.

SYLLABLE

A sound or set of sounds uttered with a single effort of articulation.

SYMBOLISM

A broad term, here applied to the expression of meaning by concrete symbols that suggest less concrete matter. We may say, "Love is like a garden" (simile) or "Love is a rose-garden" (metaphor). But, if we express the idea without saying "love" outright but only by a statement such as "We are in a rose-garden," that is symbolism. A passage in Eliot's "Burnt Norton" may suggest such a meaning:

> Footfalls echo in the memory
> Down the passage which we did not take
> Towards the door we never opened
> Into the rose-garden.

In symbolism it is usual to proceed more by implication and suggestion than outright statement.

SYNTAX

Diction consists of **VOCABULARY** (words one at a time) and syntax (patterns of arrangement). Syntax is the rule-governed arrangement of words in sentences. In Frost's lines "Something there is that doesn't love a wall" and "Whose woods these are I think I know," the vocabulary is quite common but the syntax is unusual. Syntax seems to be that level of language that most distinguishes poetry from prose. It is unlikely that any prose writer or speaker would say, "I will arise and go now, and go to Innisfree, and a small cabin build there, of clay and wattles made."

TERCET
A stanza of three lines, a triplet, in which each line ends with the same rhyme. The term is also used for a passage of three rhymed lines in a poem mostly in couplets.

TERZA RIMA
A three-lined stanza, supposedly devised by Dante (for his *Divine Comedy*) with rhyme scheme *aba bcb cdc ded* and so forth. *Terza rima* has been popular with English poets, being used by Wyatt, Milton, Shelley, Byron, Yeats, Eliot, Ransom, Auden, and Walcott.

TERZA RIMA SONNET
A fourteen-lined poem with rhymes based on the pattern of **TERZA RIMA**: *ababcbcdcdedee* is the pattern in Shelley's "Ode to the West Wind." Frost, Hardy, Nims, Larkin, Robert Morgan, and Michael McFee have written terza rima sonnets.

TETRAMETER
A line of four feet.

THICK SCANSION
Scansion compounded by certain audible effects of diction, especially syntax. Elementary scansion has to do with rhythm and meter, but the sounding of a line may also depend on certain other properties. Foreign or otherwise unfamiliar words may take longer to pronounce, and departures from ordinary subject-verb-object word order can also introduce uncertainty which leads to slowing of pronunciation and neutering of accent. "We trust in God" – the normal word order – may scan as two iambs: Wĕ trúst in Gód. The slightly unusual order of "In God we trust" may result in retardation of pace and flattening of stress, yielding two spondees: ín Gód wé trust.

TRAVESTY
A work that holds another up to ridicule by keeping a solemn subject constant while lowering the style to something less formal; much the same as burlesque. (The word means the same as *transvestite*: "a change of clothing.")

TRIMETER
A line of three feet.

TRIOLET
A French verse form consisting of eight lines, the first two being repeated as the last two, and the first line recurring also as the fourth. There are only

two rhymes, and their arrangement is **ab** *aa* *abab* (boldface indicates whole lines that are repeated.)

TRIPLE RHYME
Rhyme in which the rhyming stressed syllable is followed by two unstressed, undifferentiated syllables, as in "meticulous" and "ridiculous."

TRIPLET
Loosely, any set of three lines, especially if rhymed. Sometimes applied to a set of three lines introduced for the sake of variety into a poem in rhymed couplets.

TROCHEE
A rhythmic foot consisting of one accented syllable followed by one unaccented syllable.

UNACCENTED
Sometimes "weak": applied to a syllable that receives minimal accent, as the second of "sofa."

UNDERSTATEMENT
A common figure of speech in which the literal sense of what is said falls detectably short of (or "under") the magnitude of what is being talked about. When someone says "pretty fair" or "not too shabby" but means "splendid," that is clear understatement.

VELAR
Consonant sounds produced by contact with the soft palate: voiceless (k), voiced (g), and voiced nasal (ŋ): in *rick*, *rig*, *ring*.

VERSE
Used in two senses: (1) as a unit of poetry, in which case it has the same significance as **STANZA** or **LINE**; and (2) as a name given generally to metrical composition. In the second sense verse means rhythmical and, frequently, metrical and rhymed composition, in which case it may imply little as to merit, the term poetry or poem often being reserved for verse of high merit.

VERSE EPISTLE
A versified letter: a popular form going back to classical antiquity, with notable examples by Horace and Ovid. The verse epistle enjoyed a revival in the eighteenth century, especially in the hands of Alexander Pope. There are some later examples by Robert Browning and others.

VERSE-PARAGRAPH

A nonstanzaic, continuous verse unit, in which the lines are grouped in unequal blocks according to content. The beginning of a verse-paragraph may be indicated by indentation, as in prose. Poetry written in paragraphs is usually either blank verse or free verse. Milton's *Paradise Lost* is in blank verse paragraphs; much of Whitman's *Leaves of Grass* is in free verse paragraphs.

VILLANELLE

A fixed nineteen-lined form, originally French, employing only two rhymes and repeating two of the lines according to a set pattern. Line 1 is repeated as lines 6, 12, and 18; line 3 as lines 9, 15, and 19. The first and third lines return as a rhymed couplet at the end. The scheme of rhymes and repetitions is *abá aba abá aba abá abaá*.

VOCABULARY

That component of **DICTION** that has to do with words considered one at a time.

VOICED

Applied to consonant sounds uttered with vibration of the vocal folds, such as the sounds commonly represented by *b*, *d*, *g*, *v*, and *z*.

VOICED NASAL

Applied to voiced consonant sounds with a nasal component, such as those represented by the letters *m* and *n* and the symbol ŋ; as in *tam*, *tan*, *tang*.

VOICELESS (also UNVOICED)

Applied to consonant sounds uttered without voice. For the voiced sounds commonly represented by the letters *b*, *d*, *g*, *v*, and *z*, the voiceless counterparts are commonly represented by the letters *p*, *t*, *k*, *f*, and *s*.

VOLTA

The turn in thought – from question to answer, problem to solution – that occurs at the beginning of the sestet in the Italian sonnet and between the twelfth and thirteenth lines of the Shakespearean sonnet. The volta is routinely marked by "but," "yet," or "and yet."

VOWEL

A sound produced by vibrations of the vocal cords without audible friction or contact.

Suggestions for Reading:
A Biased Bibliography

Even in the twenty-first century, it would be conceivable for somebody completely illiterate to create a perfectly brilliant poem. Some scholars have speculated that the so-called blindness of the Greek epic poet Homer is a euphemism for illiteracy. Now, thousands of years later, literacy is not an absolute requirement for the production of poetry, though it is a functional requirement for the literal *writing* thereof. If human history has gone on for, say, 100,000 years, it is unlikely that many people have been literate for more than about 5000 of those years. As many as one-fifth of adults in the world may be technically illiterate, and a great many more are functionally so: that is, they can read but they don't.

That is a caveat: beware of thinking you can learn about creating poetry by reading about it. Maybe you can, maybe some people have done so, but it is more likely that poets have received their education by other means. Once you commit yourself to poetry, there *may* be some texts that *may* help; maybe not. You can buy books called things like *Complete Idiot's Guide to Writing Poetry*, but such titles suggest farce more than learning, and people who go in for such things may not ask enough of themselves. Just a little way from those entertaining sites, there are some items that can be recommended.

The Poetry Toolkit: For Readers and Writers, First Edition. William Harmon.
© 2012 William Harmon. Published 2012 by Blackwell Publishing Ltd.

——————————— A. Works on Language[1] ———————————

Oxford English Dictionary (1989[2]) 2nd edn, 20 vols, Oxford and New York: Oxford University Press. (See also *The Shorter Oxford English Dictionary* (2002), 5th edn, and *Concise Oxford English Dictionary* (2011), 12th edn (both Oxford University Press).)

Oxford Dictionary of Pronunciation for Current English (2003), Oxford and New York: Oxford University Press.

The American Heritage Dictionary of the English Language (2006), 4th edn, Boston: Houghton Mifflin.[3]

Webster's Third New International Dictionary (2002), Springfield, MA: Merriam-Webster.[4]

Merriam-Webster's Collegiate Dictionary (2008), 11th edn, Springfield, MA: Merriam-Webster.[5]

---

[1] Language is a useful and entertaining area that engages the attention of almost everybody. Language in one way or another is the form, the matter, and the medium of poetry, and there is very little poetry that does not involve language.

[2] The project began in the 1850s and led to the eventual publication of a twelve-volume first edition that later gained a thirteenth volume of supplementary material (1933). A twenty-volume second edition appeared in 1989 and has since been augmented by volumes of additions. Now there are electronic versions on CD-ROM and in online form made available through libraries, universities, and individual subscription. The entries provide definitions, etymologies, histories of forms and variants, with illustrative quotations that strive to indicate the earliest and latest appearance in print. Readers who detect a mistake or omission may submit suggestions through http://www.oup.com/uk/oedsubform/.

[3] A reliable one-volume dictionary that features an appendix of Indo-European roots. Here one can trace the history of a root like *bak-*, "staff used for support," which may be the ancestor of *peg*, *bacillus*, *baculiform*, *baguette*, *debacle*, *imbecile*, and *bacteria*.

[4] A basic dictionary available in many libraries and schools.

[5] Another basic dictionary.

---------------- **B. Works on Usage** ----------------

Austin, J. L. (1962) *How to do Things with Words*, edited by J. O. Urmson, Oxford and New York: Oxford University Press.[6]

Follet, Wilson (1988) *Modern American Usage*, New York: Hill and Wang.[7]

Fowler, H. W. (1926) *A Dictionary of Modern English Usage*, Oxford and New York: Oxford University Press.[8]

Garner, Bryan A. (1998) *Modern American Usage*, New York: Oxford University Press.[9]

Strunk, William and White, E. B. (2009) *The Elements of Style*, 50th anniversary edn, New York: Pearson Longman.[10]

---

[6] An important work combining philosophy with commonsense that promoted our awareness of what is called a speech act, that is, an utterance that is also an action. An ordinary locution is something like "I am sorry." A special illocution is something like "I apologize," in which the verb designates an action. Illocutions tend to be first-person present-tense utterances that have a high degree of truth value. If someone says "I'm sorry," you can respond, "No you're not." But if someone says "I apologize," you can't say "No you don't," because the apology has already been uttered.

[7] A somewhat less distinguished guide than Fowler (see following note), but still a provocation to thinking about clarity and propriety.

[8] One of the great works of twentieth-century language study. Fowler can be quirky, but his guidance is basically sound, and his style is itself a model of economy and force. "Inversion: Writers who observe the poignancy sometimes given by inversion, but fail to observe that 'sometimes' means 'when exclamation is appropriate', adopt inversion as an infallible enlivener; they aim at freshness and attain frigidity." Fowler's discussion of *cinema*, while outdated, is still valuable as evidence of how to pronounce "prose kinema" in a poem by Ezra Pound (/kaɪˈniːmə/ rather than /ˈkɪnɪmə/). What Fowler says about "Scotsman" ("…in compliment to a Scotch hearer, *Scots-* being (OED) 'the prevalent form now used by Scotch people'") refers to a superseded edition of the *Oxford English Dictionary*. Despite such shortcomings, the original "Fowler," now available as *A Dictionary of Modern English Usage: the Classic First Edition*, remains useful. Those who crave the up-to-date may consult the second edition, *Fowler's Modern English Usage* (1965), revised by Sir Ernest Gowers, or the third, *The New Fowler's Modern English Usage* (1996, revised 2004), the *Pocket Fowler's Modern English Usage*, edited by Robert Allen, second edition, 2008 (and electronic resource) or *A Dictionary of Modern English Usage: Introduction and Notes by David Crystal*, 2009.

[9] Another unobjectionable resource, good for consultation in perplexing situations; less prescriptive than old-fashioned grammars and style books.

[10] Strunk was a teacher at Cornell, where E. B. White was one of his students who turned out to be so grateful that he converted his old teacher's book of principles into an accessible best seller. (White may be more familiar as the author of *Charlotte's Web*.)

———————————— C. General Reference ————————————

Harmon, William (2011) (ed.) *A Handbook to Literature*, 12th edn, Boston: Longman.[11]

Preminger, Alex and Brogan, T.V.F. (1993) (eds) *The New Princeton Encyclopedia of Poetry and Poetics*, Princeton, NJ: Princeton University Press.[12] (Also published as an electronic resource, 2000.)

———————————— D. Scholarship and Criticism ————————————

Brooks, Cleanth (1947) *The Well-Wrought Urn: Studies in the Structure of Poetry*, New York: Harcourt Brace.[13]

Collingwood, R. G. (1938) *The Principles of Art*, Oxford and New York: Oxford University Press.[14]

Crane, R. S. (1952) (ed.) *Critics and Criticism: Ancient and Modern*, Chicago: University of Chicago Press.[15] (Abridged edition, 1957.)

[11] The first edition came out in 1936, edited by C. A. Hibbard and W. F. Thrall. They both died in the 1940s and were succeeded by Hugh Holman, who edited late printings of the first edition as well as the second, third, and fourth editions. After Holman's death in 1981, the job of editor passed to William Harmon, who, like all the earlier editors, was associated with the University of North Carolina in Chapel Hill. He has done eight editions, the latest of which is the twelfth, in 2011.

[12] A thorough encyclopedia with a lot of information on versification, especially useful with languages other than English.

[13] A key work of the New Criticism that emphasized the artwork as a free-standing creation with its own structure not dependent on the psychology of the poet or of the reader. With a wide range of poems from many periods, the book emphasizes paradox as the hallmark of poetry.

[14] A general examination of works of art of all sorts, concentrating on art as the physical expression of emotion resulting from perception and intuition. Art in a general sense is a part of everybody's daily life; with an artist, it finds a particularly durable record of complex processes of perception and expression.

[15] A set of articles from the debate between New Critics and Aristotelians as well as some more general studies. Of particular interest here are R. S. Crane's attack on Cleanth Brooks and Elder Olson's attack on William Empson. There is also a remarkable study of one small but important word in *King Lear* ("this") by Norman Maclean, a legendary teacher who went on, in retirement, to publish *A River Runs Through It* about his family's life in Montana and elsewhere.

Empson, William (1968) *Seven Types of Ambiguity,*[16] 3rd edn, New York: New Directions. (Original edition 1930, London: Chatto and Windus.)

Harmon, William (2005) (ed.) *Classic Writings on Poetry*, New York: Columbia University Press.[17]

Jakobson, Roman and Waugh, Linda R. (2002) *The Sound Shape of Language*, 3rd edn, Berlin and New York: Mouton de Gruyter.[18]

Pound, Ezra (1937) *The ABC of Reading*, London: Routledge; New York: New Directions.[19] See also the essay "How to Read" (1929) in *Literary Essays of Ezra Pound* (1968), New York: New Directions.

Wilson, Edmund (1931) *Axel's Castle: A Study of the Imaginative Literature of 1870–1930*, New York and London: C. Scribner's Sons.[20]

──────────────── E. Versification ────────────────

Bridges, Robert (1921) *Milton's Prosody, with a Chapter on Accentual Verse and Notes*, Oxford: Clarendon Press.[21] (Original edition, 1889, Oxford: Oxford University Press.)

Fussell, Paul (1979) *Poetic Meter and Poetic Form*, revised edn, New York: Random House.[22]

[16] A demonstration of what happens when a brilliant eccentric looks in detail at poetry from all ages; he was a good poet himself (as was Elder Olson, with whom he engaged in a celebrated controversy).

[17] A handy collection of the best-known critical documents from classical antiquity to the twentieth century.

[18] Studies in language and literature by a leading structuralist thinker.

[19] A vigorous examination of some of the principles of verse writing, especially some of the ways in which language can be "charged" with meaning.

[20] One of the pioneering studies of modernist literature as it continues the Symbolist movement from the nineteenth century. It provided a clear introduction for many readers who may have been unfamiliar with figures like Gertrude Stein and T. S. Eliot, who would become much more famous in the years that followed.

[21] A remarkable and refreshingly original study of the versification of a notoriously challenging poet by a Poet Laureate who was a master of his vocation.

[22] An extraordinarily subtle and sensitive study of versification, remarkable for its ability to connect sound effects with substance. When Auden, say, rhymes differently accented syllables – such as that between "afraid" and "decade," – Fussell can detect the presence of dissonance and irony.

Hollander, John (2001) *Rhyme's Reason: A Guide to English Verse*, 3rd edn, New Haven: Yale University Press.[23]

Saintsbury, George (1923) *A History of English Prosody, from the Twelfth Century to the Present Day*, 2nd edn, London: Macmillan.[24]

Saintsbury, George (1910) *Historical Manual of English Prosody*, London: Macmillan.[25]

Wimsatt, W. K. (1972) (ed.) *Versification: Major Language Types; Sixteen Essays*, New York: Modern Language Association.[26]

Wright, George T. (1988) *Shakespeare's Metrical Art*, Berkeley: University of California Press.[27]

[23] An entertaining guide to all the familiar measures and stanzas, with original examples that illustrate and explain what's being discussed. Hollander is one of the best poets of a very strong generation as well as a gifted scholar and linguist.

[24] Even though Saintsbury's "present day" is decades ago, his work on prosody – like his work on wine and beer – has not been superseded. A reader forewarned about Saintsbury's quirks and prejudices can still benefit from his extraordinarily wide reading and deep thinking – and his genial wit as well.

[25] The manual boils things down entertainingly. In some ways, the most mechanical and technical parts of poetry remain the most mysterious. Any schoolchild can immanentize an eschaton; it takes some subtlety to parse even a simple sentence and scan even a simple line.

[26] A single fairly compact volume contains in handy form the basic prosodic information about poetry in most of the major languages and literatures (Chinese, Japanese, Biblical Hebrew, Classical Greek and Latin, Germanic, Celtic, Spanish, French, English, Slavic, Italian). The chapter on Italian versification was written by A. Bartlett Giamatti (1938–1989), a prodigious polymath who was a Renaissance scholar, university president (Yale), and commissioner of baseball – all in a relatively short life (he was also the father of actors Paul and Marcus Giamatti).

[27] A basic but subtle examination of Shakespeare by a notable scholar, teacher, and composer of light verse.

—————————— F. Anthologies and Collections ——————————

Harmon, William (1998) (ed.) *The Classic Hundred Poems*, 2nd edn, New York: Columbia University Press.[28] (Original edn, 1990, Columbia University Press.)

Harmon, William (1992) *The Top 500 Poems*, New York: Columbia University Press.[29]

Larkin, Philip (1973) (ed.) *The Oxford Book of Twentieth Century English Verse*, Oxford and New York: Oxford University Press.[30]

Nims, John Frederick (1990) *Sappho to Valery: Poems in Translation*, Princeton, NJ: Princeton University Press.[31]

Nims, John Frederick and Mason, David (2005) *Western Wind: An Introduction to Poetry*, 5th edn, New York: Random House.[32]

[28] This volume was generated by an objective look at *Columbia Granger's Index to Poetry*, which since 1904 has tallied the contents of hundreds of anthologies and presented the results by title, first line, author, and subject. It was relatively easy to identify those poems that have been anthologized most often. The volume also includes biographies, commentaries, and notes.

[29] An extension of *The Classic Hundred Poems*, expanding the selection to 500 poems.

[30] Some Oxford books are as interesting for the choice of editor as for their contents. Philip Larkin was probably the greatest living poet in England for the years between 1955 and 1985, and his selection of poems for this Oxford book are entertaining and revealing. (Other Oxford books have been edited by such poets as W. H. Auden, W. B. Yeats, Kingsley Amis, A. C. Quiller-Couch, Donald Hall, and William Harmon.)

[31] John Frederick Nims was a poet, polyglot translator, editor, and teacher. His achievement continues the tradition of H. W. Longfellow, Ezra Pound, and Kenneth Rexroth, original poets who benefitted from an understanding of foreign language and literature.

[32] Probably the best all-round anthology of poetry available in the twenty-first century, and each successive edition is an improvement.

Quiller-Couch, Sir Arthur T. (1900) (ed.) *The Oxford Book of English Verse: 1250–1900*, Oxford and New York: Oxford University Press.[33] Also Gardner, Helen (1972) (ed.) *The New Oxford Book of English Verse, 1250–1950*; and Ricks, Christopher (1999) (ed.) *The Oxford Book of English Verse* (both Oxford University Press).

Yeats, W. B. (1936) (ed.) *The Oxford Book of Modern Verse 1892–1935*, Oxford and New York: Oxford University Press.[34]

---

[33] Quiller-Couch inaugurated the venerable series of Oxford books of verse and other things as well (including Death and Oxford). "Q" belonged to an older style of editors, who felt free to change poems and titles without much scholarly discipline. For example, he gave the title "A Farewell to Arms" to a poem attributed to George Peele ("His golden locks time hath to silver turned"). That seems to be where Ernest Hemingway got the ironic title of his novel about justifiable desertion in wartime. Later it turned out that the poem not really called "A Farewell to Arms" was probably not really written by George Peele but by Sir Henry Lee. "Q" was not a stick in the mud, however. When preparing *The Oxford Book of Victorian Verse*, first published in 1912, he acquired two poems from Ezra Pound, then a twenty-seven-year-old American living in London, and it turned out that the original versions of *The Oxford Book of Victorian Verse* contained twice as many poems by Ezra Pound as by Gerard Manley Hopkins (whose poetry was not well known until after 1918).

[34] Like Philip Larkin's Oxford book, this one may tell more about W. B. Yeats than about Modern Verse; but Yeats is worth knowing about, and his anthology contains many items that are now not available anywhere else. It is also noteworthy that Yeats included poems by a twenty-three-year-old George Barker.

Acknowledgments

Edgar Lee Masters: 3 lines from "Hamilton Greene" from *The Spoon River Anthology*, © 1916 Macmillan Publishing Co., Inc. Permission to reprint granted by Hilary Masters.

James Stephens: "A Glass of Beer" from *Collected Poems*, Macmillan Publishing Co., Inc. Permission to reprint granted by the Society of Authors as the Literary Representative of the Estate of James Stephens.

Ezra Pound: "Fan-Piece, For Her Imperial Lord" from *Personae*, © 1926 Ezra Pound. Reprinted by permission of New Directions Publishing Corporation.

"l(a" is reprinted from *E. E. Cummings: Complete Poems 1904–1962*, edited by George J. Firmage, by permission of W. W. Norton & Company. Copyright © 1991 by the Trustees for the E. E. Cummings Trust and George Firmage. Reprinted with permission of W. W. Norton & Company Ltd UK.

Desmond Skirrow: "Ode on a Grecian Urn Summarized" is reprinted from Amis, K. (1978) (ed.) *The New Oxford Book of English Verse*, p. 316. First printed in the *New Statesman* (30 July 1960). Reprinted by permission of the *New Statesman*.

Index

Page numbers in **bold** denote glossary reference

The Poetry Toolkit: For Readers and Writers, First Edition. William Harmon.
© 2012 William Harmon. Published 2012 by Blackwell Publishing Ltd.